NOLO *Your Legal Companion*

"In Nolo you can trust." —**THE NEW YORK TIMES**

OUR MISSION
Make the law as simple as possible, saving you time, money and headaches.

Whether you have a simple question or a complex problem, turn to us at:

NOLO.COM

Your all-in-one legal resource

Need quick information about wills, patents, adoptions, starting a business—or anything else that's affected by the law? **Nolo.com** is packed with free articles, legal updates, resources and a complete catalog of our books and software.

NOLO NOW

Make your legal documents online

Creating a legal document has never been easier or more cost-effective! Featuring Nolo's Online Will, as well as online forms for LLC formation, incorporation, divorce, name change—and many more! Check it out at **http://nolonow.nolo.com**.

NOLO'S LAWYER DIRECTORY

Meet your new attorney

If you want advice from a qualified attorney, turn to Nolo's Lawyer Directory—the only directory that lets you see hundreds of in-depth attorney profiles so you can pick the one that's right for you. Find it at **http://lawyers.nolo.com**.

ALWAYS UP TO DATE

Sign up for NOLO'S LEGAL UPDATER

Old law is bad law. We'll email you when we publish an updated edition of this book—sign up for this free service at nolo.com/legalupdater.

Find the latest updates at NOLO.COM

Recognizing that the law can change even before you use this book, we post legal updates during the life of this edition at **nolo.com/updates**.

Is this edition the newest? ASK US!

To make sure that this is the most recent edition available, just give us a call at **800-728-3555**.

(Please note that we cannot offer legal advice.)

MAR 08

Please note

We believe accurate, plain-English legal information should help
you solve many of your own legal problems. But this text is not a
substitute for personalized advice from a knowledgeable lawyer. If
you want the help of a trained professional—and we'll always point
out situations in which we think that's a good idea—consult an
attorney licensed to practice in your state.

14th edition

Living Together
A Legal Guide for Unmarried Couples

By Attorneys Toni Ihara, Ralph Warner & Frederick Hertz

FOURTEENTH EDITION	FEBRUARY 2008
Editor	EMILY DOSKOW
Cover Design	SUSAN PUTNEY
Production	MARGARET LIVINGSTON
Proofreader	PAUL TYLER
CD-ROM Preparation	ELLEN BITTER
Index	SONGBIRD INDEXING
Printing	CONSOLIDATED PRINTERS, INC.

Ihara, Toni Lynne.
  Living together : a legal guide for unmarried couples / by Toni Ihara, Ralph
Warner & Frederick Hertz. -- 14th ed.
    p. cm.
  Includes index.
  ISBN-13: 978-1-4133-0755-9 (pbk.)
  ISBN-10: 1-4133-0755-8 (pbk.)
  1. Unmarried couples--Legal status, laws, etc.--United States. 2. Unmarried
couples--Legal status, laws, etc.--United States--Forms. I. Warner, Ralph E. II.
Hertz, Frederick. III. Title.
  KF538.I35 2008
  346.7301'6--dc22

                       2007035643

Quantity sales: For information on bulk purchases or corporate premium sales, please contact the Special Sales
Department. For academic sales or textbook adoptions, ask for Academic Sales. Call 800-955-4775 or write to
Nolo, 950 Parker Street, Berkeley, CA 94710.

Acknowledgments

Recent editions of *Living Together* have benefitted from the extraordinary legal research help of Ella Hirst and Alayna Schroeder and the exceptional editing and creative input of Marcia Stewart and Kathleen Michon. Thanks, too, to Amy Ihara for her hard work and creative contributions during the manuscript preparation stage.

For the 12th and subsequent editions, thanks are due to Twila Slesnick for her edits and additions to the income tax and retirement plans material.

About the Author

Attorneys Toni Ihara and Ralph Warner have been involved in the self-help law movement since its inception in the early 1970s. Ralph Warner is a co-founder of Nolo and is author of several self-help legal books, including *Everybody's Guide to Small Claims Court*. Toni Ihara is an anthropologist turned lawyer turned graphic artist, and has been with Nolo since the beginning. After living together for nearly 20 years, Toni and Ralph are now married.

Frederick Hertz is a practicing attorney and mediator and the author of *Legal Affairs: Essential Advice for Same-Sex Couples* (Owl Books) and co-author of Nolo's *A Legal Guide for Lesbian & Gay Couples*. He lives in the San Francisco Bay Area.

Table of Contents

5 Renting and Sharing a Home

6 Buying a House Together

7 Starting a Family

Appendixes

Index

Living Together: An Introduction

Living together has never been more popular. According to the 2000 Census data, over 5.4 million unmarried couples live together (which translates into 10.8 million people). This is a whopping 72% increase since 1990. Forty percent of unmarried households have children. The number of cohabiting seniors tripled in that same period and is continuing to rise. The average American spends the majority of his or her life unmarried.

If you are part of an unmarried couple living together, it's probably comforting to know that you are far from alone. However, this doesn't mean that you can ignore how the law affects your relationship. This book explains the wide range of legal and practical rules that affect opposite-sex unmarried couples living together—from sharing money and property (contract law) to owning a house together (real estate law) or sharing an apartment (landlord-tenant law) to having a child with your partner (family law) to writing a will (estate planning).

RESOURCE

If you are part of a gay or lesbian couple living together, see *A Legal Guide for Lesbian & Gay Couples*, by Denis Clifford, Frederick Hertz, and Emily Doskow, also published by Nolo.

When you understand the law, you and your partner can make informed decisions about how to structure your life, finances, property ownership, and family relationships to best meet your needs. Failing to learn about the law and take measures to protect yourself and your partner can have negative consequences. The special rules governing married couples (such as those relating to property ownership, divorce, and inheritance rights, to name a few) don't apply to unmarried couples. In order to compensate for this, you'll have to do some extra work. For example, you may want to write a will to ensure that your partner gets your property when you die, sign paternity statements to ensure that

a father's parental rights are preserved, or create a "living together contract" to avoid protracted court battles over property if you split up.

To help you, we provide dozens of written documents (both as tear-out forms and on CD) that unmarried couples can use to spell out their individual legal and financial arrangements, including:

- living together contracts regarding your money and property—whether you want to keep everything separate, pool all assets, or something in between (such as share ownership of a car or specific item)
- house ownership agreements—whether you're sharing costs and ownership equally or not
- basic wills and estate planning forms
- parenting agreements, paternity statements, and other documents relating to children you have together (or bring into your relationship from a previous marriage), and
- property settlement agreements for use in the event you separate.

We believe that most unmarried couples can safely and easily master the majority of legal rules that affect them. However, it's also true that an experienced lawyer's advice can be invaluable when it comes to dealing with more complicated situations. We'll point out how and when a lawyer's expertise can be helpful—for example, if one of you has children or substantial assets, or you're dealing with complicated estate planning.

There are many reasons why people choose to live together without getting married. Some don't see the need for the state's approval of their commitment to each other. Many couples view it as a trial period before marriage. Some avoid marriage because they have gone through a messy divorce. Young people in expensive urban areas often live with partners in order to reduce housing costs. A growing minority choose not to marry because they don't wish to participate in an

One of the common issues faced by unmarried couples is how to introduce each other in a way that reflects the importance of your relationship—boyfriend/girlfriend, special friend, significant other, lover, or POSSLQ (Person of the Opposite Sex Sharing Living Quarters, the Census Bureau phrase for heterosexual couples who live together without getting married)—the choice is yours. Because "partner" is one of the most commonly used and neutral terms, we use it throughout this book to refer to one member of an unmarried couple.

institution that excludes same-sex couples. And the fast-increasing number of unmarried couples over 45 that live together—over one-fifth of all unmarried couples fall into this category—often have financial concerns that come into play. For example, by not marrying they don't become legally obligated for their partner's medical treatment, and they reduce the risk of paying tax on Social Security benefits. And by not marrying, many avoid tricky inheritance issues if one or both partners have children from a previous marriage or own substantial assets.

One of the most common reasons older couples choose to live together instead of marrying is to avoid joint liability for debts, especially for long-term care or medical bills. Staying unmarried also enables each partner to qualify individually for public benefits, such as Medicaid, without draining the other partner's resources. There are detailed rules about how this must be structured to avoid inadvertent triggering of joint liability, so if you are considering such a strategy, consult with an attorney specializing in elder law before you make any big decisions.

Finally, changing social attitudes and values have made living together less of a stigma; living together is not considered as rare (or immoral) as it was 25 or more years ago. In fact, the American Law Institute, an influential organization of lawyers, judges, and legal scholars, recently recommended sweeping changes in family law, including recommending that family courts and state lawmakers begin to treat living together relationships more like marriage—even recommending that laws provide for alimony-like payments when unmarried couples split up after a long time together.

Whatever your reasons for not marrying, this book arms you with information to tackle most of the legal issues that arise during unmarried partnerships, including better managing your financial affairs, protecting your property, buying a house or other property together, having or co-parenting children, planning for your death, and dealing with a breakup.

Check Out the Alternatives to Marriage Project

Laws affecting unmarried couples change from time to time. To keep up to date on a particular issue, follow our advice in Chapter 11 on doing your own legal research. Also, check the Updates section on Nolo's website, www.nolo.com, for key legal rulings that affect unmarried couples. In addition, we highly recommend that you check out the Alternatives to Marriage Project, a national organization that provides resources, support, and advocacy for unmarried people living together. For more information, and to receive their newsletter "Alternatives to Marriage Update," see the ATMP website at www.unmarried.org, or write to them at ATMP, P.O. Box 320151, Brooklyn, NY 11232, telephone 718-788-1911.

The Legal State of Living Together

This chapter provides an overview of the key legal issues affecting unmarried couples—from the laws of living together (cohabiting) to making property agreements. This chapter also explains the rules regarding common law marriages and domestic partnerships.

Sex and the Law

The United States Supreme Court finally entered the 21st century in 2003. In *Lawrence v. Texas*, 123 S.Ct. 2472 (2003), the court struck down a Texas law prohibiting "deviate sexual intercourse" (in this case, sodomy) between two persons of the same sex. The Supreme Court overruled its own opinion in *Bowers v. Hardwick*, 486 U.S. 186 (1986), which upheld a similar law in Georgia. The Supreme Court held that the Due Process Clause of the Fourteenth Amendment protects the decisions of individuals about intimate physical relationships from intrusion by the state, and that the protection extends to unmarried as well as married persons.

The legal effect of *Lawrence v. Texas* was to render all sodomy laws unconstitutional, including those directed at heterosexual couples. Of course, the laws of the states that continue to prohibit sodomy will stay on the books until they are challenged in court or repealed by the Legislature. If you live in one of those states and are prosecuted for sodomy, however, you should be able to get your case dismissed simply by raising a challenge under *Lawrence*.

Although it does not address such laws directly, *Lawrence* also calls into question all restrictions on consensual adult sexual activity, such as laws prohibiting cohabitation and fornication. (See "Legal Definitions of Prohibited Sex Acts," below.) If you and your partner are over 18 and neither of you is married to someone else, you can consider yourself fairly safe from criminal prosecution for your private, consensual sexual activity, even if your state still has laws on the books relating to cohabitation and fornication.

Adultery, however, is still illegal in many states. These laws may not be affected by the *Lawrence v. Texas* decision, because of the special public policies involved (for example, support of marriage and protection of children). Adultery laws may still find their way into divorce, alimony, and custody proceedings, or they may be invoked in cases involving property disputes. (See Chapter 8 for more on these issues.)

Legal Definitions of Prohibited Sex Acts

Fornication: Voluntary sexual intercourse between unmarried people of the opposite sex. If one of the people is still married, this is generally considered to be adultery, not fornication. In many states, adultery is technically a crime, but rarely is anyone prosecuted for it.

Cohabitation: Two people living together in an intimate sexual relationship, without being married. Some courts, especially those in states where fornication is illegal, describe a cohabitation relationship as meretricious, meaning "of an unlawful sexual nature."

Sodomy: Generally refers to oral or anal sex. Many states call it an unnatural act or a "crime against nature." Some states prohibit all sodomy, while others prohibit only specific acts.

To find out more about laws (and penalties) regarding cohabitation, fornication, or adultery, check your state laws. Chapter 11 explains how to do this kind of legal research. Also, for information on state laws involving adultery that may affect alimony or division of marital property if you're living with someone while getting a divorce, see Chapter 8.

RESOURCE

The National Gay and Lesbian Task Force (NGLTF) keeps track of sex laws affecting both heterosexuals and homosexuals. For more information, contact the NGLTF at 2320 17th St., NW, Washington, DC 20009, 202-332-6483, or check their website at www.ngltf.org. The American Civil Liberties Union also monitors sex laws. For information, see www.aclu.org.

CAUTION

Speaking of sex—don't. It is critical that you omit any references to a sexual relationship in any living together contract you write. If you do, and your contract is reviewed by an ultraconservative judge in a separate dispute, the whole contract may be thrown out. (Chapter 3 discusses this issue in more detail.)

Domestic Partners

The term "domestic partnership" has come to mean a lot of different things, depending on the circumstances. In its most general sense, the phrase refers to two people who live together in a committed relationship intending to be emotionally and financially responsible for each other. But the legal meaning of the phrase can vary widely.

Statewide Domestic Partnership Programs

In California, Maine, Oregon, and Washington, state laws allow certain couples to register as domestic partners. Except for Maine, all of those states limit registration to same-sex couples and opposite-sex couples in which at least one partner is 62 or older. Rights and responsibilities differ—in California and Oregon domestic partners have the same rights and responsibilities as married couples, but in Maine and Washington the rights are more limited. Because the partnership isn't recognized as a marriage for federal purposes such as tax benefits, very few heterosexual couples are registering, even if they qualify.

City, County, State Employee Programs

A number of cities and counties allow unmarried couples to register as domestic partners and offer domestic partnership benefits for employees. Colleges and universities, plus some states, also provide domestic partner benefits to employees. And many private employers, including the majority of Fortune 500 companies, provide benefits to unmarried partners of employees. The Alternatives to Marriage Project website (at www.unmarried.org) has links to information regarding domestic partner benefits, including a guide to getting your employer to offer domestic partner benefits.

The benefits provided and qualifications to participate in these programs vary. Common benefits include:

- health, dental, and vision insurance
- sick and bereavement leave
- accident and life insurance
- death benefits
- parental leave (for a child you co-parent)
- housing rights and tuition reduction (at universities), and
- use of recreational facilities.

The complete list of potential benefits is extensive; the typical benefits offered, however, are not. In some cases, all that a company or city offers is bereavement or sick leave. In other situations, the benefits offered are extensive—and expensive. Often, either the employee foots the bill for his or her partner, or the company pays (if it also pays for spouses). However, regardless of who pays, the employee must pay taxes on the benefits. The IRS considers benefits awarded to an unmarried partner as taxable compensation.

Here are the questions you need to ask to see how and if domestic partner benefits apply to you:

- Who qualifies as a domestic partner—are heterosexual couples covered or only same-sex couples?

- How will an employer identify your domestic partner—by registration with a local registry (a public record of domestic partners)? Some companies may require you to have registered a domestic partnership before extending company health benefits to your partner. This is usually to ensure that roommates aren't taking advantage of the system.

- Must you and your partner be together for a minimum number of years?

- Must you live together and share expenses?

- Must you be financially responsible for each other? (Usually, you must live together in an exclusive relationship and share basic living expenses, such as food and shelter, with your partner.)

CAUTION

It's important to remember that registering locally or with an employer only gives you the specific benefits of that registration, and does not change your legal relationship into a marriage.

What Are the Legal Implications of Registering as Domestic Partners?

Depending on where you live, by registering as domestic partners, you and your partner may have created an implied contract for other purposes, such as sharing income and property. This is likely to come up if one partner dies without an estate plan and the surviving partner claims to own part of the decedent's property based on an oral or implied contract.

If you are in a domestic partnership, you should make a written property ownership contract, such as one of those included in Chapter 3. This is especially important if you do not wish to share property or income beyond day-to-day expenses. A court might otherwise treat the fact that you registered as domestic partners as an indication that you had agreed to share ownership of property.

Common Law Marriage

Marriage is the legal union of two people. Once they become married to each other, their responsibilities and rights toward one another concerning property and support are defined by the laws of the state in which they live. While a married couple may be able to modify some of the rules set up by their state, they can end their marriage only by a court granting a divorce or an annulment.

Many people believe that if you live with a person for a long time you're automatically married—that you have what is called a common law marriage, with the same rights and responsibilities of a couple who has been legally married. In most states, this is not true. In these states, marriage requires a license and ceremony. A dozen or so states, however, do recognize common law marriage. (See "States Recognizing Common Law Marriage," below.) But even living together in one of these states doesn't mean you are married. You must intend to be married and "hold yourselves out" to the world as married.

There are no absolute rules or guidelines; whether or not a common law marriage exists depends on the facts of each situation. However, a common law marriage can occur only when:

- you are a heterosexual couple who lives together in a state that recognizes common law marriages

- you have lived together for a significant amount of time (not defined in any state). Despite much belief to the contrary, the length of time you live together does not by itself determine whether a common law marriage exists. No state law or court decision says seven years or ten years of cohabitation is all that is needed for a common law marriage. It's only one factor the court may consider, and

- you hold yourselves out to the community (your neighbors, friends, and coworkers) as a married couple—typically, this means using the same last name, referring to the other as "my husband" or "my wife," and filing a joint tax return. (For more on the subject of names, see Chapter 4.)

Courts most often apply the rules of common law marriage in situations where one partner dies without a will and the other claims there was a common law marriage so as to inherit property under intestate succession laws. These laws automatically give a share of property to a spouse but don't recognize an unmarried partner. (Chapter 9 provides an overview of intestate succession laws.)

If your state recognizes common law marriages where both partners are still living and your relationship meets the requirements, you may need to end your relationship by divorcing, just as you would if you had gotten married with a license and ceremony.

States Recognizing Common Law Marriage

Common law marriage is recognized only in the states listed below. If you live in any of these states and want to know the status of your relationship, you will need to read your state's law. Chapter 11 provides advice on doing legal research.

Alabama	New Hampshire
Colorado	Oklahoma
District of Columbia	Rhode Island
Iowa	South Carolina
Kansas	Texas
Montana	Utah

In a few other states, common law marriages will be recognized if they were created before the date the practice was abolished. These are Georgia (created before 1997), Idaho (created before 1996), Ohio (created before 1991), and Pennsylvania (created before 2005). Kentucky recognizes common law marriage only for purposes of awarding workers' compensation benefits.

Your Common Law Marriage in Colorado May Be Recognized in California

There's a little trick in the area of common law marriages. A state that doesn't provide for common law marriages will still recognize one if it was properly formed in a state that does provide for them. For example, if you have been living together in a common law marriage state for many years and then relocate to a non–common law marriage state soon before one of you dies, the laws of common law marriage will apply to the division of the deceased partner's estate.

EXAMPLE: Colorado allows common law marriages; California does not. If Bob and Carol started living together in Los Angeles in 1980 and are still happily coupled today (but have never gone through a marriage ceremony), they are not legally married, even if they pretend they are. If, however, they started living together in Colorado in 1985 with the intention of forming a common law marriage and moved to California in 1995, both Colorado and California will recognize their common law marriage as valid.

If you live together in a state that recognizes common law marriages and don't wish to be married, it's a good idea for you both to sign a statement making it clear that this is your joint intent. If you use the same last name and/or mix property together, it's essential that you do this. Otherwise a common law marriage may later be found to exist.

We've included a sample of this type of agreement below. You may want to use this one on its own, or integrate it into one of the living together contracts in Chapter 3.

CD-ROM

The forms CD includes a copy of the Agreement of Joint Intent Not to Have a Common Law Marriage, and Appendix B includes a blank tear-out copy of this form.

Agreement of Joint Intent Not to Have a Common Law Marriage

_____Wanda Oglethorpe_____ and _____Rich Walters_____

agree as follows:

We have been and plan to continue living together as two free, independent beings and neither of us has ever intended to enter into any form of marriage, common law or otherwise.

_____Wanda Oglethorpe_____   _____3/24/xx_____
Signature   Date
_____Rich Walters_____   _____3/24/xx_____
Signature   Date

Living Together Contracts

This section describes the basic legal rules of living together contracts and why they are so important for unmarried couples. Chapter 3 provides several different living together agreements you can tailor to your particular situation and directions for completing them. Be sure to read Chapter 10 for details on issues that may arise should you separate without having prepared a living together agreement.

Living Together Contracts— What They Are and Why Unmarried Couples Need One

A contract is no more than an agreement to do (or not to do) something. Marriage is a contractual relationship, even though the "terms" of the contract are rarely stated explicitly, or even known by the marrying couple. Saying "I do" commits a couple to a well-established set of state laws and rules governing, among other things, the couple's property rights should one spouse die or should the couple split up.

Unmarried couples, on the other hand, do not automatically agree to any state-imposed contractual agreement when they start a relationship. The couple may have a joint obligation to a landlord or to a mortgage company if they rent or buy a place together, but that obligation is no different than if they were roommates. Living together, in and of itself, does not create a contractual relationship, nor does it entitle you to a property settlement (or inheritance) should you split up (or should one of you die).

A typical unmarried couple buys property, mixes assets, and invests together, often without writing down how they intend to share the property if they split up. Then, if problems about money and property come up, they usually try to reach an understanding or a compromise. Sometimes they visit a therapist or ask their friends to help. If they split up, they quietly divide their possessions and go their separate ways, and they are not required to follow the legal rules that apply to marriage and divorce.

But some couples' relationships don't end so well. They don't quietly divide the property and move on, but instead bring their battle to court. Courts in most states have responded to these claims by trying to figure out what the couple had agreed to during the relationship and dividing their property accordingly. In doing so, courts have ruled that unmarried couples generally have the right to create whatever kind of living together contracts they want relating to financial and property concerns.

As a result, if an unmarried couple chooses to make an agreement together, or in some states if they act as though an agreement exists, that agreement will often be considered an enforceable contract—a "nonmarital agreement" in legal terms, or what we call a living together agreement in this book.

These agreements do not usually cover personal aspects of your relationship, such as who does the cooking, feeds the dog, or cleans the house. In fact, agreements on nonmonetary issues are unlikely to be enforced in court.

Sometimes living together contracts are made to protect each partner in case the relationship ends. But more often, couples enter into them to communicate their needs and expectations, define their rights, and enhance one or both partners' peace of mind at either the start of the relationship or when the couple makes a major purchase. Creating a well-crafted agreement not only helps you figure out how you really want to own your property, but also serves as a useful reminder if misunderstandings develop later or one of you dies without a will. Another important benefit of a living together agreement is that if one partner is supporting the other, or if one partner has given up a career in order to take care of the home or raise children, the agreement will protect the dependent partner by ensuring that issues of support and compensation are stated in writing. Otherwise, the dependent partner can be left with nothing after having given up a lot.

Even though some courts will enforce an oral agreement—or even an implied one—we believe that a written agreement is essential, though it's surely no substitute for trust and communication. A contract won't enable an unmarried couple to continue loving one another or prevent them from splitting up; but if times get hard, a written agreement can do wonders to reduce paranoia and confusion and help people deal with one another fairly. There are no national statistics on how many unmarried, cohabiting couples enter into living together contracts, but some lawyers say such contracts are on the rise as a result of more couples living together and new legal rulings that support the validity of living together agreements.

The Law and Living Together Contracts

Before the 1970s, couples who lived together without getting married existed in a legal vacuum. The law generally held that money and property belonged to the person who earned it or originally owned it. Contracts to share earnings or property usually weren't enforced by courts on the ground that the agreements were based on "meretricious consideration." Consideration is the price paid in a contract; meretricious means "having the nature of prostitution."

What the courts were saying was that living together contracts were illegal contracts for sex outside of marriage (cohabitation was illegal in all states until 1970), and illegal contracts cannot be enforced. This meant that unmarried couples were unable to enforce their agreements to share or divide property upon separation or death.

All this began to change in the mid-1970s, when the California Supreme Court decision in the case of *Marvin v. Marvin*, 557 P.2d 106 (1976), gave unmarried couples in California the right to make contracts to jointly own property or to support each other. (See "The *Marvin* Case," below.)

Because the *Marvin* case has often been referred to in the press as a defining event regarding the right of unmarried couples, many people assume that the decision is the law everywhere. This is an exaggeration. The California Supreme Court has no legal authority outside of California, except by way of example. However, the case's general proposition—that unmarried couples are subject to the principles of contract law—has been universally accepted (with some variations) by courts of every state.

This change in the law was significant. Now, contracts between people living together are no longer illegal.

The *Marvin* Case

The California Supreme Court decision in *Marvin v. Marvin*, 557 P.2d 106 (1976), thrust the issue of contract rights for unmarried couples into the media spotlight. This case rose to prominence partly because of the late actor Lee Marvin's fame, and partly because of the sweeping nature of the decision. The case arose from a dispute between Lee Marvin and Michelle Triola Marvin, the woman he lived with and supported for a number of years. After they broke up, Lee supported Michelle for a while, but then stopped. She sued him, claiming that they had an oral agreement—in exchange for her giving up her career as a dancer to be a full-time homemaker and companion, he said he would support her for the rest of her life.

The trial court initially ruled against Michelle, stating that living together contracts between unmarried couples were illegal and unenforceable. Michelle appealed to the California Supreme Court, which handed down the well-known *Marvin* decision, adopting several significant new legal rules for unmarried couples in California. Most importantly, it stated that unmarried couples did indeed have the right to make contracts that could be enforced in court.

The *Marvin* decision did not rule that an unmarried partner is automatically entitled to financial support (which the media termed "palimony") just as a divorcing spouse would be entitled to alimony. Instead, the unmarried partner must prove a legal basis for such a claim—such as a contract.

Palimony isn't a legal term; it was coined by journalists to describe the division of property or alimony-like support given by one member of an unmarried couple to the other after they break up.

Some General Legal Rules Regarding Living Together Contracts

Here are some of the basic principles governing living together contracts, established in the *Marvin* case and other court decisions.

Unmarried Couples Don't Have the Same Rights as Married Couples

The court in *Marvin* held that California divorce laws—alimony and the division of property—don't apply to unmarried couples. This means that a court can't use state divorce laws when your relationship ends; a court instead will divide up your property based on contract law principles. Without a contract of some kind, neither party will have any rights to the other's assets or to post-separation support—unless the couple lived in a state that recognizes common law marriage (see above) and held themselves out to be married. In this case, the relationship must be ended by divorce.

The general rule that marital property rules do not apply to unmarried couples has been widely adopted in other states. However, a few states that do not recognize common law marriage have nevertheless found ways to provide some property to a long-term living together partner when a relationship ends. For example, at least one court in the State of Washington has applied marital community property law to unmarried couples, even though the state doesn't recognize common law marriage. (*Connell v. Francisco*, 898 P.2d 831 (1995).)

Unmarried Couples May Enter Into Contracts

The court in *Marvin* stated that unmarried couples may make express contracts concerning their property, money, or other assets. An express contract is one made in words—oral or written.

This was a significant change in the law: Contracts between people living together in a sexual relationship were no longer illegal. The court added a caveat that is recognized in many other states: If the contract is explicitly based on sexual services performed by one partner, the contract is invalid. (See "Don't Mention Sex," below.)

The courts of nearly every state and the District of Columbia now enforce written contracts between unmarried partners. Most states also recognize oral (spoken) contracts. (Texas and Minnesota are the only states that have passed laws requiring contracts to be in writing, but courts in other states—including New York and New Mexico—have been unwilling to recognize implied agreements.) However, if one partner says there was an oral contract while the other emphatically denies it, a judge is unlikely to find that a contract was made, unless other evidence (such as a witness to the discussion about the contract) supports the contract claim.

In some instances, courts have recognized contracts that are implied from the circumstances of the couple's relationship (jointly contributing to purchase expensive items, for example) or the bases of their actions (supporting a partner while you're living together) if they can be proved. In these cases, the court finds not that the couple explicitly agreed to a contract, but that the couple acted as if a contract existed—that there was an unspoken agreement. Courts have found such implied contracts even when the cohabitation was part-time. For example, in a case involving the famous lawyer, Johnnie Cochran, the court ruled that even though Cochran spent as little as one night per week with a woman to whom he was not married, there could still be a valid and enforceable agreement for lifetime support. (*Cochran v. Cochran,* 89 Cal.App.4th 283 (2001).) In that case, Johnnie Cochran lived with Patricia, to whom he was not married, and their son, on a part-time basis for many years. During some of those years, Cochran was married to other women. Cochran provided Patricia and their son with monetary support. When Cochran stopped the support, Patricia

sued. Cochran argued that even if there was an implied agreement for lifetime support, it couldn't be enforced because the *Marvin* case only applied to cohabiting couples, and he and Patricia never cohabited. The court disagreed, ruling that even part-time living together was enough to meet the "*Marvin*" standards of cohabitation—and sent the case back to the trial court to hear evidence as to whether there was, in fact, an implied agreement for lifetime support.

CAUTION

Illinois, Georgia, and Louisiana couples beware. These states are all exceptions to the general rule of acceptance of contract rights for unmarried couples. There the courts still hold that the "immoral" nature of living together prevents a couple from forming a contract. (*Hewitt v. Hewitt,* 394 N.E. 2d 1204 (1979).) However, some progress has been made: At least one Illinois court has held that contracts not based entirely on living together, and not resembling marriage claims, may be enforced. (*Spafford v. Coats,* 118 Ill. App. 3d 566 (1983).)

Concepts of Fairness (Equity) Sometimes Protect the Rights of Members of Unmarried Couples

The courts of some states, including the California Supreme Court in the *Marvin* case, have recognized that the legal concepts of "unjust enrichment" and "implied contract" can apply to disputes between unmarried couples. In this context, unjust enrichment means that if one person contributes something (usually labor, such as housework) to make the other's property more valuable, with the reasonable expectation of receiving a benefit in return, that expectation will be honored. The legal notion of implied contract is somewhat different. If the circumstances of a couple's property dealings look like a contract to share ownership—like an unspoken agreement—the court will find an implied contract.

Janet works to repair and refinish Todd's boat for nine months, expecting a share of the resulting increased value. After they split up, Todd refuses to give her a cent. If Janet sued Todd to recover her share of the boat she would probably argue that Todd had been unjustly enriched by her work and that she should be paid for her labor.

Although the legal theory of unjust enrichment has been recognized by many states besides California, including Arizona and Florida, other states, such as New York, reject it. (*Morone v. Morone,* 50 N.Y. 2d 481 (1980).) Even in states that do recognize it, the practical problems inherent in trying to win a lawsuit based on unjust enrichment mean that it's rarely worth the trouble to file suit, unless large amounts of money are at stake.

The lesson to be learned: Unmarried partners should record all important understandings (contracts) in writing and never rely on courts to bail them out later.

To Be Safe, Write It Down

By now, one thing should be clear: You can avoid a host of legal problems by putting your living together agreement in writing. A written contract covering who owns what is the only way to protect yourself and honor your collective intentions— whether you want to keep all your property separate or share some or all of it. Without some type of written agreement, you may face serious and potentially expensive battles if you separate and can't agree on how to divide what you have acquired.

After they break up, Miriam sues Eric. She demands $100,000, an amount she claims Eric agreed to pay her if they should break up within one year of Miriam's moving 500 miles to live with Eric. When Eric emphatically denies that he had made any such agreement and Miriam can produce no evidence to back up her claim, the court rules for Eric.

Putting your contract in writing needn't be time-consuming or dreary (and it's certainly better than having a judge write one for you as part of an expensive court fight). Approach the task in the spirit of clarifying your understanding and preserving the shared memory of two fair-minded people. The details of how to accomplish this are in Chapter 3.

Sometimes one or both partners can be reluctant to sign a contract, believing it demonstrates a lack of trust in the other partner's word. To the contrary, we believe it's a healthy dose of realism, recognizing that over time memories fade and feelings change, and a written contract can make you feel secure that your intentions at the time you made it won't be forgotten. Without a written contract, it is almost impossible to enforce a claim of an oral contract in court. If your partner isn't willing to sign an agreement, don't rely on the oral promise—it's best to consider yourself to be without a contract at all.

Cases Based on Implied Contracts and Unjust Enrichment

Oregon. *In re Raimer and Wheeler*, 119 Or. App. 118, 849 P.2d 1122 (Or. Ct. App. 1993). The couple in this case lived together for six years and jointly operated several businesses, including a ranch. Shirley Wheeler owned the ranch and did the bookkeeping for the ranch. Rondal Ray Raimer worked the ranch, installed an updated irrigation system (which Wheeler reimbursed him for), brought additional acres under irrigation, and spent a substantial amount of his money on ranching supplies and equipment. When they split up, the Oregon courts awarded Raimer one-half of the appreciation of the ranch and reimbursement for the items he had purchased for the ranch because both parties had jointly operated it and treated it as a joint asset while living together.

Wisconsin. *Watts v. Watts*, 137 Wis.2d 506, 405 N.W.2d 303 (1987). Here, one partner gave up a career to move in with the other and become a full-time homemaker and mother. The court said she could sue under any theory available to non-cohabitants, including implied contract (they had an unspoken agreement that she'd be paid for her services), unjust enrichment (he benefited from her efforts and should compensate her), or partition of the jointly held property.

North Carolina. *Suggs v. Norris*, 364 S.E.2d 159 (1988). As in the *Watts* case above, the court allowed one partner to sue the other's estate under any legal theory available to non-cohabitants. She chose unjust enrichment, claiming that they had a joint business, all the proceeds went to him, and she should be paid for her work. She was.

California. *Byrne v. Laura*, 52 Cal. App. 4th 1054 (1997). After Byrne died, his living together partner sued his estate for a division of property. The trial court rejected Laura's claims as an effort to get marital support. The Court of Appeal reversed, finding that if Laura could prove, as she alleged, that Byrne promised to take care of her for the rest of her life, she might be entitled to half of his assets based on an oral or implied contract.

Connecticut. *Boland v. Catalano*, 202 Conn. 333, 521 A.2d 142 (1987). This couple lived together for nine years, pooling assets and earnings. The court found an implied contract to share income and the "fruits of joint labor."

Indiana. *Turner v. Freed*, 792 N.E.2d 947 (2003). A couple lived together on and off for more than five years, during which time the woman did all of the housework and raised the couple's son as well as taking care of her partner's son from a previous relationship. In addition, she helped her partner with his work for less-than-market rate pay. All of this allowed the partner to build his water-softening business, and when the couple broke up, the court found that the woman was entitled to a payment on the basis that, otherwise, the man would be unjustly enriched by her help.

New Jersey. *In re Estate of Roccamonte*, 174 N.J. 381, 808 A.2d 838 (2002). In another, more recent case, a Court of Appeal held that evidence showing the two parties had a marital-type relationship supported an argument that the male partner had promised to support the female cohabitant for life, and the promise was enforceable against the man's estate. The court also held that it wasn't necessary for the woman to be completely economically dependent on the man in order for a valid palimony agreement to exist—the promise itself was enough.

Don't Mention Sex

A living together contract that is explicitly based on sexual services performed by one partner may be ruled invalid if you end up in court. Explicit does not mean you used sexually explicit language in your agreement. It means that you made reference somewhere in your agreement to the fact that the two of you are having sex. The courts are very sensitive to any implication that they are legitimizing any act of prostitution (what is sometimes called "meretricious consideration"). If a court can imply from the wording of your contract that either party agreed to perform any sexual acts in order to receive a benefit from the contract, it may not be enforced. Even referring to one's partner as a "lover" has been held sufficient grounds to throw out a living together contract.

EXAMPLE: Dianne and Val lived together for many years in a state that didn't recognize common law marriages. Dianne died without leaving a will, and Val sued the estate for a share of the accumulated property, alleging that he gave up his career as a mountain-climbing guide to live with Dianne and be her lover, companion, and homemaker in exchange for a share in the property. Because the word "lover" implies that sexual services are an inseparable part of their agreement, many courts would rule that Val can't recover a share of the property.

However, some courts have ruled that, in some situations, a word such as "lover" can be deleted from the contract, while the rest of the agreement is enforced.

What Happens to Your Written Living Together Agreement If You Get Married?

Let's suppose you take our advice and write your own living together contract (using one of the forms in Chapter 3). Several years later you decide to tie the knot. Is your living together contract enforceable after marriage? Only if it was created shortly before your marriage or at a time when you both planned to be married, and only if it meets your state's standards for a premarital agreement. To be enforceable, premarital (prenuptial or premarriage) contracts must be made in contemplation of marriage. That means that most couples who prepared living together agreements will have to sign a new premarital agreement if they decide to marry and want to keep the same arrangements they've had.

Premarital agreements allow people who plan to marry to modify the contract imposed by state marital law. You can establish your own property ownership rules, different from the state's marital property laws, in a premarital agreement. So if you do want the property ownership terms of your living together agreement to apply during your marriage—for example, if you're an older couple and want to keep property separate—you can normally do this by rewriting your agreement as a premarital agreement. You can also agree in advance as to how much support one person will pay the other in case of divorce by using a prenuptial agreement.

Twenty-seven states have adopted the Uniform Premarital Agreement Act, which lets couples make premarital written contracts concerning ownership, management, and control of property; disposition of property at separation, divorce, and death; alimony; wills; and life insurance beneficiaries. (See "States That Have Adopted the Uniform Premarital Agreement Act," below, for the list.) The states that haven't adopted the Act have other premarital agreement laws, which often differ in only minor ways from the Act. In every state, couples are prohibited from including provisions about child custody or support—the court, not the couple, must make these decisions.

Premarital agreements are usually upheld by courts unless one person shows that the agreement is likely to promote divorce (for example, by including a large alimony amount in the event of divorce), was written and signed with the intention of divorcing, or was unfairly entered into (for example, a spouse giving up all rights to the other's future earnings without the advice of an attorney).

Here are the main provisions of the Uniform Act.

(a) *Parties to a premarital agreement may contract with respect to:*

  (1) *the rights and obligations of each of the parties in any of the property of either or both of them whenever and wherever acquired or located;*

  (2) *the right to buy, sell, use, transfer, exchange, abandon, lease, consume, expend, assign, create a security interest in, mortgage, encumber, dispose of, or otherwise manage and control property;*

  (3) *the disposition of property upon separation, marital dissolution, death, or the occurrence or nonoccurrence of any other event;*

  (4) *the modification or elimination of spousal support;*

  (5) *the making of a will, trust, or other arrangement to carry out the provisions of the agreement;*

  (6) *the ownership rights in, and disposition of, the death benefit from a life insurance policy;*

  (7) *the choice of law governing the construction of the agreement; and*

  (8) *any other matter, including their personal rights and obligations, not in violation of public policy or a statute imposing a criminal penalty.*

(b) *The right of a child to support may not be adversely affected by a premarital agreement.*

States That Have Adopted the Uniform Premarital Agreement Act

Arizona	Montana
Arkansas	Nebraska
California	Nevada
Connecticut	New Jersey
Delaware	New Mexico
District of Columbia	North Carolina
Hawaii	North Dakota
Idaho	Oregon
Illinois	Rhode Island
Indiana	South Dakota
Iowa	Texas
Kansas	Utah
Maine	Virginia
	Wisconsin

If you wish to marry and convert your living together contract into a premarital agreement, follow these steps:

1. Use your upcoming marriage as an opportunity to take another look at your agreement; make any agreed-upon updates and changes.

2. Rewrite your agreement. Call it a prenuptial or premarital agreement, and state that it is made in contemplation of marriage and does not take effect until you marry.

3. Because even a small mistake can result in a court later refusing to enforce your agreement, have your new agreement reviewed by an attorney experienced in this area. In most cases, each partner should have an attorney review the agreement.

4. Sign your agreement in front of a notary public.

For more information about premarital agreements, see *Prenuptial Agreements: How to Write a Fair & Lasting Contract*, by Katherine E. Stoner and Shae Irving (Nolo).

Special Issues for Seniors

The fastest-growing demographic group among unmarried couples is seniors (one source says that over the past decade, the number of unmarried partners over the age of 65 has increased by 70%). All of the same reasons that younger couples give for not marrying may apply to seniors as well—not wanting to repeat experiences from a bad marriage or not wanting the state involved in the relationship, for example—but for many seniors, finances are the biggest issue preventing legal matrimony. There are a number of common concerns that seniors have about tying the knot.

Social Security and Pensions. If you are divorced and you remarry before age 60, you'll lose Social Security income from a previous marriage to which you would have otherwise been entitled. (However, you may get more from your new spouse's Social Security payment, so use the calculator available from the Social Security Administration at www .ssa.gov to figure out whether this is a real problem for you.) The same is often true of pension benefits awarded to you as part of a divorce settlement.

Marriage can also affect the amount of taxes you're required to pay on your Social Security benefits when you begin receiving them. A single person can earn $25,000 per year before being taxed on those benefits, while a married couple can have total income of only $32,000 before taxes are levied.

Estate Planning. If you have college-age children, marriage may mean that your new spouse's income is counted for financial aid purposes, which in turn may reduce the aid your child is eligible for. And if you have adult children and want them to inherit the bulk of your estate, you must use careful estate planning to ensure that your wishes are carried out. Spouses have certain inheritance rights in many states, and if you want to do something that limits those rights you must make sure your documents are in good order.

Alimony. If you were in a long-term marriage that ended in divorce and you're receiving alimony, you'll most likely have to give that up when you remarry—check your divorce order.

Medical Expenses. When you marry, you take on responsibility for your partner's support and care. If your new spouse has serious health concerns, you may not want to take on that financial responsibility. Unmarried couples, no matter how intimately connected in personal and financial ways, don't take on this same responsibility.

With all of these potential concerns, it's no wonder seniors are cohabiting in droves. If you are considering getting hitched, we'd recommend seeing an attorney or tax professional who can advise you about the pros and cons of marriage in your particular circumstances.

Living Together Agreements: Why and How

In case you didn't get the message from Chapter 2, it's extremely important to spell out your financial and property arrangements in a written agreement—what we call a living together contract or living together agreement. Among other things, an agreement can help avoid problems when you commingle money and property; make clear what your intentions and expectations are regarding property ownership, caring for children, covering household expenses, and the like; and ease the division of property during a breakup. Examples of problems unmarried couples face if they don't have a living together agreement are discussed throughout the remainder of this book. For example, in Chapter 4, you'll learn why it's important to put in writing your agreement to commingle or keep your property separate. Chapter 6 discusses why you should have a contract if you plan to jointly own a home, and Chapter 10 explains how *not* having a written agreement can cause major problems if you break up.

Of all the reasons to write out your agreement, avoiding a court fight is probably the most important. From a practical perspective, little gets resolved in court without costs and legal fees eating up the lion's share of the money and property in dispute. Those of you who have been through a contested divorce already know this. Once you add up the time, emotional pain, and bitterness that are always a part of our adversary process, you should be reaching for your pen (or keyboard).

Obviously, you don't need a living together contract if you have no assets or are in a brief relationship. But in a long-term and serious relationship, whether you're basking in the glow of just having "joined forces" or you've been together 20 years, you should consider the legal consequences of how you live.

This chapter on living together contracts is designed to help you clarify your understanding about your life as a couple. Talking out (and writing down) your intentions should bring you closer, and help you overcome any fears or concerns you may have about money, property, and your future. And if you do split up, having an agreement helps you avoid litigation. If a lawsuit is filed, the judge will focus on interpreting your written agreement, not on trying to infer an implied contract from your behavior, or determining who's right if one of you claims you had an oral contract and the other disagrees.

Your living together contract need not be like the fine-print monsters forced on you by car salesmen or insurance agents. A simple, comprehensive, and functional document using common English is much better than one loaded with "heretofores," "pursuants," and other legalese. You can, and should, design your agreement to say exactly what you both want, in words you both understand.

This chapter shows how to do just that, and includes a variety of contracts for different situations. All of our contracts are written in plain English and easy to follow. Please read (or at least skim) all the contracts in this chapter before deciding which one to use. You may choose to copy the contract verbatim, customize one to meet your specific needs, or use our contract as a starting point for your own agreement.

CROSS REFERENCE

Chapters in this book provide agreements covering other aspects of your relationship, including:

- Renting a home together (Chapter 5): How to prepare an agreement spelling out your responsibilities to each other as tenants, covering who pays what portion of the rent and expenses, who gets the place if you split up, and the like

- Buying or owning a house together (Chapter 6): How to write a contract for owning a house together, including sharing costs and ownership, what happens to the house if you break up or one of you dies, and how to deal with disputes over the house

- Having children together: How to prepare paternity statements (Chapter 7) or custody agreements (Chapter 8)
- Preparing a will and other estate planning documents (Chapter 9)
- Drafting a settlement agreement should you separate (Chapter 10).

Ten Tips for Writing a Living Together Agreement

The rest of this chapter provides specific instructions and forms you will need to prepare a living together agreement. Here are some basic tips to keep in mind as you go:

1. Talk it out and reach an understanding. Before you can prepare a written agreement covering ownership of your property, the two of you must agree on how you will conduct your financial affairs. This is especially true if one of you makes sacrifices for the relationship, such as moving a long distance or giving up a job to care for small children. How you reach an understanding about money and property issues is up to you. We suggest that before trying to reach an agreement, you carefully read the rest of this chapter (and if real property is involved, Chapter 6) so you understand your options.

Many people find that creating a contract forces them to deal with the very guts of their relationship. This is a healthy thing to do now and then—but it can also be trying. Take your time; don't expect to finish in an evening. A good contract often involves compromise and accommodation. Preparing your contract should be an affirmative act, but it's up to you to make it so. If you get bogged down in trading this for that and wonder why you're dealing with all of this legal mumbo-jumbo, take a break and get back to it when you're both feeling more cheerful.

2. Cover the basics—property and money. A living together contract can be comprehensive, covering every aspect of your relationship, or it can be specific, covering only your new car purchase. Living together contracts can include a wide variety of economic arrangements. You can keep all property separate, or agree that what belongs to one belongs to both. Or perhaps your agreement will be somewhere in between—such as keeping property brought into the relationship separate, but agreeing to share expenses equally and make joint purchases after you start living together. But regardless of how detailed your contract is or how much you decide to include, you must deal with two basic issues: money and property.

3. Don't try to cover everything in one contract. Relationships and people are complicated. If you try to cover too much ground in one contract, you'll get bogged down and never figure it all out. It's often better to have several smaller agreements covering specific issues. For example, your property agreement should be separate from whatever agreement you have to support a partner who's in school. Your agreement on sharing housing costs and ownership should also be separate, as explained in Chapters 5 and 6.

4. Don't get personal. As we've explained in Chapter 2, agreements between unmarried partners are generally enforceable to the extent they cover property, payment for services (excluding sex), or payment in exchange for a person giving something up, such as a job or a house. A court is unlikely to enforce an agreement that covers nonmonetary issues. The contracts included in this chapter pertain only to property and finances. They do not cover the day-to-day details of your relationship, such as who will do the dishes, who will walk the dog, how many overnight guests you'll allow, and whose favorite painting goes in the living room. A court won't—and shouldn't be asked to—enforce these kinds of personal agreements. If your agreement includes personal as well as financial clauses, a court might declare the entire contract illegal or frivolous and refuse to enforce any of it—including the more important financial clauses. Obviously, you need to be clear with your partner on things such as housecleaning and cooking. Just don't mix up these day-to-day issues with the bigger legal issues of living together.

5. Don't mention sex. A living together agreement that is explicitly based on sexual services performed by one partner—even a reference somewhere in the agreement to the fact that the two of you are having sex—may be ruled invalid if you end up in court.

6. Don't prepare a living together agreement about sharing property if one or both of you are married to someone else. In many states, if the partner who is still married is permanently separated from his or her spouse, it may be possible to create a legally valid living together contract to share property. Unfortunately, however, little is certain in this legal gray area where there are few court rulings. Therefore, if one of you is still married to someone else, it's best to agree in writing to keep all your property separate until the divorce is final. Then you can write a new agreement, pooling your property if you both wish to do so. For more on legal issues that arise when you live with someone while you're still married, see Chapter 8.

7. Get legal advice before signing an agreement if a lot of money or property or complicated estate planning is involved. This is just common sense—particularly if one partner has substantially more assets than the other.

8. Get legal help if bargaining power isn't equal. A living together contract might not be enforced if a judge concludes that one person has taken unfair advantage of the other. For example, a court is unlikely to uphold a one-sided living together contract between an experienced lawyer and an unsophisticated, but wealthy, 19-year-old who just moved to America and speaks little English, under which the immigrant agrees to support the lawyer.

9. Get legal help if you live in Illinois. In Illinois, it's doubtful that any living together contract is enforceable. As explained in Chapter 2, courts in Illinois remain an exception to the general acceptance of contract rights for unmarried couples. You may be able to create a legal living together contract in Illinois by stating, in writing, that your agreement is simply a contract to share the ownership of certain property and has nothing to do with your personal relationship. See a lawyer for advice.

10. Agree in advance to mediate disputes that may arise over your agreement. We recommend mediation because it is cheaper, faster, and usually less painful than litigation. All of the contracts in this chapter include a general clause stating that you agree to bring in a third party to mediate any dispute that may arise out of the contract. (For an example, see Clause 6 in the Agreement to Share Property, below.) The same clause provides that one partner may request formal arbitration should mediation prove unsuccessful. To learn what's involved with mediation or arbitration be sure to read Chapter 10, which provides detailed information on dispute resolution.

What Happens to Your Living Together Agreement If You Get Married?

Your living together contract will be enforceable after marriage only if it was created shortly before your marriage at a time when you both planned to marry. To be enforceable, prenuptial (or premarital) contracts must be made in contemplation of marriage and they must meet the applicable state standards for premarital agreements wherever you live. For more details, including how to turn your living together contract into a prenuptial agreement, see Chapter 2.

Property Agreements

This section includes two living together agreements designed to cover the major areas of concern to most unmarried couples—ownership of property (car, house, furniture, and the like) and assets, and sharing of income and expenses. You have several options. You can keep the property that each of you owned before your agreement separate or you can share it. You can transfer ownership of none, some, or all property to your partner. You can agree to split income and expenses in many different ways, some equal, some not. You can keep separate bank and checking accounts, credit cards, and insurance, or create joint accounts. You can decide in advance who gets what should you separate, or agree to a process for resolving any disputes that come up should you separate.

We suggest you start with one of our basic contracts:

- Agreement to Keep Property Separate, or

- Agreement to Share Property.

Read both contracts and see which one works better for you, editing as appropriate as discussed in "Signing a Property Agreement or Other Living Together Contract," below.

CD-ROM

The forms CD includes copies of both the Agreement to Keep Property Separate and the Agreement to Share Property as well as Attachment A (Separately Owned Property) and Attachment B (Jointly Owned Property). Appendix B includes blank tear-out copies of all these forms.

Agreement to Keep Property Separate

Especially in the first year or two after they get together, most unmarried couples keep all or most of their money and property separate—with the occasional exception of a joint account to pay household bills or an agreement to purchase one or more items jointly.

You may think that keeping your property ownership separate is so simple that you don't need a written agreement. Think again. Because most states recognize oral contracts between unmarried couples (as discussed in Chapter 2), the lack of a written agreement can be an invitation for one partner to later claim the existence of an oral property-sharing agreement. This is what commonly occurs in the so-called palimony cases that regularly hit the headlines.

To avoid the possibility of future misunderstandings concerning property ownership, use the Agreement to Keep Property Separate form shown below to confirm that each of you plans to keep your property and income separate unless you make a specific written agreement otherwise. This agreement keeps all of your property separate, including property you brought into the relationship as well as property you purchased with your own money or received by gift or inheritance while living together.

TIP

Be sure to read "Buying and Investing Together" in Chapter 4 for other ways to maintain your financial independence.

Here are a few things to keep in mind if you're using the Agreement to Keep Property Separate.

Clause 2 states that you will attach a separate list of major items you own to the Agreement. Prepare an attachment, such as the sample Separately Owned Property form shown here, listing the personal property each of you owns. If this is the first attachment to your contract, label it Attachment A as shown here. (See "How to Edit or Modify a Living Together Agreement," below, for advice on preparing attachments.) This sample is just a partial list of what most couples own. You should be very specific—at least list all items worth $100 or more. Be sure to update your list from time to time—once a year is a good period.

Agreement to Keep Property Separate

_____ Rose Jackson _____ and _____ Alan Lewis _____

agree as follows:

1. This contract sets forth our rights and obligations toward each other. We intend to abide by the provisions in a spirit of cooperation and good faith.

2. All property owned by either of us as of the date of this agreement will remain the separate property of its owner and cannot be transferred to the other person unless this is done in writing. We have each attached a list of our major items of separate property to this contract. (See Attachment A, Separately Owned Property.)

3. The income each of us earns—as well as any items or investments either of us purchases with our income—belongs absolutely to the person who earns the money unless there is a written joint ownership agreement as provided in Clause 6.

4. We will each maintain our own separate bank, credit card, investment, and retirement accounts, and neither of us will in any way be responsible for the debts of the other (if we register as domestic partners in a community that makes this option available and, by so doing, the law requires us to be responsible for each other's basic living expenses, we agree to assume the minimum level of reciprocal responsibility required by the law).

5. Expenses for routine household items and services, which include groceries, utilities, rent and cleaning supplies, will be shared equally.

6. From time to time, we may decide to keep a joint checking or savings account for a specific purpose (for example, to pay household expenses), or to own some property jointly (for example, to purchase a television). If so, the details of our joint ownership agreement will be put in writing (either in a written contract or a deed, title slip, or other joint ownership document).

7. Should either of us receive real or personal property by gift or inheritance, the property belongs absolutely to the person receiving the gift or inheritance and cannot be transferred to the other except in writing.

8. In the event we separate, each of us will be entitled to immediate possession of our separate property.

9. Any dispute arising out of this contract will be mediated by a third person mutually acceptable to both of us. The mediator's role will be to help us arrive at a solution, not to impose one on us. If good faith efforts to arrive at our own solution to all issues in dispute with the help of a mediator prove to be fruitless, either of us may make a written request to the other that the dispute be arbitrated. In that case, our dispute will be submitted to arbitration under the rules of the American Arbitration Association, and one arbitrator will hear our dispute. The decision of the arbitrator will be binding on us and will be enforceable in any court that has jurisdiction over the controversy. By agreeing to arbitration, we each agree to give up the right to a jury trial.

10. This agreement represents our complete understanding regarding our living together and replaces any and all prior agreements, written or oral. It can be amended, but only in writing, and any amendments must be signed by both of us.

11. If a court finds any portion of this contract to be illegal or otherwise unenforceable, the remainder of the contract is still in full force and effect.

_____ Rose Jackson _____   _____ March 2, 20xx _____
Rose Jackson   Date

_____ Alan Lewis _____   _____ March 2, 20xx _____
Alan Lewis   Date

Attachment A
Separately Owned Property

The following is the separate personal property of _____ Rose Jackson _____:

Living room furniture: blue sofabed, red armchair, oak rocking chair, and glass coffee table

Dell personal computer

King-size bed

Cuisinart food processor

The following is the separate personal property of _____ Alan Lewis _____:

Oriental rugs in living room and dining room

Pine dining room table and six chairs

Stereo system, TV, and VCR

Kitchen table and matching chairs

Making an agreement about the property you bring into the relationship may seem unnecessary, but it's not. Think about trying to separate it all ten years from now, when you've both been referring to everything around the house as "ours."

TIP

A property inventory will also come in very handy for insurance purposes should your property be stolen or damaged in a fire, flood, or other natural disaster.

Clause 4 of the Agreement to Keep Property Separate specifies that if you register as a domestic partner in a program that makes you responsible for each other's basic living expenses, you agree to only the minimal level of reciprocal financial responsibility. We include this language because, as discussed in Chapter 2, registering as domestic partners may imply that you intend to share ownership of property unless you include this type of disclaimer. Of course, if no domestic partnership programs are available to you or you do not intend to register as domestic partners, you can delete this sentence of Clause 4.

Clause 5 provides that you will share expenses for household items and services equally. If you have a different arrangement, or want to spell out how you will split expenses of nonhousehold items, such as insurance or car repairs, you can edit Clause 5 accordingly.

Clause 6 refers to a joint ownership agreement that you may prepare from time to time—for example, if you purchase a television or computer together. There's a sample agreement below that you can use for this purpose. It covers issues such as what happens to the jointly owned property if you separate.

Agreement to Share Property

Especially if you have been together several years or more and have begun to purchase property jointly (a new car or bed, for example), you may want to do what a fair number of unmarried couples do—abandon your agreement to keep property separate, and instead treat property that either of you purchases as jointly owned. If this is your understanding, write it down. Use the Agreement to Share Property form to establish that all newly acquired property—except that given to or inherited by one partner, or that which is clearly specified in writing as separate property—is to be jointly owned by both, and equally divided should you separate.

To complete the Agreement to Share Property, simply fill in your names, fill in the blank in Clause 2, and sign the agreement.

Note that Clause 3 assumes that you will attach a list of the property each of you owned prior to the date of your agreement. (See sample Attachment A, Separately Owned Property, above.) Clause 3 also assumes you will attach a list of jointly owned property. (See sample Attachment B, Jointly

Owned Property.) You may be as detailed as you want in preparing these separate property lists, but at least include major items (valued at $100 or more). Be sure to update your lists from time to time—either when you make a major purchase or at least once a year.

Signing a Property Agreement or Other Living Together Contract

Whether you use one of our living together contracts or design your own, photocopy (or print an extra copy of) the final draft (including all attachments) so you and your partner each have a copy. If you alter one of our forms by writing or typing in changes, be sure that you and your partner initial each change before signing the agreement.

Sign and date both copies of your agreement. It makes no difference who keeps which—both are "originals."

Keep your agreement in a safe place, along with copies of other important documents, such as insurance papers, title slips to jointly held property, lease, copies of wills, important financial papers, and the like.

TIP

Notarization is optional. Usually, having your agreement notarized isn't necessary. However, in some states you must notarize the agreement if it covers issues affecting real estate. If that is the case, sign the agreement before a notary. Then if you wish, you can record the agreement at your county records office. (Chapter 6 explains how to notarize and record a house ownership contract.) Notarization doesn't make a contract legal or enforceable. It simply proves that your signatures aren't forged, which can never hurt.

Agreement to Share Property

_____Beth Spencer_____ and _____Rich Portman_____

agree as follows:

1. This contract sets forth our rights and obligations toward each other. We intend to abide by this agreement in a spirit of cooperation and good faith.

2. All earned income received by either of us after the date of this contract and all property purchased with this income belongs in equal shares to both of us with the following exceptions: _____

   _____

3. All real or personal property earned or accumulated by either of us prior to the date of this agreement (except jointly owned property listed in Attachment B of this agreement), including all future income this property produces, is the separate property of the person who earned or accumulated it and cannot be transferred to the other except in writing. Attached to this agreement in the form of Attachments A, Separately Owned Property, and B, Jointly Owned Property, are lists of the major items of property each of us owns separately and both of us own jointly as of the date of this agreement.

4. Should either of us receive real or personal property by gift or inheritance, that property, including all future income it produces, belongs absolutely to the person receiving the gift or inheritance and cannot be transferred to the other except in writing.

5. In the event we separate, all jointly owned property will be divided equally.

6. Any dispute arising out of this contract will be mediated by a third person mutually acceptable to both of us. The mediator's role will be to help us arrive at a solution, not to impose one on us. If good faith efforts to arrive at our own solution to all issues in dispute with the help of a mediator prove to be fruitless, either of us may make a written request to the other that the dispute be arbitrated. In that case, our dispute will be submitted to arbitration under the rules of the American Arbitration Association, and one arbitrator will hear our dispute. The decision of the arbitrator will be binding on us and shall be enforceable in any court that has jurisdiction over the controversy. By agreeing to arbitration, we each agree to give up the right to a jury trial.

7. This agreement represents our complete understanding regarding our living together and replaces any and all prior agreements, written or oral. It can be amended, but only in writing, and any amendments must be signed by both of us.

8. If a court finds any portion of this contract to be illegal or otherwise unenforceable, the remainder of the contract is still in full force and effect.

_____Beth Spencer_____   _____September 15, 20xx_____
Beth Spencer   Date

_____Rich Portman_____   _____September 15, 20xx_____
Rich Portman   Date

Attachment B
Jointly Owned Property

The following property is jointly owned by _____ Beth Spencer and Rich Portman _____
in equal proportions except as otherwise noted:

_____ Sony video camera _____

_____ Electric lawn mower _____

_____ Deck furniture including table, umbrella, and six chairs _____

_____ Blue ceramic dinnerware from Pottery Barn (set of six) _____

_____ All linens and towels _____

How to Edit or Modify a Living Together Agreement

One of the property agreements or other living together contracts in this book may meet your needs perfectly. However, it's more likely you'll want to make some changes to fit your circumstances—either the first time you prepare an agreement or sometime down the road.

Editing a form in this book. Many unmarried couples will be able to use one of our living together agreements as is, simply filling in a few blanks and signing it. You may decide to edit or delete part or all of a particular clause. Or you may want to add a clause. Changing an agreement is obviously no problem if you use the forms CD (see "How to Use the CD-ROM," Appendix A of this book).

But if you need to change a tear-out copy of a property agreement or other living together contract, take the following steps:

1. If you want to delete all or part of a clause, simply cross out the words or clauses you want to delete—then each of you must intial each deletion. If you want to delete several provisions, you'll need to renumber the clauses, or redo the entire contract to avoid confusion.

2. If you want to add words to a clause, you must insert the new language into the specific clause of the agreement, or refer to it as an attachment, by adding the words: "Clause [number] continued on Attachment A [or B, C, and so on] of [name agreement]."

   EXAMPLE: "Clause 2 continued on Attachment A of Agreement to Share Property."

   Similarly, if you want to add a new clause, insert the words "Agreement continued on Attachment B of [name agreement]" after the last clause of the agreement and before the place where the agreement gets signed.

3. Make your own attachment form, using a sheet of blank paper. At the top, write "Attachment A [or B, C, and so on] to [name the agreement] between [insert your names]—Page 1 of 1."

   EXAMPLE: "Attachment A to Agreement to Share Property Between Beth Spencer and Rich Portman—Page 1 of 1."

   If you need more than one page, the first page of the attachment should be labeled "Page 1 of 2," the second "Page 2 of 2," and so on.

4. Begin the attachment with the words "a continuation of Clause [number]" and then add the clause number. Or, if you're adding a new clause, simply write the new clause number.

5. Type or print the new information or agreement.

6. Both you and your partner should initial the attachment at the bottom of each page.

7. Staple the attachment to your agreement.

Changing a form after you've signed it. Modifications of a contract should always be in writing. This is because ancient, but still applicable, legal doctrines make most oral modifications of a written contract invalid. In addition, our contracts expressly state that any changes must be in writing. A modification can simply state that you agree to change your contract, and then set out the change. Date and sign all modifications. But if you're making really major changes, tear up the old agreement and start over.

You should evaluate your living together agreement from time to time (maybe once a year on your anniversary) as your relationship or your situation changes.

SEE AN EXPERT

See a lawyer if you're making major changes to a living together agreement—or if lots of money is at stake. By the time you finish modifying one of our agreements, your changes may pretty much replace the original. If that's the case, and especially if it refers to significant amounts of money or if property is involved, have a lawyer look at your living together agreement.

Optional Clauses to Add to Living Together Agreements

Here are some clauses you may want to add to your property agreement or other living together contract.

Property Division at Death. It's legal (but not required) to include a clause stating that if one partner dies, the survivor keeps the jointly owned property. We include this type of provision in some, but not all, of our contracts, depending on whether we think it's likely to be desired. (For example, see Clause 6 of the Sample Joint Purchase Agreement, below.) If a contract does contain a clause stating that the survivor becomes the sole owner of a particular piece of property when the first partner dies, it takes precedence over any provision in a will that says otherwise.

If there is no mention of what happens to property at death in a living together agreement that covers jointly owned property, each person can leave his or her portion by will or other estate plan to anyone (including, of course, one's partner). We discuss how to do this in Chapter 9. The one major exception to this rule is for property (such as a house) held in joint tenancy with right of survivorship, which automatically goes to the surviving joint tenant(s) when one joint tenant dies. (Chapter 6 discusses this issue in detail, and Chapter 9 covers wills and estate planning.)

If a clause covering property division at death is not in an agreement and you want it to be, or if you want to delete this language from a form, modify your agreement accordingly.

Agreement to Attend Counseling Before Separating. None of the agreements in this book contain a provision requiring that a couple attend counseling together if one of them wishes to separate. Unless both partners are willing to participate at the time the problems arise, making this commitment in advance serves little purpose. However, if you want to include such a provision, here is sample language you can use (or modify) as part of your living together agreement:

If one of us wants to end the living together relationship and the other doesn't, before splitting up we agree to participate in good faith in at least three conciliation sessions with a mutually acceptable third party. If, after a minimum of three sessions, one of us still wants to end our living together relationship, it will end.

Agreement to Share Ownership of a Joint Purchase

Many people make purchases item by item, understanding that whoever makes the purchase owns the property. George buys the kitchen table and chairs, and Edna buys the lamp and stereo. If they split up, each keeps the property he or she bought. In this situation, George and Edna would use the Agreement to Keep Property Separate, above.

Purchases also can be pooled. Edna and George can jointly own everything bought during the relationship, and divide it all 50-50 if they separate. In this case, the Agreement to Share Property, above, would be appropriate.

While these types of consistent approaches to property ownership may simplify things, they are required by neither law nor logic. Edna and George could choose a combination of the two methods. Some items may be separately owned, some pooled 50-50, and some shared in proportion to how much money each contributed toward the purchase price or how much labor each put into upkeep.

How to Prepare an Agreement for a Joint Purchase

Many unmarried couples opt for a basic keeping-things-separate approach, at least when they first get together. However, an unmarried couple will often want to own one, or sometimes several, major items together, as would be the case if they pool income to buy a car and an expensive sound system. Clause 6 in the Agreement to Keep Property Separate allows you to easily do this.

You can prepare an Agreement for a Joint Purchase using the form shown below. Simply fill in the details of your joint purchase, including the item or property bought, the percentage of ownership (such as 50-50 or 60-40) each of you has, and how you will deal with the property should you split up. For example, you may specify that one person automatically has the right (of first refusal) to buy out the other's share. You may agree to do a simple coin toss or come up with your own approach depending upon the particular property.

CD-ROM

The forms CD includes a copy of the Agreement for a Joint Purchase, and Appendix B includes a blank tear-out copy of this form.

You can edit this Agreement for a Joint Purchase as you see fit, or use it as a starting point to prepare your own agreement. For example, if one of you purchased the jointly owned item by credit card, you may want to add details to Clause 2, clarifying that one person made the purchase, but that the item is jointly owned. See the Sample Joint Purchase Agreement When One Partner Is the Legal Borrower, for ideas.

CAUTION

Only the partner whose name is on the credit card is legally obligated to pay, even if you have an agreement splitting the cost. If only one of you signs a credit agreement to purchase an item, only that person is legally obligated to pay the creditor. This is true even if you and your partner sign an agreement to share ownership and payments. The creditor will accept money from anyone and properly credit the account, but if a payment isn't made, the creditor will pursue only the person whose name is on the account. Thus, Karen doesn't have to pay Racafrax if Marcus stops paying the bill for the furniture he purchased with Karen but charged to his account. Karen has a legal contract with Marcus, but not with Racafrax. Of course, the store doesn't care who pays the bill. Karen can send the money and the store will credit Marcus's account.

Buying a Car Together

It's not uncommon for unmarried couples to purchase a car together. If you do so, be aware that buying a car means entering into a series of agreements with third parties (for example, a car dealer, a bank, and an insurance company) that are binding regardless of the status of your relationship.

It pays to understand all of your options and choose an arrangement that is financially viable.

Sole Ownership. If you intend that the vehicle will belong to only one partner, but the other partner will advance part or all of the down payment in the form of a loan, the borrower should sign a written contract to repay. This contract is a called a "promissory note." A sample promissory note and directions for use are included in Chapter 6. If you choose this option, you should register the vehicle in the borrower's name only.

If you decide that only one of you will own the car, you can include the other partner as an "additional driver" on the car insurance. One advantage to sole car ownership: If the car is involved in an accident, only the partner who owns the car can be sued. (But if the other partner was driving, that person could be sued for negligent actions.)

Joint Ownership. If you intend to own the vehicle jointly, you'll need a written agreement outlining the details. This is especially important if only one

Agreement for a Joint Purchase

_____ Amy Randolph _____ and _____ Brett Bow _____

agree as follows:

1. We will jointly acquire and own a _____Sony flat-screen television set_____ (the Property) at a cost of $ __1850__ .

2. We will own the Property in the following shares [fill in]:

    _____Amy_____ will own _50_ % of the Property and _____Brett_____ will own _50_ % of the Property.

3. Should we separate and cease living together, one of the following will occur:

    a. If one of us wants the Property and the other doesn't, the person who wants the Property will pay the other the fair market value (see Clause 4) of his or her share of the Property.

    b. If both of us want the Property, the decision will be made in the following way [choose one]:

    ☒ (1) Right of First Refusal. _____Amy_____ shall have the right of first refusal and may purchase _____Brett's_____ share of the Property for its fair market value (see Clause 4). _____Amy_____ will then become sole owner of the Property.

    ☐ (2) Coin Toss Method. We will flip a coin to determine who is entitled to the Property. The winner, upon paying the loser for his or her share of ownership, will become the sole owner of the Property.

    ☐ (3) Other. _____ .

4. Should either of us decide to end the relationship, we will do our best to agree on the fair current value of the Property. If we can't agree on a price, we will jointly choose a neutral appraiser and abide by that person's decision.

5. Should we separate and neither of us wants the Property—or if we can't agree on a fair price—we will advertise it to the public, sell it to the highest bidder, and divide the money according to our respective ownership shares as set forth in Clause 2.

6. Should either of us die while we are living together, the Property will belong absolutely to the survivor. (If either of us makes a will or other estate plan, this agreement shall be reflected in that document.)

7. This agreement can be changed, but only in writing, and any changes must be signed by both of us.

8. Any dispute arising out of this contract will be mediated by a third person mutually acceptable to both of us. The mediator's role will be to help us arrive at a solution, not to impose one on us. If good faith efforts to arrive at our own solution to all issues in dispute with the help of a mediator prove to be fruitless, either of us may pursue other legal remedies.

9. If a court finds any portion of this contract to be illegal or otherwise unenforceable, the remainder of the contract is still in full force and effect.

_____Amy Randolph_____   _____February 17, 20xx_____
Amy Randolph   Date

_____Brett Bow_____   _____February 17, 20xx_____
Brett Bow   Date

Sample Joint Purchase Agreement When One Partner Is the Legal Borrower

Marcus Lyons and Karen Moore agree as follows:

1. Marcus has entered into an agreement with Racafrax Company to purchase a bedroom set consisting of one king-size bed, one double dresser, two night stands, and two lamps at a total cost of $2,500.

2. Marcus has agreed to pay to Racafrax that sum in monthly installments of $240, including interest, for 12 months, due on the first of every month beginning January 1, 20xx.

3. We intend that this bedroom set will be owned equally by both of us and that we each will pay one-half the cost.

4. Karen will pay Marcus $120 per month at least one week before each monthly payment is due. Marcus will pay the entire installment due to Racafrax in a timely manner.

5. Should either of us fail to make his or her share of the payment, the other will have the right to do so, and the ownership percentage of this person will be proportionately increased. If, for example, Karen makes sixteen payments (all of hers and four of Marcus's), she'd own $^{16}/_{24}$, or $^{2}/_{3}$, of the furniture.

6. Each of us shall keep a record of payments made. All payments shall be made by check.

7. If we stop living together, Marcus may buy the bedroom set from Karen by agreeing to be solely responsible for the rest of the monthly payments to Racafrax and by paying Karen one-half of the difference, if any, between the bedroom set's current resale value, and the amount of money still owed to Racafrax.

8. If Marcus does not want the furniture under the terms set out in Paragraph 7, Karen may buy the bedroom set by paying the full amount still owed to Racafrax, so that Marcus no longer is obligated to make payments to Racafrax, and by paying Marcus one-half of the difference, if any, between the bedroom set's current resale value and the amount of money still owed to Racafrax. Alternatively, Karen may enter into an arrangement with Racafrax to take over the payments herself, and pay Marcus one-half of the difference between the bedroom set's current resale value and the amount of money still owed.

9. If neither person wants the bedroom set, the furniture will be sold. The balance owed Racafrax shall be paid from the proceeds of sale, and any remaining money will be divided between us equally or, if either of us has made extra payments under Paragraph 5 of this agreement, according to our ownership share.

10. Should either of us die while we are living together, the furniture will belong absolutely to the survivor. If either of us makes a will or estate plan, this agreement will be reflected in that document.

11. This agreement can be changed, but only in writing, and any changes must be signed by both of us.

12. Any dispute arising out of this contract will be mediated by a third person mutually acceptable to both of us. The mediator's role will be to help us arrive at a solution, not to impose one on us. If good faith efforts to arrive at our own solution to all issues in dispute with the help of a mediator prove to be fruitless, either of us may make a written request to the other that the dispute be arbitrated. If such a request is made, our dispute will be submitted to arbitration under the rules of the American Arbitration Association, and one arbitrator will hear our dispute. The decision of the arbitrator will be binding on us and will be enforceable in any court that has jurisdiction over the controversy. By agreeing to arbitration, we each agree to give up the right to a jury trial.

13. If a court finds any portion of this contract to be illegal or otherwise unenforceable, the remainder of the contract is still in full force and effect.

Marcus Lyons	*February 3, 20xx*
Marcus Lyons	Date
Karen Moore	*February 3, 20xx*
Karen Moore	Date

of you signed for the loan but both of you will be contributing toward its repayment. When you register the vehicle with the state, put it in both names. Depending on state law, you often have three options with car registration:

Option 1. "Thomas Finnegan or Keija Adams." This creates a joint tenancy in many states; if one person dies, the other automatically inherits the car without going through probate. However, depending on state law (see Option 3, below), the "or" form of ownership lets either party sell the vehicle without the knowledge or consent of the other.

Option 2. "Thomas Finnegan and Keija Adams." This establishes a tenancy in common; both signatures are required to transfer title of the vehicle. At death, however, each person can leave his or her share to anyone he or she wishes. If no estate plan is made, the nearest blood relative inherits the deceased person's share by intestate succession. If you want your partner to inherit your interest in the car, include it in your will (discussed in Chapter 9), or consider Option 3, below.

Option 3. "Thomas Finnegan and Keija Adams, as Joint Tenants With Right of Survivorship." Not only does this let the survivor automatically inherit the car without going through probate if one of you dies, but it also requires both signatures to transfer title while you're both alive.

CAUTION

State vehicle ownership rules can vary. Before relying on the general vehicle ownership rules described above, check with your state's motor vehicle department. Most have information online. Your state's rules regarding the words that should be used to establish the different types of joint ownership of motor vehicles may be slightly different from those outlined above.

How to Transfer Ownership in Property

If one of you already owns property, such as a car, you may want to give the other a full or partial interest in your property. If the property comes with a title slip (for example, a car or boat), you can change the names on it to reflect the new joint or transferred ownership. If you don't have a title slip, simply make one up. A sample is shown below. Be sure to include the names, dates, and any amount paid, and sign and date it.

It's particularly important to create a title slip (or change a state-provided slip) when you transfer or change ownership of valuable property. If you split up, having clear records of who owns what will make your financial disentanglement much easier.

TIP

Transferring ownership of real property has its own special rules and is usually, but not always, handled in a separate, written agreement. Several samples are included in Chapter 6. Be particularly careful in this area, as there may be significant tax consequences to a transfer.

Sample Title Slip

I, Shirley Letterman (owner), give one-half of my right, title, and interest in MegaBoom VII Sound Experience Home Theater System, model number 123456789, to Fred Leno, for the sum of $150.

Shirley Letterman
Shirley Letterman

September 2, 20xx
Date

Fred Leno
Fred Leno

September 2, 20xx
Date

Agreement Covering Joint Projects

John and Martha live together. They have no property to speak of, but they have a dream—to build a boat and sail around the world. They know it will take a lot of time, energy, and cooperation, and they want to protect their vision should any of life's disappointments affect their relationship.

A Sample Agreement Covering a Joint Project is shown below. You can use this as a guide in crafting your own agreement. (If you're building a house, many of the ownership and financing issues are the same as if you were buying a house together. See Chapter 6 for advice.)

In making your own agreement for a joint project, be sure you spell out completely:

- what the project is—for example, construction of a sailboat (Clause 1)

- how much each partner will contribute in terms of income, labor, or something else (Clauses 2 and 3)

- how the joint project will be divided should you separate (Clauses 4, 5, and 6); for example, in Clause 4 of the Sample Agreement Covering a Joint Project, you could reverse the provision giving Martha the first option to keep the boat, or include a provision that you will flip a coin for that right, and

- the effect on the agreement if one partner fails to contribute his or her promised share to the project (Clause 7).

You can add other relevant terms to your agreement—for example, you may want to cover contingencies such as what happens if the project costs more than originally estimated.

SEE AN EXPERT

If your project is a business, consider seeing a lawyer. If you and your partner are opening a business together, you will be investing a great deal of your time—and probably your money. To begin, you'll need a formal partnership agreement. We recommend *Form a Partnership: The Complete Legal Guide*, by Denis Clifford and Ralph Warner (Nolo), to do this. You should also have your agreement checked by a lawyer with experience in small business issues.

Sample Agreement Covering a Joint Project

John Ito and Martha Silver agree as follows:

1. We both want to construct a 30-foot sailboat to be jointly owned upon completion.

2. We each will contribute $12,000 for the purchase of necessary supplies. This money will be kept in a joint bank account and both signatures will be required to withdraw money from this account.

3. We each will work diligently on the boat (this means at least 20 hours per month). We will each keep records of all hours worked.

4. Should we separate, Martha will have the opportunity to buy out John's share for an amount of money equal to John's actual cash investment plus $25 per hour for each hour he has worked on the boat.

5. If we separate and Martha decides not to buy out John's share under the terms of Paragraph 4, John will have the opportunity to buy out Martha's share on the same terms.

6. Should neither of us elect to purchase the other's share of the boat at separation, we will sell the boat and divide the proceeds equally.

7. If either of us fails to work on the boat at least 20 hours per month for three consecutive months, the other may buy out the nonworker's share under the terms of Paragraph 4.

8. Should either of us die while we are living together, the survivor becomes sole owner of the boat. (If either of us makes an estate plan, this agreement will be incorporated in that document.)

9. This agreement can be changed, but only in writing, and any changes must be signed by both of us.

10. Any dispute arising out of this contract will be mediated by a third person mutually acceptable to both of us. The mediator's role will be to help us arrive at a solution, not to impose one on us. If good faith efforts to arrive at our own solution to all issues in dispute with the help of a mediator prove to be fruitless, either of us may make a written request to the other that the dispute be arbitrated. If such a request is made, our dispute will be submitted to arbitration under the rules of the American Arbitration Association, and one arbitrator will hear our dispute. The decision of the arbitrator will be binding on us and will be enforceable in any court that has jurisdiction over the controversy. By agreeing to arbitration, we each agree to waive the right to a jury trial.

11. If a court finds any portion of this contract to be illegal or otherwise unenforceable, the remainder of the contract is still in full force and effect.

John Ito
John Ito

July 2, 20xx
Date

Martha Silver
Martha Silver

July 2, 20xx
Date

Agreement Covering Homemaker Services

In some relationships, one person works outside the home while the other cooks, cleans, shops, and otherwise takes care of the place. This sort of division of labor can raise questions such as whether the homemaker should be compensated. One suggestion is to pay the stay-at-home partner a weekly salary.

Let's take the example of Ted and Joanne. Ted is 45, divorced, and has custody of his two children. He's a physician with an annual after-tax income in excess of $350,000. Joanne is 38, also divorced, with custody of her child. Her ex-husband only occasionally pays child support. Ted and Joanne decide to live together and agree that Ted will earn the money and Joanne will take care of the children and of the household full-time. They want to write a contract that will provide Joanne with fair compensation for housework and child care, but not give her any rights to Ted's property should they separate.

One preliminary problem Ted and Joanne face is valuing Joanne's services. Should her pay be based on what the cheapest local domestic workers charge or what a high-quality teacher gets paid, or should it be based on Ted's income? Also, should Joanne have some responsibility to provide some of the household and child care services without compensation? After all, she and her child live there too.

Although there is no one answer to these questions, it often helps to list all factors that either feels ought to go into deciding how much the stay-at-home worker should be paid, and then to work out a compromise agreement that feels good to both. In our view, the two most important factors are that:

- the household worker have enough income (money of his or her own) to achieve a substantial measure of financial independence, and

- both members of the couple feel the amount is more or less reasonable.

The Sample Agreement Covering Homemaker Services shown below provides one model you can follow for this type of situation.

CAUTION

IRS warning. Make sure you give some thought to the tax implications of your arrangements, however. Giving your partner more than $12,000 per year can trigger a gift tax obligation, and paying "wages" to a partner for domestic services can trigger Social Security and income tax withholding obligations. In some instances, therefore, it may be more prudent simply to have the higher-earning partner pay more of the joint expenses.

Sample Agreement Covering Homemaker Services

Ted Corbett and Joanne Lewis agree that they plan to live together. They hope to be in a committed, long-term relationship that will provide love and nurturing for both themselves and their children. In a spirit of fairness, and to help this come about, they agree that:

1. Ted will continue to work as a physician. He and Joanne expect that he'll work 50–60 hours a week and will have little time or energy to care for the home.

2. Joanne will work in the home raising the children and doing most of the domestic chores including the cleaning, laundry, cooking, and gardening. Ted will pay Joanne $800 a week for her services, over and above the costs of running the home as set out in Paragraph 7. These payments will be adjusted from time to time to reflect changes in the cost of living.

3. Ted will make Social Security and other legally required employer payments for Joanne as his employee and will pay for medical insurance coverage for her and her son, Tim.

4. All real and personal property owned by either Ted or Joanne prior to the date of this agreement will remain the separate property of its owner and cannot be transferred to the other person unless this is done in writing. We have each attached to this contract a list of our major items of separate property.

5. As of the date of this agreement, all property owned, earned, or accumulated by Ted or Joanne will belong solely to the person earning or accumulating it. The home and furnishings will be provided by Ted and owned solely by him. All property purchased by Joanne with her earnings will belong to her.

6. The separate property of either Ted or Joanne, owned now or acquired in the future, cannot become the separate property of the other, or the joint property of both, except under the terms of a written agreement signed by the person whose separate property is to be reclassified.

7. Ted will provide reasonable amounts of money each month to provide food, clothing, shelter, and recreation for the entire family as long as he and Joanne live together. By doing this, Ted assumes no obligation to support Joanne or her son upon termination of this agreement.

8. Either Ted or Joanne can end this agreement by giving the other two months' written notice. No reason is necessary. During the two-month notice period, Ted will continue to provide Joanne with a home and continue to pay her salary.

9. Any dispute arising out of this contract will be mediated by a third person mutually acceptable to both of us. The mediator's role will be to help us arrive at a solution, not to impose one on us. If good faith efforts to arrive at our own solution to all issues in dispute with the help of a mediator prove to be fruitless, either of us may make a written request to the other that the dispute be arbitrated. If such a request is made, our dispute will be submitted to arbitration under the rules of the American Arbitration Association, and one arbitrator will hear our dispute. The decision of the arbitrator will be binding on us and will be enforceable in any court that has jurisdiction over the controversy. By agreeing to arbitration, we each agree to give up the right to a jury trial.

10. This agreement represents Ted and Joanne's complete understanding regarding their living together and replaces any and all prior agreements, written or oral. It can be changed, but only in writing, and any changes must be signed by both parties.

11. If a court finds any portion of this contract to be illegal or otherwise unenforceable, the remainder of the contract is still in force and effect.

Ted Corbett	*April 24, 20xx*
Ted Corbett	Date
Joanne Lewis	April 24, 20xx
Joanne Lewis	Date

Agreement for Artists and Inventors

Terri and Chris have been together for three years. Terri is a toy inventor and Chris a photographer, but both have other part-time jobs to make ends meet. They recently moved in together and decided to alternate earning an income and taking time off. This way, they can both be creative and they can also pay their rent and groceries.

Terri and Chris prepare their own agreement for this purpose. (See the Sample Agreement for Artists and Inventors shown below.)

A variation of this Sample Agreement for Artists and Inventors can be used for any situation where one partner wants to take time off—for example, to work on an invention, make a film, or write the Great American Novel. If one partner is taking time off to raise a child, you may not need an "equal time off" agreement or a loan, as both partners are contributing to the relationship in different ways.

TIP

A loan and promissory note is another option. If only one person wants to take time off, the working partner may simply lend the other money, using a promissory note such as the one shown in Chapter 6. No matter what you arrange, you must specify how much time equals how much money and, if appropriate, set a method of repayment.

Sample Agreement for Artists and Inventors

Terri McGraw and Chris Macklin agree as follows:

1. Each of us will keep as our separate property, all property (and any income generated by that property) each of us owns as of the date of this agreement. We have each attached a list of our major items of separate property to this contract. (See Attachment A, Separately Owned Property.)

2. Starting as of the date this agreement is signed and continuing for as long as we live together, any property or income, including salaries or financial returns from artistic pursuits, earned by either of us (except for inheritances and gifts—see Paragraph 3) belongs equally to both of us. All joint funds will be kept in joint bank or securities accounts.

3. Money or property inherited by either of us or gifts given to either of us during the time we live together will be and remain the separate property of the person inheriting it. Separate property belonging to one of us cannot become the separate property of the other or the joint property of both without a written agreement signed by the person whose separate property is to be reclassified.

4. We agree to take turns working at regular full-time jobs in order to earn enough money for the two of us to live on. While one person works, the other will be free to pursue his or her creative endeavors. Terri will work for the first six months, Chris the next six months, and so on, alternating six-month periods of work and creative time for the duration of this agreement.

5. All our household expenses and personal and medical expenses will be paid by the one of us who's employed at the time the expense is incurred.

6. Should our living together relationship end at a point when one partner has been employed for a longer period of time than the other, the partner employed for less time will reimburse the other partner for one-half of the living expenses incurred during the extra months that the other partner has worked.

7. Should our living together relationship end, each of us will keep our separate property (property we owned prior to living together, income from that property, and any property inherited or received as a gift while we are together). All property, other than intellectual property, that was acquired or created while we lived together will be considered to be jointly owned and will be evenly divided.

8. All works created by either partner during our living together relationship that can be protected by copyright, patent, trade secret, or trademark laws (intellectual property), will be owned by the creating partner. All income from the sale, license, or exploitation of any of this intellectual property will be shared equally between the partners as long as we continue in a living together relationship. Should our living together relationship end, all income from the intellectual property will be shared for a period of three years from the date of separation. In the event that both partners jointly create a work, we will try to enter into a separate co-ownership agreement that establishes each partner's ownership interest based upon their contribution.

9. This agreement represents our complete understanding regarding our living together and replaces any and all prior agreements, written or oral. It can be changed, but only in writing, and any change must be signed by both of us.

10. If a court finds any portion of this contract to be illegal or otherwise unenforceable, the remainder of the contract is still in full force and effect.

11. Any dispute arising out of this contract will be mediated by a third person mutually acceptable to both of us. The mediator's role will be to help us arrive at a solution, not to impose one on us. If good faith efforts to arrive at our own solution to all issues in dispute with the help of a mediator prove to be fruitless, either of us may make a written request to the other that the dispute be arbitrated. In that case, our dispute will be submitted to arbitration under the rules of the American Arbitration Association, and one arbitrator

---

Sample Agreement for Artists and Inventors (continued)

will hear our dispute. The decision of the arbitrator will be binding on us and will be enforceable in any court that has jurisdiction over the controversy. By agreeing to arbitration, we each agree to give up the right to a jury trial.

Terri McGraw	*October 15, 20xx*
Terri McGraw	Date
Chris Macklin	*October 15, 20xx*
Chris Macklin	Date

Special Problems of Artists, Writers, and Inventors

Creative people often work on inventions, software programs, artwork, or books for a long time. While the work is in progress—and even when it's done—it is usually unclear how much monetary value, if any, the finished product will have. If you keep all your property and income separate, valuing creative works won't be a problem. Each person owns what he or she has created.

If you agree to pool the property you accumulate while living together, however, valuing creative work—if you split up—can be a real problem. Suppose, for example, you're a successful writer who's been working on a novel for two years. Who knows whether this yet-to-be-published book will sell 5,000 copies, a million copies, or some number in between? If you and your partner break up, even if you easily agree to divide your property, you may have real difficulty doing it fairly.

If you're determined to share all of your property, you will face some important issues when it comes to creative works protected by copyright, trade secret, or patent laws (also known as intellectual property laws). For example, co-owning a painting is quite different from co-owning the copyright in that painting. The owner of the painting makes money when the painting is sold; the owner of the copyright makes money when the image is licensed for use on postcards, books, posters, or other merchandise. If

you are an inventor, the rules can be even more complex. Under patent law, for example, each co-owner has the right to license the invention without paying the other co-owner.

If you and your partner wish to share in the income from artistic or inventive property, we recommend that you create an agreement that establishes: (1) that ownership in any intellectual property rights will be retained by the partner who created the work; and (2) that income from the sale or licensing of the works will be shared equally between the partners for a fixed time period, after which the owner no longer has to share the income with the other partner.

This arrangement provides for sharing of income but allows the creator of the creative work to control the sales and licensing deals—an important factor for every writer, artist, or inventor. The use of a fixed time period guarantees that the split will not go on forever; keep in mind that copyright protection, for example, lasts over 100 years.

The Sample Agreement for Artists and Inventors, above, includes the options discussed above. This is just one of many ways that intellectual property can be divided. If you and your partner are concerned about the rights and income associated with a creative work, have a lawyer familiar with intellectual property law review any agreement you prepare before you sign on the dotted line.

Agreement for People in School

It's common for one partner to help the other with educational expenses or support while he or she is in school. It is important to have a written agreement in this situation.

Agreements providing that one member of an unmarried couple will help support the other while he or she goes to school can take many different forms. Usually, the aim of such an agreement is to make clear that the person going to school will owe the other partner (who pays all or some of the school bills and supports the student while in school) a certain amount of money. That way, if the couple breaks up shortly after the student finishes school, the nonstudent partner won't have paid school bills and supported the student for nothing.

One way to plan for a fair monetary result is to provide that the person going to school owes the other partner any money expended for tuition and living expenses. This can take the form of a simple promissory note for all money paid out, plus reasonable interest. (See Chapter 6 for a sample promissory note.) Assuming the student goes to school for several years, the amount owed will have to be updated periodically.

EXAMPLE:

Soon after Alvin and Siena move in together, they agree that Siena will attend pharmacy school while Alvin works, supports them both, and pays a portion of Siena's tuition. (Siena will take out a student loan for the rest.) Alvin and Siena agree in writing that if they break up while Siena is in school or within three years after she graduates, she will owe Alvin $10,000 for each year he has supported her, with no interest to be charged until she graduates, at which point interest will be figured at a rate of 10%. They also agree that Siena will have five years to repay Alvin in equal monthly installments.

Of course, more complicated agreements are possible. In the Sample Agreement for People in School, below, Carol plans to become a veterinarian, and Bill is an aspiring dentist. To maximize both career opportunities and their personal relationship, they provide that each shall help the other finish his or her education.

Agreement to Protect Person Who Moves a Long Distance or Gives Up a Job

Occasionally, one partner moves a considerable distance to be with the other. Sometimes, doing this is a welcome adventure. Other times, however, it's more traumatic, especially if the person who is moving must give up a good job and a supportive network of family and friends. And there's always the fear that the relationship won't work out and the person who moved will either have to return to his or her original location or cope with being alone in a new town. Obviously, these concerns increase if the mover has small children.

To deal with this potential problem, some couples agree that the person who moved or gave up a job will be compensated if the relationship dissolves within a relatively short time. Here are two slightly different clauses that can be included in any living together contract in this book:

As a condition of Sarah giving up her job and moving with John to Chicago, John agrees that if, for any reason, they cease living together before September 1, 20xx, John shall immediately pay Sarah $5,000 to help her establish a separate household.

or

John and Sarah agree that as a condition of John giving up his present employment and moving to New York to live with Sarah, she will immediately pay him the sum of $2,500.

Sample Agreement for People in School

Carol Thayer and Bill Fujimoto agree as follows:

1. We are living together and plan to continue to do so indefinitely.

2. All property owned by either of us prior to the date of this agreement (including all future income earned from this property) shall be the separate property of its owner. We have attached a list of our major items of separate property to this contract. (Attachment A, Separately Owned Property.) In addition, all money or property inherited by or given to either of us shall be his or her separate property.

3. We will take turns going to school so that the one not in school can support the other until he/she gets a degree. We will flip a coin to decide who goes first. The "loser" will be responsible for a portion of the "winner's" educational expenses, up to a total of $18,000 per year, for three years. At the end of three years, the person who has already attended school will assume these responsibilities for the other, for three years, up to a total of $20,000 per year.

   If we split up during the first three-year period, all agreements by either of us to provide the other with future education expenses will be at an end. The student shall sign a promissory note agreeing to repay the full amount the other partner has expended for the student's education at the rate of $800 per month. However, if we live together for more than three years, our continuing financial obligations to support each other while in school shall not be affected by subsequent separation. Thus, if a separation occurs during the fourth, fifth, or sixth year, the nonstudent still must pay the other's tuition and other school-related expenses up to a total of $20,000 for that year. All tuition is to be paid in the month due.

4. During the first six years we live together, beginning with the date we sign this agreement, all income and property acquired by either of us (excluding inheritances, gifts to one of us, and income produced by previously owned separate property) shall be jointly owned. The person who is the primary income producer at the time will manage the funds and pay all necessary household bills. After six years, we will inventory our accumulated property and divide it equally. Thereafter, each person's earnings shall be his or her separate property and neither of us will have any interest in the present or future property of the other.

   If we separate before the end of six years, all jointly owned property shall be divided according to the fraction of time each of us has provided the primary support (if Carol supports Bill for three years and Bill supports her for two, Carol is entitled to three-fifths of the property).

5. Should we separate, neither will owe any continuing financial obligation to the other except as set out in Paragraph 3.

6. Any change in the ownership status of any property (from the separate property of one person to joint property, or from the separate property of one person to the separate property of the other) shall be made in writing and signed by the person making the transfer.

7. This agreement is our complete understanding regarding our living together and replaces any and all prior agreements, written or oral. It can be amended, but only in writing, and any writing must be signed by both.

8. If a court finds any portion of this contract to be illegal or otherwise unenforceable, the remainder of the contract is still in full force and effect.

9. Any dispute arising out of this contract will be mediated by a third person mutually acceptable to both of us. The mediator's role will be to help us arrive at a solution, not to impose one on us. If good faith efforts to arrive at our own solution to all issues in dispute with the help of a mediator prove to be fruitless, either of us may make a written request to the other that the dispute be arbitrated. In that case, our dispute will be submitted to arbitration under the rules of the American Arbitration Association, and one arbitrator will hear our dispute. The decision of the arbitrator will be binding on us and will be enforceable in any court that has jurisdiction over the controversy. By agreeing to arbitration, we each agree to give up the right to a jury trial.

Bill Fujimoto
Bill Fujimoto

January 2, 20xx
Date

Carol Thayer
Carol Thayer

January 2, 20xx
Date

Debt, Credit, Taxes, and More:
Practical Aspects of Living Together

When you and your partner decide to live together, you are probably acting on romantic impulses. Unfortunately, practical problems inevitably tag along in the wake of romance.

Although most of these problems aren't legal and don't involve lawyers, some day-to-day issues are connected with law. This chapter focuses on the everyday legal situations unmarried couples face—from the pros and cons of joint accounts to legal rules about discrimination against unmarried couples to paying income taxes.

CROSS REFERENCE

Related topics covered elsewhere in this book include:

- How to write living together agreements covering property, cars, and other joint purchases: Chapter 3
- Renting or buying a home together: Chapters 5 and 6
- Having or adopting a child together: Chapter 7
- Writing wills and planning your estates: Chapter 9
- Handling disputes regarding property when separating: Chapter 10.

Debt and Credit

While most of us aspire to rise above crass material concerns, the reality is that all couples benefit from clearly agreeing who will pay for the rent, car installments, or groceries. When you live together, you must also decide whether to pool your money and the property you buy with that money, or keep it all separate. Sharing a home doesn't mean your financial lives must become one. If you want to combine finances, be sure you really know and trust your partner. Don't feel pressured to combine everything when you're just starting out simply because the unmarried couple upstairs—who have been together 15 years—have only one bank account.

This section provides an overview of an unmarried couple's rights and responsibilities when it comes to debt and credit. Once you understand these, you'll be better prepared to write out your agreement about sharing money and property—equally, partially, or not at all. Chapter 3 shows how to do this.

Property, Assets, and Debts Defined

Virtually anything one can own is considered property. Generally, we think of items that have monetary value as **property**—including both tangible things you can see and touch (furniture, houses, cars, and jewelry) and intangible items (such as business goodwill or the right to receive future pensions). **Assets** is another term for property of all kinds. A **debt** is a sum of money owed to someone else.

Debts

Unlike marriage, living together does not make you responsible for your partner's debts. Should your partner declare bankruptcy or face other debt problems, you won't lose your property as long as you've kept it separate. Your wages cannot be attached and your property cannot be taken to pay for your partner's overdue bills or debts, and your credit rating will not be negatively affected by your partner's financial problems.

But this financial independence may suddenly disappear if:

- you sign a joint purchase agreement
- you cosign a loan with your partner obligating yourself to pay the debt if the person taking out the loan fails to do so
- your partner's debt is charged to a shared or joint account, or
- you register as domestic partners, in some situations.

Joint Bank Accounts

There are many different ways to pool money—not at all, completely, or on a limited basis. It's up to you. You might decide to combine all of your finances, to keep them entirely separate, or to shoot for something in between.

You should have no problem opening a joint checking or banking account under both your names. In general, joint accounts are sensible if you limit their purpose (for example, for specific household expenses or for travel) and keep adequate records. Many unmarried couples have peacefully maintained joint bank accounts for years.

But a joint account is still a risk. Each person has the right to spend all the money. Both partners are responsible for all activity involving the account. You're equally liable for bounced checks, overdrafts, and all the rest. This can cause big problems if one of you is a habitual overspender.

You can prevent your partner from bouncing checks and the like by requiring both signatures on checks and withdrawals. But this is usually cumbersome and inconvenient.

Record keeping can pose another problem with joint accounts. It's often difficult to keep track of how much money is in the account when two people are writing checks and making withdrawals. You'll have to set up a reliable method of tracking these things and then resolve to stick to it.

CAUTION

Transfers of assets between unmarried partners may be taxed. Be careful if you are shifting valuable property or a lot of money to your living together partner. If the asset is worth more than $12,000, you will likely need to file a federal gift tax return. So, get some good tax advice in advance. See Chapter 9 for more on this issue.

Joint Accounts May Imply a Contract to Share Income

As we discuss in Chapter 2, in some states, including California, enforceable contracts between unmarried couples to share earnings and other property can be made orally or sometimes even implied from the circumstances of a relationship. Sharing credit and bank accounts might be a factor a court would consider in deciding whether a couple had an implied contract to share income and other property. So if you want to do everything possible to keep property ownership separate, it's best not to open joint accounts. If you do, sign an agreement, such as the Agreement to Keep Property Separate in Chapter 3.

Joint Credit Accounts

As with bank accounts, you may want to keep your credit accounts separate and each deal with creditors on your own terms. In that way you don't have to worry about the other person's purchases and any potential damage to your credit rating. Nevertheless, many unmarried couples open joint credit card accounts in which both partners are authorized by the credit lender to charge up to a credit limit.

You can open a joint account for broad purposes, such as paying household expenses or to fund a distinct project—for example, remodeling a kitchen, saving for a vacation, or making a joint investment. Or you may use a joint card solely for household purchases, and use your individual cards for all other expenditures. You can get a joint charge account where you pay the entire monthly balance at once, like American Express, or a credit account where you are only obligated to pay a monthly minimum, such as a Visa or department store account.

How (and Why) to Check Your Credit Report

If you've lived together for a long time or have had joint credit card or bank accounts, it's possible that your credit report has become intertwined with that of your partner or has information on it that belongs only to him or her, and not to you. This is usually not to your advantage, especially if your partner has bad credit.

Your credit report contains your credit history. Credit reports are maintained by credit bureaus—companies that collect information related to your creditworthiness, including your bank and credit card accounts, loans (such as mortgages, car loans, and student loans), payment history on those loans and accounts, delinquencies on accounts, bankruptcy filings, criminal arrests and convictions, current and previous employers, lawsuits and judgments against you, and tax or other liens. Creditors, landlords, employers, banks, and collection agencies can request and review your credit report.

Unfortunately, many credit reports contain inaccurate or outdated information. If you have some joint accounts with your partner or have been living together for a long time, the credit bureaus may have included information on your credit record about your partner's separate accounts. Information about separate accounts should only appear on the report of the partner responsible for that account. Information about joint accounts should appear on both reports.

Each partner should request a copy of his or her credit report and review it for errors or outdated information. It's a good idea to do this every year. Contact one of the three major national credit bureaus to get your report.

The federal Fair Credit Reporting Act (FCRA) now requires each major national credit bureau—Equifax, Experian, and Trans Union—to provide you one free copy of your credit report each year. You can request your free report by one of these means:

- Telephone—877-322-8228

- Internet—www.annualcreditreport.com, or

- Mail—Annual Credit Report Service, P.O. Box 105281, Atlanta, GA 30348-5281.

You must provide your name, address, Social Security number, and date of birth when you order. You also may be required to provide information that only you would know, such as the amount of your monthly mortgage payment.

You may be entitled to additional free copies of your credit report in any of the following circumstances:

- you have been denied credit or insurance because of information in your credit file (In that case, you are entitled to a free copy of your report from the credit bureau that reported the information. A creditor that denies you credit or insurance will tell you the name and address of the credit bureau reporting the information that led to the denial.)

- you are unemployed and planning to apply for a job within 60 days following your request for your credit report

- you receive public assistance, or

- you believe that your credit file contains errors due to fraud, such as identity theft.

If you find errors on your report (for example, a car loan for which your partner is the only signatory) or outdated information, notify the credit bureau in writing. The bureau is required by law to correct your report. If the bureau investigates the item and disagrees with you, at the very least you can include a brief explanation on your report about the disputed item.

For more information on what information can appear on your credit report and for how long, how to correct errors, and how to rebuild credit after a financial setback, see *Credit Repair*, by Robin Leonard and John Lamb (Nolo).

It's fairly easy to put two names on a credit card. You simply fill out a joint credit card application. Many companies have changed the blanks from "spouse" to "co-applicant" or "co-applicant/ spouse." If the application form only says "spouse," cross off the word "spouse" and write in "co-applicant." Don't claim to be a spouse—that term has a specific legal meaning (having to do with liability and responsibility), and lying on a credit application is fraud.

As long as one of you has sufficient income or savings to be considered a good credit risk—that is, you appear to be able to pay the bills—you'll probably get the credit card. Creditors are generally willing to open joint credit accounts—and why shouldn't they be? A joint account means more people are responsible for a debt. For example, if Roger and Jane have a joint credit card, and Roger lets his sister Fiona charge $2,500 on it, Roger and Jane are both legally obligated to pay the bill—even if Jane didn't know about Fiona using the card or knew about it but opposed it. Similarly, if Jane retaliates by leaving Roger and going on a buying binge, Roger is legally responsible for all the charges Jane makes.

If one of you has a poor credit history, you may be denied a joint card, even if the other's credit is perfect. The partner with better credit may have to reapply in his or her name only.

> **! CAUTION**
>
> **If you break up, immediately close all joint bank and credit accounts.** All too often, one person feels depressed about a breakup and tries to pamper himself or herself with "retail therapy." Don't just divide up the cards, each keeping a few. You're both still liable for all accounts—and you could get stuck paying for your partner's "therapy" bill. And if a joint account becomes delinquent, your credit record will suffer—even if you didn't incur the charges. Chapter 10 discusses important breakup tasks such as closing a joint account.

Buying and Investing Together

Many couples make purchases and investments together, such as houses and cars (issues covered in Chapters 3 and 6). Here we cover joint ownership of and investment in other assets.

Property Acquired Before Getting Together

Each person retains complete ownership of all property (TV, furniture, dishes, CDs, books, cars, and the like) owned before getting together. In several of the property agreements set out in Chapter 3, we provide a section for each person to list his or her separate property. It isn't legally necessary to do this (the property is already separately owned), but it's a good way to avoid later confusion. You can, of course, give your partner an equal or partial interest in some or all of your property. We also explain how to do this in Chapter 3.

Property Acquired After Getting Together

As an unmarried couple, you have the choice of either keeping your property separate or merging it (what lawyers call commingling). Whatever you decide, be sure to put it in writing, using the property agreements in Chapter 3. This will help avoid confusion if you separate.

How to Keep Your Property Separate

It is imperative to keep property separate if one of you is having debt problems or is not covered by comprehensive medical insurance. But even if you and your partner both have excellent credit ratings and good medical coverage, you can avoid potential complications by keeping property separate.

Here's how to maintain your financial independence and keep most of your assets and debts separate:

- Write a simple property agreement, such as the one in Chapter 3, outlining your intention to keep your income and property separate.

- Don't open joint accounts or make joint purchases unless absolutely necessary or for limited purposes. Keep the bulk of your money in your own name and don't add extra signatures to your account.

- Don't cosign a loan or credit agreement for your mate unless you're willing to pay the entire debt in full if your partner can't, or won't.

- Don't pass yourselves off as husband and wife or use the same name—especially if you live in a state that recognizes common law marriage.

- It's not a good idea to register as domestic partners (if this is an option), as some registration forms declare that you will be financially responsible for each other's basic needs and living expenses. If you want to take advantage of the benefits and protections of a domestic partner ordinance, check your state law or consult with an attorney to see what effect registration will have on keeping your property separate.

How to Mix or Commingle Your Property

It's fairly common for unmarried partners to pool income to purchase a car, furniture, or other expensive item. Even if only one of you takes out a loan to finance the purchase or uses separate money to buy it, you can both be legal owners, if that's what you want.

If you intend to own an item jointly, you'll need a written agreement outlining the details, especially if only one of you signs for a loan but both of you will be contributing funds toward the repayment. Again, Chapter 3 includes sample agreements for owning property jointly. The contracts cover important issues, such as how property is to be paid for, your joint ownership or investment percentages, what happens to the property if you break up, and whether the survivor becomes the sole owner if one of you dies.

How to Share Costs, But Not Ownership, of Property

In some situations, one partner may lend the other money for a major purchase, such as a car, without intending to share ownership of the property. In this case, the partner borrowing the money should sign a promissory note agreeing to repay the loan. Chapter 6 includes a sample promissory note you can use for this purpose. To keep the property separate, register the car in the borrower's name only.

Discrimination

This section covers various forms of discrimination you may face as an unmarried couple.

CROSS REFERENCE

Chapter 5 covers legal rules regarding discrimination in rental housing. Chapter 6 covers discrimination in house purchases.

Credit Discrimination

A credit grantor generally will provide credit to anyone who is a good financial risk. A person with no apparent source of income, with a history of long periods of unemployment, who regularly pays bills late or misses payments, or who has recently declared bankruptcy, isn't a good risk. A person with a low income and many dependents and expenses also may not be a good risk. These are legitimate considerations for a lender. However, creditors are not permitted to consider factors that are unrelated to income or ability to pay, such as marital status.

The Equal Credit Opportunity Act (ECOA) prohibits creditors from discriminating on the basis of marital status (and on the basis of race, national origin, religion, sex, age, or because all or part of a person's income comes from public assistance). (15 U.S.C. §1691.) Ability to pay should be the criterion used.

Specific federal regulations say that a creditor:

- cannot inquire about marital status for individual unsecured credit unless the applicant lives in a community property state or is using as collateral property located in a community property state

- cannot require the use of a married name, but must allow credit to be issued in either your given name or a combined surname

- can require you to reveal alimony and child support payments for which you are responsible, but not payments you receive, unless you rely on them to establish your income for credit purposes

- may not ignore your income from child support or alimony payments in determining your creditworthiness, but may consider how likely it is that you will actually receive that income

- may not ignore income from a part-time job

- may not ask questions about your birth control practices, or whether you intend to have children

- may not terminate your account or require a reapplication if you change your name or marital status unless there is evidence that you're unwilling or unable to pay your bill, and

- must inform you of any reason you are denied credit.

A creditor that illegally discriminates in extending credit may be liable for up to $10,000 plus any money that's actually lost as a result of the discrimination.

But the law is not completely cut and dried. Under the ECOA, asking a person's marital status is not discrimination if the inquiry is made in order to determine "the creditor's rights and remedies

applicable to a particular extension of credit"—for example, whether the creditor will require a co-signer or guarantor, or whether property you are claiming as an asset for purposes of your credit application is jointly owned. However, the inquiry is illegal if it is made solely for the purpose of discriminating on the basis of your status. In addition, because the ECOA allows a creditor to consider state property laws in its decision to extend credit, in some states a creditor may be able to ask about marital status in certain situations. For example, if a loan will be secured by real property, and state law gives the applicant's spouse an interest in the property, the creditor can ask if the applicant is married.

Few cases have tested the Equal Credit Opportunity Act. Since its passage, however, unmarried couples have had fewer obstacles in opening joint accounts.

To read the text of the ECOA, visit the Federal Trade Commission's website (www.ftc.gov) and look in the Consumer Protection area.

 CROSS REFERENCE

Questions about credit-related discrimination? If you feel you have been the victim of discrimination, contact the consumer affairs division of one of these federal agencies for advice:

Non-bank-related problems.
Federal Trade Commission
Website: www.ftc.gov
Phone: 877-FTC-HELP (382-4357)

Bank-related problems.
Federal Reserve Board
Website: www.federalreserve.gov
Phone: 202-452-3693, 888-851-1920
TTY: 877-766-8533.

Discrimination in Employment

It's unlikely that a private employer will care about your marital status. The exception might be if you're in an extremely important or politically or culturally sensitive position—for example, you're an unmarried, pregnant private school teacher. In situations like this, some courts have allowed employers to fire employees based on their unmarried status. (For example, the court supported the employer when an unmarried pregnant North Carolina woman who lived with her lover was fired from her job at the YWCA because she was "setting a bad example." *Harvey v. YWCA*, 533 F. Supp. 949 (N.C. 1982).) In other cases, they haven't. (In Virginia, a school forced an unmarried pregnant teacher to take a leave of absence. A court found that the school violated the teacher's constitutional rights. *Ponton v. Newport News School Bd.*, 632 F. Supp. 1056 (E.D. Va. 1986).)

If you work for one of the rare employers that does object to your cohabitation and threatens to fire or demote you because of it, whether you have protection depends on several things: (1) whether your employer is a federal agency, private company, or local or state government agency; and (2) the law in your state.

Private Companies and Local or State Government Agencies

There is no federal law that prohibits firing or job discrimination against people because they are unmarried and living with a partner. However, many states have passed laws that prohibit this type of discrimination. If you work for a private company or a local or state government agency and you live in a state or locality that prohibits employment discrimination based on marital status, you probably cannot be fired for cohabiting.

Keep in mind that many of these state and local laws only apply to employers with a minimum number of employees, such as five or more. Also, some state courts have ruled that the "marital status" provisions do not protect cohabitors, only employees who are married or single. Finally, state laws change all the time, so before you assume your state does or doesn't protect

> **States That Prohibit Employment Discrimination Based on Marital Status**
>
> States that have nondiscrimination laws include Alaska, California, Connecticut, Delaware, District of Columbia, Florida, Hawaii, Illinois, Maryland, Michigan, Minnesota, Montana, Nebraska, New Hampshire, New Jersey, New Mexico (with 50 or more employees), New York, North Dakota, Oregon, Virginia, Washington, and Wisconsin.

you, check with the state agency that governs employment discrimination—this is often the state fair employment practices agency. Or, do some legal research on your own. (See Chapter 11 for information on legal research.)

If your state doesn't have a statute that prohibits marital status discrimination in employment, you may still get protection from the courts. For example, federal district courts in Michigan and Arkansas have upheld the right of police officers to cohabit. (*Biggs v. North Muskegon Police Dept.*, 563 F. Supp. 585 (Mich. 1983); *Swope v. Bratton*, 541 F. Supp. 99 (Ark. 1982).) However, other courts have allowed employers to fire employees because they cohabited. For example, a court in Texas allowed a police department to take disciplinary action against officers for off-duty dating and cohabitation. (*Shawgo v. Spradlin*, 701 F.2d 470 (5th Cir. 1983).) And in 1977, a Pennsylvania court held that a public library employee's living in "open adultery" was reason enough to warrant firing. (*Hollenbaugh v. Carnegie Free Library*, 436 F. Supp. 1328 (W.D. Pa. 1977).)

Finally, don't forget to check your employer's personnel manual. Many employers have internal policies prohibiting discrimination on the basis of marital status. If your employer has such a policy, it must follow it, even if state law doesn't prohibit marital status discrimination.

Federal Government Agencies

Federal law states that most federal agencies aren't allowed to discriminate on the basis of marital status in hiring, firing, assignments, or discipline. And court decisions involving federal employees usually give cohabitants protection on the job.

Discrimination When Traveling Together

In most parts of the country, an unmarried couple will encounter no problems when traveling together. Many hotels and motels require only one name and signature on the register, though you'll have to state the number of people that will be occupying the room. Even if you both must sign the register, you are still very unlikely to have problems. Clerks, after all, are used to the fact that many married women do not adopt their husband's last name.

A very few places may hassle you if you register under two different surnames, and refuse to provide lodging if you say you're unmarried. But this is very unlikely, especially if you stay in a name-brand hotel or motel.

CAUTION

Don't register under a false name or false pretext of marriage. In some jurisdictions (like Maine and the District of Columbia) it is illegal to register in a hotel under a false name. (Me. Rev. Stat. Ann. tit. 30, § 3822; D.C. Code Ann. § 22-3224.) And, if you are in North Carolina or Arkansas and a hotel does inquire as to your marital status, you might want to think twice before claiming that you are married. Under those states' laws, it's illegal to falsely register or represent yourself as a married couple when you are not in fact married. (N.C. Gen. Stat. § 14-186; Ark. Code Ann. § 20-26-203.) The only reported case of prosecution under the Arkansas statute dates back to 1947. But the North Carolina statute was revisited and amended as recently as 1994.

Sometimes travel discount rates are available only to married couples. Most are extended to any two adults traveling together, but occasionally you may be able to save a few dollars by saying you're married. Do you run any legal risk by doing this? Probably not. For purposes of tours, tickets, and the like, you're pretty safe in claiming the status that will get you the cheapest rate. Again, because many married couples use different last names these days, no one is likely to ask for proof that you're married.

CAUTION

Legal remedies for discrimination. What happens if a hotel or motel discriminates against you because of your marital status? Do you have any legal recourse? Unless there is a local ordinance prohibiting discrimination in public accommodations on the basis of marital status (these exist in many major cities and university towns), the answer is usually no. For more information on researching local ordinances, see Chapter 11.

Sharing Your Last Name

Normally, each partner in an unmarried couple keeps his or her own last name. It's easy, legal, and creates few, if any, practical problems. Occasionally, however, members of an unmarried couple want to use the same last name—his name, her name, a hyphenated version of the two names, or a completely new name for both.

This can be done with little difficulty, as it's fairly simple to change your last name by getting a court order.

Bear in mind that you cannot change your name to defraud creditors, for any illegal purpose, to benefit economically by the use of another person's name, or to invade someone's privacy (don't name yourself Madonna or Bill Clinton). Also, you can't take on a name that is likely to incite violence (such as a racial epithet) or is inherently confusing (such as a string of numbers). Otherwise, you can change your name for any reason and assume any name you wish.

> **CAUTION**
>
> **Using the same last name may have undesired legal repercussions.** In some states, it can show intent to establish a common law marriage. If your state recognizes common law marriage (see Chapter 2) and you use the same last name, you may create an implication that you intend to be married—especially if you tell others that you are married. If you live in a common law marriage state and want to use the same name, but don't want to be married, it's a good idea to sign a brief Agreement of Joint Intent Not to Have a Common Law Marriage, like the one included in Chapter 2. Also, don't hold yourselves out to family and friends as a married couple.

Using the same last name combined with other factors, such as a claim by one of you that you orally agreed to pool income, may imply that you intend to share your earnings and property. If you wish to keep all property separate but share your last name, it's an extremely good idea to sign an agreement to keep your property separate by using one of the living together agreements included in Chapter 3.

Change of Name by Usage

In some states, it is legal to change your name by simply using a new name and gradually changing your official documents to match the name you are using. However, given the rising incidence of identity theft and the focus on security after the terrorist attacks of September 11, 2001, we no longer recommend the usage method of changing your name, even if you live in a state that allows it. Most government agencies will no longer just take your word for the fact that you've changed your name, but will require a court order with a judge's signature. And you don't want to run afoul of the Patriot Act or any other new "homeland security" rules by having documentation in two different names. It's far better to just spend the few hundred dollars and take the time to change your name legally through the court petition method.

Change of Name by Court Order

The second way to change your name is by court order. Getting a court order is usually pretty simple: You fill out, and file at the courthouse, a short petition, publish legal notice of your intention to change your name in a local legal newspaper, and attend a routine court hearing.

Once you obtain the court order changing your name, you must still change your records, identity cards, and documents. All you need to do is show the various bureaucrats the judge's order.

> **CAUTION**
>
> **Each state has its own laws governing the court order method.** While the procedures are similar, if you're serious about changing your name by court order, check your state laws (Chapter 11 shows how). *How to Change Your Name in California*, by Lisa Sedano and Emily Doskow (Nolo), will help you do the job quickly and efficiently in that state.

> **TIP**
>
> **Rather not say why you're changing your name?** If you live in a state where you must give a reason for the change and you'd rather not tell the judge that you're changing your name to your partner's, you don't have to. You can state that your new name will make it more convenient for business or simply say that you like the new name better.

Income Taxes

In most cases, being unmarried does not negatively affect the amount of taxes you pay. In fact, some unmarried couples pay less in federal income taxes than do married couples. In addition, some unmarried partners can claim the other partner as a dependent, which qualifies them for an additional exemption. And when it comes to selling your home, if you and your partner are unmarried and you each own half the home, you can often reap the same tax benefits as married couples, although the eligibility requirements are a little tougher to satisfy.

Common law marriage counts as a real marriage as far as taxes are concerned. If you live in a state that recognizes common law marriage and you hold yourself out to be married, you are also married for federal tax purposes and should file accordingly. (See Chapter 2 for a list of states recognizing common law marriage.) However, if you and your partner live together with no intent to be married, you may (and should) file as single individuals even if you live in a state recognizing common law marriage.

Tax Rates and the Standard Deduction

For many years, unmarried couples that lived together paid less in federal income tax—often substantially less—than did their married counterparts. This was especially true for higher-income couples. If both people worked, getting married often was expensive. For example, two single wage-earners, each with net taxable income of $50,000 per year, would have been in a 28% tax bracket in 2000. But if these people were married, their combined $100,000 net taxable income would have put them in a 31% bracket.

Compounding this so-called "marriage penalty" was the standard deduction, which disproportionately favored single people. An individual who filed as a single person in 2000 could claim a standard deduction of $4,400 (and two single people living together would get $8,800). The same couple, if married and filing jointly, was entitled to a combined standard deduction of only $7,350.

This discrepancy (why wasn't the married couple entitled to a standard deduction of $8,800?) didn't lead to an actual revolt by married taxpayers, but

their vocal displeasure eventually brought about some changes, and the marriage penalty was largely eliminated beginning in 2003. This was accomplished by making the standard deduction for married taxpayers exactly twice that of single taxpayers. Lawmakers also widened the 15% tax bracket for married couples. This relief is scheduled to last through 2010 and may be extended.

Income Tax and Social Security

When it comes to taxing Social Security, the marriage penalty is very much alive and well. Older married couples in which the partners have modest incomes and receive Social Security benefits must pay tax on a portion of their benefits if their "base amount" is more than $32,000. (The "base amount" is the married couple's combined adjusted gross income, as reported on their tax return, plus interest from tax-exempt investments, plus 50% of their combined Social Security benefits.) In contrast, each partner in an unmarried couple pays taxes on Social Security benefits only if his or her "base amount" is more than $25,000. That would mean that, as a couple, their base amount could be as high as $50,000 before they had to pay taxes on Social Security benefits.

RESOURCE

For information on tax rules relating to older people, see IRS Publication 554, *Older Americans Tax Guide*, available from the IRS at 800-829-1040 or www .irs.gov.

Dependents and Taxes

In some circumstances, one partner in an unmarried couple can claim a cohabiting partner as a dependent and qualify for an additional exemption ($3,400 in 2007). The IRS defines dependents as either close relatives or unrelated persons who live in the taxpayer's household as the principal place of abode and are supported by the taxpayer.

Claiming Your Partner as a Dependent

Your partner may qualify as a dependent if you provide over one-half of his or her total support (for food, shelter, clothing, medical and dental care, education, and the like) during the year, he or she has earned less than $3,400 in 2007 (not including tax-exempt income, such as welfare or Social Security benefits), and he or she is a U.S. resident or citizen who has lived with you the entire year. In addition, your partner cannot file a joint return with someone else (for example, a spouse if he or she is still married).

TIP

For more details on these requirements, see IRS Publication 501, *Exemptions, Standard Deductions and Filing Information.* **To get this publication, contact the IRS at 800-829-1040 or visit its website at www.irs.gov.

Claiming Child Household Members as Dependents

Unmarried partners may also claim "head of household" filing status when they support a dependent other than an adult with whom they are living. So, for example, if your child lives with you and your partner, you could file as head of household and get many of the same credits available to married filers, such as the earned income credit for the working poor, and child and dependent care credits. By filing as head of household, an unmarried taxpayer could claim both the child and the other adult as dependents, for a total of three exemptions.

When parents are divorced or just live apart, the question of who gets to take the dependency exemption for federal income tax purposes often arises. Section 152 of the Internal Revenue Code provides that if the parents were once married, the parent who has physical custody for the greater part of the year gets to claim the exemption. You can change this by waiving your right to claim the exemption in a written agreement (for example, in a divorce, separation, or child custody agreement)

or by filing a declaration with the IRS. For more information on how to handle this situation, see IRS Publication 504, *Divorced or Separated Individuals,* which you can download for free at www.irs.gov.

If you were never married, the child qualifies by living with you for more than half the year as long as the child didn't provide more than half of his or her own support.

Income Tax on the Sale of Your Home: Capital Gain Exclusion

Current tax law allows married couples to avoid taxes on the first $500,000 of capital gain (usually the difference between the original purchase price and the selling price) when they sell their home, as long as at least one spouse has owned the home, and both spouses have resided in the home, for two out of the five years preceding the sale.

Unmarried individuals are each entitled to a $250,000 gain exclusion on their portion of the home owned with someone else. However, in the case of an unmarried couple, both individuals must have owned and lived in the home for two of the five years preceding the sale.

TIP

For more information on the capital gain tax break, see "Check Out Legal and Tax Issues Before Transferring a Share of Your House" in Chapter 6. For advice on tax rules and to get the IRS publications mentioned above, contact the IRS at 800-829-1040 or visit the IRS website at www.irs.gov. If you claim your partner as a dependent, the IRS objects, and you want to fight it, we recommend that you get a copy of *Stand Up to the IRS,* by Frederick W. Daily (Nolo).

Social Security

Unmarried couples that live together are often at a disadvantage when it comes to Social Security benefits—especially if one partner stays at home caring for children or running the household.

Typically, you qualify for Social Security benefits based on your own earnings record. If you don't work at a job that requires payment of Social Security tax, you don't earn credit towards Social Security benefits. But married couples get a benefit—spouses are eligible for certain Social Security benefits based on the *other* spouse's earnings record. These are called dependents' benefits (which you get if your spouse qualifies for retirement or disability benefits) and survivors' benefits (which you get if your deceased spouse or ex-spouse qualified for retirement or disability benefits). So, for example, if a husband stays at home and takes care of the kids for a number of years, he may still be able to collect Social Security benefits based on his wife's earnings record. Adults who live together, but are not married, are not eligible for their partner's dependents' or survivors' benefits although their children are dependents of both. This presents an obvious disadvantage when one partner in a living together arrangement works outside the home and the other works in the home caring for kids or taking care of the household.

A stay-at-home partner could earn Social Security credits, however, if the other partner employed him or her to take care of the home and children. The "employer partner" would pay wages to the stay-at-home partner and pay Social Security tax on the stay-at-home partner's behalf. Both partners would have to comply with other requirements. For example, the stay-at-home partner would have to pay state and federal income tax on the wages. And in many states, the "employer partner" would also have to pay disability insurance and other types of insurance or taxes. (See the "Agreement Covering Homemaker Services" in Chapter 3 for a contract that provides for this type of arrangement.)

CROSS REFERENCE

Unmarried elderly couples may avoid taxes on their Social Security benefits. For information on how some unmarried couples can benefit tax-wise when it comes to Social Security benefits, see "Income Taxes," above.

TIP

A common law marriage is valid for purposes of receiving Social Security. Common law marriage is just as valid as a formal marriage for Social Security purposes. This means if you lived with someone covered by Social Security in a state that recognizes common law marriage (see Chapter 2) and your partner has recently died or become disabled, you may be able to claim you were married and, as a result, qualify for benefits.

TIP

Living with someone doesn't end Social Security benefits derived from a former marriage. If your spouse has died and you are receiving survivor's benefits or if you are divorced, you can get benefits on your ex-spouse's Social Security account if your marriage lasted at least ten years and, in some cases, if you have been divorced for at least two years (it makes no difference whether a former spouse has remarried or you are living with someone). Similarly, if you qualify for benefits as a divorced spouse and your ex has died, you can receive survivor's benefits as early as age 60 (50 if you're disabled).

RESOURCE

For advice on Social Security rules and benefits, contact a local office of the Social Security Administration or check their website at www.sss.gov. For a clear explanation of Social Security benefits—what's available and how to claim them—see *Social Security, Medicare & Government Pensions: Get the Most Out of Your Retirement & Medical Benefits*, by Joseph Matthews with Dorothy Matthews Berman (Nolo).

Retirement Plans

Many people are surprised—and pleased—to discover upon retirement that the bulk of their wealth is sitting in one or more retirement plans. These valuable assets provide security to the retiring worker, of course, and can also provide for a surviving spouse if the worker dies prematurely.

Unmarried couples can use retirement plans in much the same way—to provide for a surviving partner. But unmarried couples need to jump through a few more hoops to accomplish the same thing.

Naming a Beneficiary

Whether you have an IRA, a 401(k), or another type of retirement plan, you may name any beneficiary you want. But you must do exactly that—name the beneficiary by filling out a beneficiary designation form that states your wishes. Generally, your financial institution will require you to complete a beneficiary designation form when you first open an IRA. But in the case of an employer's plan, you might have to request a form from your plan administrator.

Many employer plans name a surviving spouse as a default beneficiary in the event a worker fails to designate a beneficiary in writing. However, unmarried partners will not be default beneficiaries, so it is important that you complete a form, then keep a copy of the form in your files and give one to the plan administrator.

Naming a beneficiary of your retirement plan accomplishes several things. First, it ensures that the assets are distributed to the people you intend. Second, designating a beneficiary might protect the retirement plan from probate. (In many states, retirement plan assets are not subject to probate, provided there is a clear designation of beneficiary. Without such a designation, assets might be forced through probate to identify the appropriate heir.) Third, when you name a beneficiary of your

retirement plan, the individual or individuals who inherit the plan will have more control over how quickly the assets are distributed, potentially saving your beneficiary a bundle in taxes.

Bear in mind that naming a beneficiary is not an irrevocable action. You may change your beneficiary at any time by completing a new beneficiary designation form.

Your Will Doesn't Govern Your Retirement Plan

Some people make the mistake of failing to name a beneficiary or simply naming "my estate," believing their will should take care of everything. But in the case of a retirement plan or IRA, it is the beneficiary designation form, not the will, that governs what happens to the assets. So, for example, if your beneficiary designation names your brother as beneficiary of your IRA, but in your will you indicate that you want your IRA assets to go to your partner, the IRA assets will go to your brother, because his name is on the beneficiary designation form. Similarly, if you fail to name a beneficiary on the beneficiary designation form, you are deemed not to have named a beneficiary of the plan, even if you try to leave the retirement funds to someone in your will.

Rollovers

Married couples enjoy some advantages over unmarried couples when it comes to inherited retirement plans. For example, and perhaps most important, a spouse who inherits a retirement plan is permitted to roll it over into a retirement plan of his or her own. Having done so, the spouse can then treat those assets as if they had always been part of his or her own retirement account.

In comparison, the surviving partner in an unmarried couple cannot roll over his or her deceased partner's retirement assets into the survivor's retirement plan. If the survivor attempts to make such a transaction, the assets would immediately be subject to tax and penalties.

The picture is not completely bleak, however. If you inherit an IRA from your partner, you are not required to take all the money out immediately and pay taxes on it (although you may if you wish). Instead, you are permitted to spread distributions over your life expectancy, thereby reducing the tax burden.

Thanks to a new law that took effect in 2007, you can achieve much the same result if you inherit your partner's interest in an employer's retirement plan. You may roll over your partner's retirement plan assets into an IRA and then take distributions over your life expectancy. For this to work, you must satisfy the following conditions:

- You must have the retirement plan assets transferred to a new IRA, not an existing one.

- The new IRA must be in your partner's name, not your name. (This allows the IRS to distinguish between IRAs inherited by a nonspouse and those belonging to the original owner or a spouse; different distribution rules apply so the IRS needs to know which is which.)

- The transfer must take place as a trustee-to-trustee transfer, meaning you can't take the money out and then put it into a new IRA—it has to be rolled over directly from one savings vehicle into the other.

- The employer plan must allow the rollover.

There's more good news. Even if the plan provides that your partner's interest must be paid out within five years (the five-year rule), you can void that requirement by taking your first required distribution from the employer plan on or before December 31 of the year after your partner's death and rolling over the balance into a new IRA in your partner's name—usually it will be titled to include your name as well; for example, it might say: "John Doe (deceased) IRA, for benefit of Jane

Doe." If you roll over the assets into the new IRA in the year of death, you may roll over the entire amount and take the first required distribution the following year. But again, for all of this to work, the employer's retirement plan has to permit the rollover to an IRA.

RESOURCE

For more information about inheritance and taking money out of retirement plans and IRAs, see *IRAs, 401(k)s & Other Retirement Plans: Taking Your Money Out,* **by Twila Slesnick (Nolo).**

Public Benefits

People who receive public benefits often worry that they will be cut off if their partner moves in. If you receive benefits based on your financial condition *and* a physical or mental condition—aid to the aged, blind, or disabled, for example—you don't risk any loss. Broadly speaking, these programs function like Social Security—once you qualify, you're largely left alone. When it comes to benefits based on financial condition alone (and not on a physical condition), however, living with someone may affect your food stamp eligibility or the amount of aid you receive. This issue usually arises when a woman with children who is receiving welfare wants to live with her boyfriend. In large part because the federal government now delegates welfare rules to the states, which in turn are experimenting with all sorts of policies, the best advice we can give you is to call your local social service department and make sure you understand the rules that affect you.

Depending on where you live, here is what you may find:

- Cash contributions made by a living together partner may reduce the amount of a welfare grant—but it can depend on how much is contributed and the purpose of the contribution.

- Contributions towards household expenses—such as paying the rent or buying the food—made by someone you are living with will not affect the amount of your grant.

- In a few states, a legal responsibility for all living together partners to contribute to the so-called "Welfare Unit" is presumed. This means if you live with someone in these states, your welfare grant will be reduced even if the person doesn't, in fact, chip in on expenses.

- If you have registered as domestic partners, you may have signed a statement saying you will provide for one another. This could, in theory, be used to deny one of you public benefits, especially if the other person earns substantial income.

Insurance

Generally speaking, unmarried couples can purchase most types of insurance at competitive rates. This is usually easy to do, especially if you co-own property. Be sure to shop around, because prices can vary dramatically.

This section won't help you decide whether or not you need a particular type of insurance, but will help you sort out some of the issues involved when buying insurance with a partner.

Life Insurance

Many people get life insurance as a benefit of employment or buy their own insurance policy. Either way, you can name your partner as beneficiary.

> **CAUTION**
>
> **Don't claim to be married if you aren't.** If you have a life insurance policy in which you've incorrectly stated that you are married, change it.

See Chapter 9 for more details on life insurance as it relates to estate planning.

Homeowners' Insurance

Homeowners' (or hazard) insurance is sold to homeowners when they buy a house. It insures the house against fire, flood, and other acts of destruction. It used to be difficult for unmarried couples to buy homeowners' insurance together, but this is no longer true. Many companies now write policies for unmarried couples at the same rates offered to married couples.

However, if you're the sole owner of the house, your partner's belongings won't be automatically covered by your policy. If your partner has valuable personal property, check with your homeowners' insurance company to see whether he or she can be added as an occupant and covered under the same terms as you are. Otherwise, your partner should purchase a separate renters' insurance policy.

Renters' Insurance

Renters' insurance protects tenants against the loss of their property due to theft or some act of destruction. Like homeowners' insurance, renters' insurance is easy for an unmarried couple to obtain together. Insurance companies insure the property, not the owners of the property. And the rates are related to the age and security of your building, the neighborhood you live in, and how well your landlord maintains the building. Shop around. You should be able to find one policy that covers both of you, although a few companies may try to charge you more or require that you each buy your own policy.

Automobile Insurance

Purchasing automobile insurance can be a problem for unmarried couples, but not to the extent it once was. If you each own a car, you should have no trouble getting separate insurance. For unmarried couples who jointly own one vehicle, obtaining one policy will be cheaper than getting two (one for each partner). But you may have to shop around to find an agent and company that will allow you to do this.

If you jointly own two or more cars, it's often cheaper to get one policy covering all your cars. Married couples are always allowed to do this—and thereby get discounts and other special benefits. But again, not all insurance agents or companies will offer these benefits to unmarried couples. Shop around.

If all else fails, consider transferring ownership of both cars to one person (call your department of motor vehicles and ask how you can change the title slip) and listing the other person as a secondary driver. Also, see Chapter 3, which covers joint ownership of cars.

Health Insurance

Unmarried couples often cannot get employer-paid health insurance coverage for their partner. This is changing, however. Some cities and states are offering domestic partner benefits to their employees, and more and more private employers are doing the same. A majority of the country's largest corporations offer domestic partner benefits. You can find a list of Fortune 500 companies that provide domestic partner benefits, as well as other information on benefits, at the Human Rights Campaign website, www.hrc.org.

If your employer doesn't provide domestic partner health benefits, and your partner doesn't get benefits through a job (or doesn't work), see whether your employer will agree to cover your partner on its health plan if you pay for the premiums. Group plans available through employment are usually less expensive, and often provide better coverage, than individual plans.

Even if your employer does provide domestic partner health benefits, the premium paid to cover the domestic partner will be considered taxable income, not a pre-tax deduction from income as it is when the employee is covering a spouse. Also, be aware that the federal COBRA (Consolidated Omnibus Budget Reconciliation Act) health insurance rules don't apply to your partner if you lose or leave your job. Under COBRA, your employer must allow you to continue health insurance coverage for a certain period of time, as long as you pay the premiums, but your partner is not entitled to continue domestic partner benefits as would be the case if you were married.

Workers' Compensation Insurance

In some states, the dependent of a worker who is killed on the job can obtain death benefits from the state workers' compensation insurance program. Because "dependent" is often broadly defined, in several instances courts have allowed unmarried partners to recover these benefits. For example, a Maryland court awarded workers' compensation benefits to a woman who lived with the deceased worker for a number of years—giving up her job to take care of the house and raise the children while the deceased provided financial support. (*Kendall v. Housing Auth.*, 76 A.2d 767 (Md. Ct. Spec. App. 1950).) In California, a court awarded benefits to a woman who lived with the deceased worker because she was a "good faith" member of his household, even though she was married to someone else. (*State v. Workers' Compensation Appeals Bd.*, 94 Cal. App. 3d 72 (Ct. App. 1979).) And in Oregon, the Workers' Compensation statute itself states that unmarried cohabitants are entitled to compensation as long as the couple had children together and lived together for more than one year before the worker was injured. (Or. Rev. Stat. § 656.226 (1991).)

However, not all courts have been so generous. In South Carolina, a woman living with and dependent on a deceased worker was denied workers' compensation benefits because she was married to another man. (*Palm v. General Painting Co.*, 370 S.E. 2d 463 (S.C. Ct. App. 1988).) And in Nevada, a court denied death benefits to the unmarried cohabitant of a deceased worker, even where the cohabitant had previously been married to the deceased worker, because she no longer had a "legally recognizable relationship" with him. (*Banegas v. State Indus. Ins. System*, 19 P.3d 245 (2001).)

Unemployment Insurance

In many states, an employee may obtain unemployment insurance benefits for quitting a job for "good cause." Often, the unemployment board will consider a spouse's decision to leave employment in order to accompany the other spouse to a new home to be "good cause." In several cases, this benefit has been extended to unmarried partners as well. For example, the Massachusetts Supreme Court ruled that a woman who left her job in order to remain with her living together partner of 13 years who was relocating his business had compelling reasons to quit and was entitled to unemployment insurance benefits. (*Reep v. Commissioner of Dep't of Employment & Training*, 593 N.E. 2d 1297 (Mass. 1992).) The California Supreme Court also awarded unemployment benefits to an unmarried woman who quit her job in order to follow her partner to another state. (*MacGregor v. Unemployment Ins. Appeals Bd.*, 37 Cal. 3d 205 (1984).) However, in that case, the court's decision was based in large part on the fact that the unmarried couple had a child together. It's unclear whether the California Supreme Court would rule the same way if an unmarried couple did not have children together.

Liability for Medical Care of a Mate

Generally, one member of a married couple is liable to pay for all, or at least a substantial portion of, health and nursing home care for the other, over and above what is reimbursed by public or private insurance. (State laws allow a healthy spouse of modest means to keep (exempt) a portion of the combined property.)

Fortunately, the legal situation is far better for unmarried couples. If one partner has large medical bills or moves to a nursing home, the other's property is not at risk of being grabbed to pay the bills—unless the couple has voluntarily mixed their property together, as with a joint bank account. If the institutionalized person exhausts his or her property, including that person's half of jointly owned property, Medicare pays the rest, and the other member of the couple need not exhaust any savings or sell property to raise money. For more information, see *Long-Term Care: How to Plan & Pay for It*, by Joseph Matthews (Nolo).

Making Medical and Financial Decisions for Your Partner

If you ever become unable to make your own health care decisions or manage your own finances—because of injury, serious illness, or advanced age—you probably want your partner to step in and take care of you. Unfortunately, unmarried couples, unlike their married counterparts, often aren't permitted to handle medical or financial decisions for each other without signed authorization.

There are a few simple legal documents you should prepare if you want to ensure that critical decisions stay in the hands of your partner. These are called health care directives and durable powers of attorney for finances. Without these documents, your partner may face substantial obstacles to acting for you in the event of a medical emergency or handling a simple financial transaction on your behalf. At worst, your health care and finances may be placed in the hands of a biological relative who won't consider your partner's input, and may well make decisions contrary to what you want.

Fortunately, the documents you need are straightforward and usually easy to complete.

Health Care Directives

Every state has laws authorizing individuals to create simple documents setting out their wishes about the type of medical treatment they do (or do not) want to receive if they are unable to communicate their preferences. These documents may also name someone to make medical decisions on the signer's behalf. These documents are particularly important for unmarried partners. If you don't take the time to prepare them and you become incapacitated, doctors will turn to a family member designated by state law to make medical decisions for you. Most states list spouses, adult children, and parents as top-priority decision makers, making no mention of unmarried partners.

Registered domestic or civil union partners are always given priority as surrogate decision makers. And a few states that don't offer registration make room for unmarried partners on their list of potential decision makers, though they are not always given priority. No matter what state you live in, you can save your partner a great deal of time and trouble by planning ahead.

There are two documents that permit you to set out your health care wishes, both grouped under the broad label "health care directives." First, you need a written statement you make directly to medical personnel that spells out your wishes for medical care if you become incapacitated. Your statement functions as a contract with your treating doctor, who must either honor your wishes for health care or transfer you to another doctor or facility that will honor them.

The second document is usually called a "durable power of attorney for health care." In this document you appoint the person you choose—most likely your partner—to see that your doctors and other health care providers give you the kind of

medical care you want to receive. You can also use your durable power of attorney for health care to give your partner (who may be called your "attorney-in-fact," "agent," or "proxy" depending on where you live) other rights to participate in your medical care, including:

- directing your health care under any circumstances that you don't specifically address in your declaration
- hiring and firing medical personnel
- visiting you in the hospital or other facility even when other visiting is restricted
- having access to medical records and other personal information, and
- getting court authorization to enforce your health care wishes if a hospital or doctor refuses to honor them for any reason.

In some states, your statement of wishes and appointment of a proxy will be combined into a single document, often called an "Advance Health Care Directive."

A Health Care Directive by Any Other Name...

Depending on the state, your health care documents may be called by one of several different names: Advance Health Care Directive, Medical Directive, Directive to Physicians, Declaration Regarding Health Care, Designation of Health Care Surrogate, or Patient Advocate Designation. A health care directive may also be called a "living will," but it bears no relation to the conventional will used to leave property at death.

You can make valid health care directives if you are at least 18 years old and of sound mind. Being of sound mind essentially means that you are able to understand what the document means, what it contains, and how it works. Physically disabled people may make valid health care documents;

they can direct another to sign for them if they are physically unable to do so.

As long as you are of sound mind, you can change or revoke your health care directives at any time.

Durable Powers of Attorney for Finances

A durable power of attorney for finances allows you to name someone you trust (called your "attorney-in-fact" or "agent") to handle your finances if you become unable to take care of yourself. Every state recognizes this type of document.

As with documents directing medical care, you should seriously consider making a durable power of attorney for finances if you want your partner to manage your money if you can't. If you don't prepare the document and you later become incapacitated, your partner or other family members will have to ask a court for authority over your financial affairs. These proceedings, called "conservatorship proceedings," can be time-consuming and expensive—and they can be disastrous for unmarried couples if the court names another family member to take over, especially if your finances have been intertwined with those of your partner for a long time.

You can make your financial power of attorney effective immediately or you can specify that it should go into effect only if you become incapacitated; the latter is called a "springing" power of attorney. While some people are more comfortable making a springing document, an immediately effective document holds a potential advantage for unmarried couples in a long-term trusting relationship. If you make your document effective immediately, your partner can handle financial transactions for you at any time, even when you are not incapacitated. This can be useful if you are out of town, under the weather, or temporarily unavailable for any other reason.

When you make a durable power of attorney for finances, you can give your partner (or other attorney-in-fact) as much or as little control over your finances as you wish. The powers you grant may include:

- using your assets to pay your bills and everyday expenses
- buying, selling, maintaining, paying taxes on, and mortgaging real estate and other property
- collecting benefits from Social Security, Medicare, or other government programs or civil or military service
- investing your money in stocks, bonds, and mutual funds
- handling transactions with banks and other financial institutions
- buying and selling insurance policies and annuities
- filing and paying your taxes
- operating your small business
- claiming property you inherit or are otherwise entitled to
- hiring someone to represent you in court, and
- managing your retirement accounts.

Whatever powers you give your attorney-in-fact, he or she is legally required to act in your best interests.

Like health care directives, you can make a durable power of attorney for finances if you are at least 18 years old and of sound mind. And as long as you continue to be of sound mind, you can change or cancel your document at any time.

RESOURCE

Where to get the forms you need. There are a number of ways to find the proper health care and power of attorney forms for your state. You don't usually need to consult a lawyer to obtain or prepare them. Here are some likely sources for forms and instructions:

Quicken WillMaker Plus (Nolo) is software for Windows that allows you to prepare a health care directive and a durable power of attorney for finances.

It also lets you make a will, living trust, and many other useful legal documents.

Partnership for Caring offers health care forms for every state. You can download forms for free at www.partnershipforcaring.org. Or you can order them for a small fee by writing or calling the organization at 1620 Eye Street NW, Suite 202, Washington, DC 20006, 800-989-9455.

You may also be able to obtain health care forms from local senior centers, hospitals, your regular physician, or your state's medical association.

Wrongful Death and Loss of Consortium Lawsuits

When a person is killed as a result of a negligent or intentional act, the law of every state recognizes the right of a spouse and relatives to file suit and recover money and other economic benefits they would have received from the deceased person if the person had lived. Called "wrongful death statutes," these laws have traditionally not allowed unmarried partners to sue, even where the relationship has lasted many years. The unfair result can be that a blood relative who you don't even live with may be compensated, while a person you have lived with for 20 years—and who may have suffered both emotional and economic losses as a result of your death—can't be.

More recently, however, many legal commentators have agreed that it's time for the wrongful death law to catch up with social reality. And in a closely related area of the law, a few courts have granted so-called "bystander" rights—traditionally limited to spouses and blood relatives—to unmarried couples. (*Dumphy v. Gregor*, 642 A.2d 372 (N.J. 1994) and *Binns v. Fredendall*, 513 N.E. 2d 278 (Ohio 1987).) Bystander rights come into play to compensate a person who suffered emotional distress as a result of witnessing a loved one being killed or seriously injured.

New Mexico recently became the only state in which an unmarried cohabitant can make a claim for "loss of consortium"—usually defined as the loss of the companionship of a spouse as a result of injury. (*Lozoya v. Sanchez*, 133 N.M. 579, 66 P.3d 948 (2003).) The court ruled that factors to be considered in determining whether an unmarried partner's claim should be granted include the length of the relationship and the degree to which the partners' lives are intertwined. ●

Renting and Sharing a Home

If you're going to live with someone and you're both renters, you have to get a place. That means renting an apartment or house together, or having one partner move into the other partner's rental. Here we focus on the special legal problems encountered by unmarried couples renting together.

RESOURCE

Other landlord-tenant questions? For complete details on your rights as a tenant and landlord-tenant law, including security deposit rules, privacy rights, habitability requirements, occupancy limits, rent control, roommates, and how tenancies end, see *Every Tenant's Legal Guide,* by Janet Portman and Marcia Stewart. Californians should see *California Tenants' Rights,* by Janet Portman and David Brown. Both are published by Nolo.

CROSS REFERENCE

Related topics in this book include:

- States with laws prohibiting cohabitation by unmarried couples: Chapter 2

- Buying a house together, or moving into your partner's house: Chapter 6

- Dealing with problems regarding rental property— and each other—if you separate: Chapter 10.

Discrimination on the Basis of Marital Status

Most landlords are interested in your money, not your morals. As long as you pay rent on time, keep the rental clean, and don't fight with the neighbors, they don't care in which beds you sleep. There are, of course, exceptions—people who still refuse to rent to unmarried couples. Some landlords (despite the divorce statistics) believe that unmarried couples are inherently less stable than married ones. Others may refuse to rent to you on religious grounds. Unfortunately, in most states, landlords can get away with these kinds of choices.

This section summarizes the law on housing discrimination against unmarried couples and provides practical tips on avoiding problems with landlords.

Housing Rights of Unmarried Couples

Do you have a legal right, as an unmarried couple, to rent a place? Not under federal law. The Federal Fair Housing Acts (42 U.S. Code §§ 3601–3619) prohibit discrimination on the basis of race or color, religion, national origin, gender, familial status (having children and pregnancy), and physical or mental disability. Marital status is not one of the protected categories under federal law. (Public housing is an exception. Several courts have interpreted federal law to protect unmarried couples from discrimination there.)

State law is not much better. The majority of states don't have any legal provisions protecting people from discrimination based on marital status, meaning landlords may legally ask questions about your relationship and may refuse to rent to you if you are an unmarried couple.

While some 20 states ban discrimination on the basis of marital status, most of these states' laws extend protection to married couples only (meaning that landlords cannot treat married tenants differently from single tenants). Only a few states—California, Massachusetts, Michigan, and New Jersey—have clearly ruled that the term "marital status" refers to *unmarried* couples. Oddly, courts in Maryland, Minnesota, New York, and Wisconsin have ruled that the term "marital status" protects *single* people from being treated differently from married people, and vice versa, but does not protect unmarried couples.

Some landlords resist renting to unmarried couples on the grounds that cohabitation violates their religious beliefs. Courts in Alaska, California, Massachusetts, and New Jersey have refused to allow landlords to reject unmarried couples as tenants for this reason.

Your best protection against discrimination may be a city or county ordinance prohibiting discrimination on the basis of sexual orientation. Although usually passed to protect the housing rights of gay and lesbian tenants, most local laws forbidding discrimination based on sexual orientation also protect unmarried heterosexual couples as well.

If you suspect (or know for sure) that a landlord won't rent to you because you're not married, first find out whether your city or state has a law that has been interpreted to prohibit discrimination against unmarried couples in rental housing. If the answer is yes, you have a decent chance of winning if you fight back.

TIP

Remember that landlords are allowed to discriminate for legitimate business reasons. Even if you live in a state that prohibits discrimination on the basis of marital status, it's no guarantee you'll get the place you want. Landlords may reject you for legitimate business reasons, such as a bad credit history or negative references from other landlords.

RESOURCE

For up-to-date information on housing discrimination rules in your area, call your local city attorney's office or check your state laws and local ordinances. (Check under the heading "Housing Discrimination.") See Chapter 11 for advice on doing this type of legal research. For information on federal fair housing laws, visit the website of the Department of Housing and Urban Development (HUD) at www.hud.gov.

Practical Tips for Dealing With Potential Landlords

If your state or city has no law prohibiting discrimination on the basis of marital status, you'll have to decide how open you want to be with your landlord. Here are some suggestions:

- Act in a highly responsible and respectable manner. Be ready to present financial and credit information and personal references, especially from former landlords. If you convince a landlord that you'll be excellent tenants, other factors, such as your marital status, will be less important.
- Don't flaunt the fact that you're not married. In an age when many married women use their own last name, many landlords will assume you are married and won't ask. Most won't care.
- In conservative parts of the country particularly, it may help to go with the flow. In every city, and most large towns, there are neighborhoods with lots of unmarried people. This often tends to be true near universities. If you are new to an area, ask around.

You may not want to rent from a landlord who obviously disapproves of unmarried couples living together. This is especially true if the landlord lives nearby. Life is too short for all the hassles you're inviting by renting from someone who's inappropriately interested in tenants' private lives. If at all possible, look elsewhere.

Leases and Rental Agreements

Before signing a lease or rental agreement, carefully examine every clause. Many lease provisions are extremely restrictive and some are downright illegal and out-of-date. For example, a rental agreement form may purport to give the landlord the right to evict you without getting a court order if you fail to pay the rent. This is illegal—only a judge can order that you be evicted.

We don't have room to list all the possible illegal lease provisions, but in particular, unmarried couples should look out for any clause prohibiting "immoral behavior." If living together is legal in your state, this clause can't be used to evict you. But if cohabitation is still illegal where you live (see

Chapter 2), a landlord may attempt to use a clause prohibiting "immoral behavior" to evict you. If you are worried about this, ask the landlord to cross out "immoral behavior" language. If the landlord refuses, it's probably a signal that you'd be happier renting elsewhere.

Likewise, state laws tend to be very restrictive about the landlord's right of access to an occupied rental. If you live in one of these states, but your lease gives the landlord open-ended access to your rental, you'll know that the landlord either doesn't know the law or is deliberately breaking it. Check the laws of your state regarding rights of access (see Chapter 11 for information on how to do legal research). If your landlord offers you a lease or rental agreement that is in violation of state law, ask the landlord to revise it to comply with the law. If the landlord doesn't want to do this, once again, you've learned that your prospective landlord isn't willing to comply with the legal requirements that come with owning rental property, and you should reconsider your rental application.

Moving In Together

It's essential that you are clear as to whether you are both renting the place as cotenants or whether only one of you is the tenant and the other person is a subtenant (someone who rents from the tenant). When you are both cotenants, you have legal obligations vis-a-vis the landlord and each other that are different than the legal obligations of a tenant and a subtenant. Let's consider each of these separately.

Cotenants' Legal Obligations to the Landlord

Renting a place together and signing the same lease is the most common way that two people become cotenants. But you and your partner can become cotenants in another way, too. If you have a place and your landlord approves of an additional occupant, your partner can sign your original lease and become a cotenant. And suppose your partner moves into your rental and is openly acknowledged as a resident by the landlord—the landlord knows he's there, accepts rent from him, responds to his requests for repairs, and in every other respect treats him just like he treats you. In many states, this behavior on the part of the landlord will make your partner a cotenant, just as if he had formally signed a lease. This means, for example, that the landlord can expect your partner to pay the entire rent if you don't, as explained below, and it also means that you cannot evict your cotenant. If you want eviction rights, you'll have to keep your sweetie a subtenant, as explained below.

If you and your partner are cotenants, you're each on the hook for all rent and all damages to the rental—it doesn't matter how you split the rent or who caused the damage. You are each independently liable to the landlord for all of the rent and for complying with all terms of the lease or rental agreement.

Landlords often remind cotenants of this obligation by inserting into the lease a chunk of legalese that says that the tenants are "jointly and severally" liable for paying rent and adhering to the terms of the agreement. If one tenant (your partner) can't pay his or her share of the rent in a particular month, or simply moves out, you (the other tenant) must still pay the full rent.

EXAMPLE 1:

Clem and Julie sign a month-to-month rental agreement for $1,500 a month. They agree between themselves to each pay one-half of the rent. After three months, Clem moves out with no notice to Julie or the landlord. Julie is liable for all the rent. Clem, of course, is equally liable, but if he's unreachable, the landlord will come after Julie for the entire amount. Julie can cut her losses by legally ending the tenancy (this typically requires giving the landlord 30 days' written notice). When she moves out at the end of that period, her liability ends.

EXAMPLE 2:

This time, Clem just hangs about the place, refusing to pay or leave. Even if Julie gives the landlord a 30-day written notice and moves out, leaving Clem in the rental unit, she is still liable for the rent for as long as Clem remains. The landlord will eventually evict Clem, but is likely to try to collect all unpaid rent from Julie if she's the one with a job, including the rent for the period after she moved out. In short, Julie's best bet is to persuade Clem to get out when she does.

EXAMPLE 3:

The same facts as Example 1, but the couple has a one-year lease. Again, Clem and Julie are both liable for all the rent. If one won't pay, the other must, unless the landlord approves someone new to take over the lease. If Clem and Julie both leave, in most states the landlord must attempt to limit losses (called "mitigation of damages") by renting to a suitable new tenant. If the landlord doesn't make this effort, the landlord loses the right to collect lost rent from Julie and Clem. But if the landlord can't find a new tenant (or can only find one at a reduced rent), both Clem and Julie are independently liable for the difference between the amount called for in the lease and the amount the landlord actually collects.

TIP

Small claims court can be an effective way to collect from a former living together partner. If you pay the landlord more than your fair share of the rent, you have a legal right to recover from your partner only if you had an agreement, separate from your lease or rental agreement, that you would pay rent equally. If you break up and are shortchanged, try small claims court. (*Everybody's Guide to Small Claims Court*, by Ralph Warner (Nolo), shows how.) However, it usually doesn't make sense to sue unless you have a rent-sharing agreement in writing, and are pretty sure you can collect the judgment (this normally means that your former partner has a job or savings). In short, if your ex is a determined deadbeat, getting a small claims judgment won't put any money in your pocket.

Cotenants' joint and several liability is broader than just rent. The landlord can hold all cotenants responsible for the negative actions of just one, and terminate both of your tenancies with the appropriate notice. For example, you can be evicted if your partner seriously damages the property, moves in a dog (contrary to the landlord's no-pets rule), or otherwise violates the lease or rental agreement.

If your landlord approves your request to add a roommate, he or she will probably ask both you and your partner to sign a new lease or month-to-month rental agreement. From your landlord's point of view, this is far more than a formality, as it makes the new arrival a cotenant who is 100% liable to pay rent and make good on any damage (as discussed above). It's also desirable from your perspective, because it makes it completely clear that you and your partner share the same legal rights and responsibilities.

Cotenants' Obligations to Each Other

People sharing a rental unit usually have certain expectations of each other as roommates. We recommend that you write them down. After all, you sign an agreement with a landlord almost as a matter of course—why not do the same with each other? It's a good way to make sure you're both clear as to your responsibilities to each other as tenants—who pays what portion of the rent and utilities, who gets the place if you split up, and the like.

If your relationship ends down the line, memories may have blurred and questions such as "Whose apartment is this, anyway?" may turn into serious disputes. To avoid later problems, write down your understanding when you first move in together. A sample Agreement Covering Rented Living Space is shown below.

CD-ROM

The forms CD includes the Agreement Covering Rented Living Space, and Appendix B includes a blank tear-out copy of the form.

This agreement can stand alone or be incorporated into a more comprehensive living together contract, such as the ones discussed in Chapter 3. You can edit this agreement—for example, you can include paragraphs about living expenses, cleaning responsibilities, or anything else that is important to you. As with all the contracts in this book, the Agreement Covering Rented Living Space includes a clause requiring you and your partner to participate in mediation.

The Tenant and Subtenant Arrangement

Instead of being cotenants, you and your partner may have a tenant-subtenant arrangement. In this situation, the tenant rents directly from the landlord, and the subtenant rents from the tenant. You're likely to have this kind of arrangement if one of you moves in with the other and the landlord does not put the newcomer on the lease or otherwise acknowledge the second resident as a coequal of the original tenant, as explained above.

The main difference between the cotenant and tenant-subtenant arrangement lies in the tenant's ability to evict a subtenant. If your roommate is a cotenant, you cannot evict him or her. If your roommate is a subtenant, however, you do have eviction powers. But landlords in the know will usually object to allowing you to set up a tenant-subtenant situation. They want to retain the power

to evict either or both of you, and they also want everyone living on the property to be subject to the "joint and several" liability rule described above (in a tenant-subtenant situation, the landlord cannot demand the entire rent from the subtenant, though he or she can evict both of you if the rent isn't paid).

Let's see how these rules play out. In the Clem and Julie situation, suppose Julie has not signed a rental agreement and Clem wants to move out and Julie wants to remain; Julie and the landlord's legal relationship needs to be clarified. Clem should give written notice of his intent to leave (at least 30 days is usually required under state law) before he moves out. If he has a rental agreement, he owes no rent after the 30 days, assuming Julie is willing and able to pay. But to avoid possible problems later, should Julie be unable to pay the rent, Clem should contact the landlord and request that his name be removed from the rental agreement and Julie's officially substituted. See the Sample Tenant's Notice of Intent to Move Out and Substitute New Tenant, below.

If Clem has a lease and leaves before it expires, he still should be okay because the landlord must make reasonable efforts to limit his losses by finding a new tenant. In many states, your landlord is legally bound to accept a suitable tenant or find one without your help. Because Julie, presumably a reasonably solvent and nondestructive person, wants to stay, the landlord suffers no loss. The result is that if the landlord refuses Julie without good reason, Clem still owes no money, and any loss is the landlord's problem for refusing to limit his financial loss by letting Julie remain.

Even if you don't both sign a lease or rental agreement, you should definitely sign an agreement with each other, such as the one shown below, clarifying what happens to the rental should you separate.

Dealing With Objections When Moving Into the Rental Home of One Partner

Almost as common as two people looking for a home together is one person moving in with the other. This can be simple and smooth where the landlord is reasonable, but can raise tricky problems (and isn't recommended) if the landlord disapproves of unmarried couples or clearly doesn't want another person to move in. Don't try to argue with someone whom you know you can't convince. Use the time and energy to look for a place where the landlord is pleasant.

Sometimes, especially if the landlord lives far away or isn't likely to make waves, it seems sensible to have your partner move in and worry about the consequences later. But isn't a tenant required to get the landlord's permission before another person moves in? Usually the answer is yes, because leases and rental agreements typically limit the number of people allowed in the apartment or require landlord approval for additional roommates.

Even if your lease or rental agreement doesn't have a specific requirement that the landlord must approve additional tenants, it's normally wise to notify your landlord before moving in another person. Your landlord will almost surely figure it out anyway, and it's especially important to avoid looking sneaky if you have a month-to-month tenancy in a non-rent-control area where the landlord can evict for any reason. On the other hand, if the landlord accepts rent knowing that you have a roommate, the landlord has probably waived the legal right to enforce the "only one occupant" clause.

Getting the Landlord's Permission

If one of you plans to move into the other's rented space, whether as a cotenant or subtenant, here's our advice:

- Read the lease or rental agreement to see how many people may live on the premises and whether you need the landlord's permission to add a roommate.

- To help assure your landlord's approval, make sure your partner will meet your landlord's good-tenant criteria in terms of credit and financial status and rental history with other landlords. If you're afraid that your partner does not, in fact, meet the good-tenant requirements, it's still a good idea to let your landlord know you are adding a roommate, and try to work it out. If the landlord is really strict, you may end up needing to find another place with your partner. But even that will be better than having your landlord find out that you had someone new move in without notifying the management.

- Contact the landlord as far in advance as possible to explain your desire to add a roommate. Unless you are on fairly close personal terms with your landlord, it's a good idea to do this in writing. See the sample Letter Requesting Permission to Add a Roommate, below.

CD-ROM

The forms CD includes the Letter Requesting Permission to Add a Roommate, and Appendix B includes a blank, tear-out copy.

If you are a good tenant and regularly pay rent on time, it's more likely that your landlord will approve your request to add a roommate, even if he prefers renting to married couples.

Agreement Covering Rented Living Space

_____Julie Renoir_____ and _____Clem Lawrence_____ agree that:

1. We will jointly rent __Apartment # 4 at 1500 Peanut St., Dallas, Texas__. We have both signed a __month-to-month rental agreement__ with the landlord, __Reuben Shaw__ , and have each paid $ _750_ towards the security deposit of $ _1,500_ .

2. Each of us will pay one-half of the rent and one-half of the utilities, including the basic monthly telephone, cable, and DSL charges. We will each keep track of and pay for our own long distance calls. Rent will be paid on the first of each month and utilities within ten days of when the bill is received. Utilities will be in the name of __Clem Lawrence__ .

3. If either of us wants to move out, the one moving will give the other and the landlord 30 days' written notice and will pay his/her share of the rent for the entire 30-day period even if he/she moves out sooner.

4. No third person will be invited to stay in the apartment without the agreement of both.

5. If one of us no longer wishes to live with the other, but both want to keep the apartment, the following will occur [check one]:

   [X] _____Julie_____ has first rights to stay in the apartment and _____Clem_____ will move out.

   ☐ We will ask a third person to flip a coin to see who gets to stay.

   ☐ The person who needs the apartment most will retain it. Need will be determined by a third party whom we agree is objective, within two weeks of the date when one informs the other that he/she wishes to separate. In making this decision, the third party will consider each person's relative financial condition, proximity to work, the needs of any minor children, and _____[list any other important factors]_____ .

   ☐ Other. _____ .

   The person who is to leave will do so within _____two weeks_____ of when that decision is made, and will have an additional ___ten days___ to pay his/her obligations for rent, utilities, and any damage to the apartment.

6. Any dispute arising out of this agreement will be mediated by a third person mutually acceptable to both of us. The mediator's role will be to help us arrive at a solution, not to impose one on us. If good faith efforts to arrive at our own solution with the help of a mediator prove to be fruitless, either of us may make a written request to the other that the dispute be arbitrated. If such a request is made, our dispute will be submitted to arbitration under the rules of the American Arbitration Association, and one arbitrator will hear our dispute. The decision of the arbitrator will be binding on us and will be enforceable in any court that has jurisdiction over the controversy. By agreeing to arbitration, we each agree to give up the right to a jury trial.

7. Additional agreements: _____ .

8. This agreement represents our complete understanding regarding our living together and replaces any prior agreements, written or oral. It can be amended, but only in writing, and any amendments must be signed by both of us.

9. If a court finds any portion of this contract to be illegal or otherwise unenforceable, the remainder of the contract is still in full force and effect.

____*Julie Renoir*____   ____*March 7, 20xx*____
Julie Renoir   Date

____*Clem Lawrence*____   ____*March 7, 20xx*____
Clem Lawrence   Date

Letter Requesting Permission to Add a Roommate

1500 Peanut Street, #4
Dallas, Texas
June 2, 20xx

Smith Realty
10 Jones Street
Dallas, Texas

Dear Smith Realty :

I live at the above address and regularly pay rent to your office. I would like to add a second person, Julie Renoir , to my lease beginning July 1, 20xx . ~~He~~/She will be glad to complete a rental application and provide a recent copy of ~~his~~/her credit report and references.

I will call you soon to discuss this further. Thank you very much for considering this request.

Very truly yours,

Clem Lawrence

More Roommates, More Rent

A landlord who agrees to an additional cotenant may ask for a rent increase on the theory that more people means more wear and tear. By signing a new lease or rental agreement that creates a cotenancy, you are, in effect, starting a new tenancy, so the landlord can increase rent immediately, rather than give you the usual 30 days' notice (for a month-to-month rental agreement) or wait until the lease ends.

Unless your rental unit is covered by rent control —or if the landlord is using a big rent increase as a not-so-subtle way to discriminate against you for an illegal reason—your landlord can ask for as much extra money as the market will bear.

TIP

Negotiate the rent increase. Just because your landlord asks for a big rent increase doesn't mean you have to say yes. One good approach is to counteroffer a lower amount. Let the landlord know that you may rethink adding a roommate, or even move out yourself, if you can't reach an acceptable compromise.

Security Deposit Increases

The landlord also has the legal right to change other conditions of your tenancy when you add a cotenant and sign a new agreement. One change that is particularly likely is an increase in the security deposit. However, this is one area where the sky is not the limit, because many states limit the amount of security deposits. Usually the limit is a multiple of the monthly rent. Keep in mind that if the deposit is already at the maximum, but the landlord raises the rent for the new occupant, the maximum security deposit goes up, too.

Sample Tenant's Notice of Intent to Move Out and Substitute New Tenant

(For use if you have a
month-to-month rental agreement)

1500 Peanut Street, #4
Dallas, Texas
June 27, 20xx

Smith Realty
10 Jones Street
Dallas, Texas

Dear Smith Realty:

I live at the above address and regularly pay rent to your office under a month-to-month rental agreement. On July 31, 20xx, I will be moving out. As you know, my friend Julie Renoir also resides here. She wishes to remain and will continue to pay rent to your office on the first of each month.

We'll be contacting you soon to arrange for the return of my security deposit of $750, at which time Julie will give you a similar deposit. I would also like to have my name taken off the rental agreement and Julie's substituted. If you have any questions, or if there's anything we can do to make the transition easier, please let us know.

Very truly yours,

Clem Lawrence
555-1234

Sample Tenant's Notice of Intent to Move Out and Substitute New Tenant

(For use if you have a lease)

1500 Peanut Street, #4
Dallas, Texas
June 27, 20xx

Smith Realty
10 Jones Street
Dallas, Texas

Dear Smith Realty:

I live at the above address under a lease that expires on October 30, 20xx. A change in my job makes it necessary that I leave on the last day of August. As you know, for the last six months my friend Julie Renoir has been sharing this apartment. Julie wishes to either take over my lease or enter into a new one with you for the remainder of my lease term. She's employed, has a stable income, and will, of course, be a responsible tenant.

We will soon be contacting your office to work out the details of the transfer. If you have any concerns, please give us a call.

Very truly yours,

Clem Lawrence
555-1234

Getting Your Security Deposit Back

Getting your apartment security deposit back is a concern for all tenants—married couples, unmarried partners, and roommates. But special issues arise when one person moves out and the other remains. If you and your partner sign a lease or rental agreement together and only one of you moves out, your landlord does not have to return the security deposit to you. After all, one of you is still living there. It is up to the couple to work out a fair arrangement in this situation. Perhaps the remaining tenant pays the moving tenant half of the deposit. Or maybe a replacement roommate will pay the moving tenant a portion of the security deposit. It's best to decide how this will be handled before the situation arises. For example, include it in your agreement covering rented living space.

If both you and your partner are moving out of the apartment and want to ensure that you get your full (or close to full) security deposit back, follow this advice, which applies to all tenants (married or not):

Step 1: Document, in writing and with photographs, any problems that exist when you move in. Note dirty conditions, damaged rugs or appliances, faulty plumbing, and scratched, chipped, or cracked walls and floors. Get the landlord to sign your written list of problems. If the landlord refuses, have friends check the place over and sign your list.

Step 2: Thoroughly clean the apartment before you leave. Keep receipts for all cleaning supplies or services used (such as rental of a carpet cleaning machine).

Step 3: Document, in writing and with photographs, the condition of the apartment after you remove your belongings and clean the place.

Step 4: Do a final inspection of the apartment with your landlord. Get the landlord to sign the document you created in Step 3. If the landlord refuses, have friends inspect the apartment and take photos.

Step 5: Understand what can and cannot be deducted from your security deposit. Your landlord cannot charge you for normal wear and tear to the apartment. However, you are responsible for any other damage. You are entitled to your full security deposit less the cost of the damage over and above normal wear and tear.

Step 6: If your landlord doesn't return your security deposit within the time period specified by your state (usually between 14 and 30 days after moving out), send a demand letter to your landlord. If you get no response, you can sue the landlord in small claims court.

RESOURCE

Information on tenants' rights. For detailed information about your rights and obligations as a tenant, including how to get your security deposit back, see *Every Tenant's Legal Guide*, by Janet Portman and Marcia Stewart (Nolo). California tenants should see *California Tenants' Rights*, by Janet Portman and David Brown (Nolo). You can also obtain free information on a variety of issues affecting tenants at Nolo's website at www.nolo.com.

RESOURCE

Information on small claims court. If you have to go to small claims court, be sure to check out *Everybody's Guide to Small Claims Court*, by Ralph Warner (Nolo), or, for California residents, *Everybody's Guide to Small Claims Court in California*, by Ralph Warner (Nolo).

Buying a House Together

There may come a time when you and your partner decide to purchase a house together. That means that you'll have lots to do—locating an affordable house that meets your needs isn't always easy. And once you find your dream house, you must bargain with the seller for a favorable price, arrange for a good deal on a mortgage, have the house inspected for physical defects, and make decisions on dozens of other issues.

This chapter provides an overview of the most important aspects of housebuying. This generally involves four steps:

1. Finding the house.
2. Financing the purchase.
3. Transferring ownership (taking title to the house).
4. Working out a sensible ownership agreement between you and your partner (the buyers).

This chapter provides the legal information and sample agreements you'll need if you and your partner decide to purchase a house together. We focus on how best to take title to real property and on the specific provisions you'll want to include in an agreement for owning a house together, such as how you will share costs and what will happen to the house if you break up. Our goal is to help you create a legally binding agreement that truly meets both of your needs.

CROSS REFERENCE

Related topics covered in this book include:

- Writing living together contracts: Chapter 3
- Naming beneficiaries for real estate in a will: Chapter 9
- Dealing with the house if you break up: Chapter 10
- Working with a lawyer and researching real estate law: Chapter 11.

RESOURCE

For more information on buying a house and a guide to the best online real estate services—from financing to house inspections—see the Real Estate topic of Nolo's website at www.nolo.com. If it's your first house, check out *Nolo's Essential Guide to Buying Your First Home*, by Ilona Bray, Alayna Schroeder, and Marcia Stewart (Nolo). Californians should see *How to Buy a House in California*, by Ralph Warner, Ira Serkes, and George Devine (Nolo), for all aspects of home buying in the Golden State.

May Sellers Discriminate Against Unmarried Buyers?

Few, if any, sellers will care about your marital status. But if a seller does refuse to sell to you simply because you aren't married, you may have little or no legal recourse in most places. In a growing number of states and in some cities, discrimination on the basis of marital status in the sale of real property is illegal. However, in many of these states, courts have ruled that "marital status" applies to married couples (or sometimes single people) but not unmarried couples. If you run into problems buying property as an unmarried couple, contact your city attorney's office, state fair housing office, or the U.S. Department of Housing and Urban Development (HUD) for advice.

TIP

How to avoid discrimination. If you face a serious threat of discrimination, consider presenting the house purchase offer in one name alone, and then add the second name only when you are ready to close escrow.

In a few areas, you may face an unexpected obstacle: zoning ordinances aimed at barring unrelated people from living together. Most of these laws prohibit groups of people from living together, but a few also prohibit two unrelated adults from living together. Several state courts, including those in Michigan, New York, and California, have interpreted their own constitutions to prohibit local communities from discriminating against unrelated adults. But unfortunately, other states' courts have been less open-minded. For example, one Missouri court evicted an unmarried couple and their children from a neighborhood zoned for single family residences, stating that "there is no state policy which commands that groups of people may live under the same roof in any section of a municipality they choose." (*City of Ladue v. Horn*, 720 S.W. 2d 745 (1986).) And a Maryland court allowed a co-op to restrict residents to the immediate family of the co-op member, stating that it would provide "a more stable community." *(Maryland Commission on Human Relations v. Greenbelt*, 475 A.2d 1192 (1984).) Although it's very unlikely you'll run into this sort of problem, it still makes sense to check that the city—or neighborhood—in which you plan to buy isn't zoned only for people related by "blood, marriage, or adoption." Also, if you're buying a co-op or a property subject to a community association, check the rules for any restrictions.

How to Find and Work With a Real Estate Agent

Most homebuyers use a real estate broker (or an agent who works for a broker) to help find a home and negotiate the house purchase contract. A good agent can give you advice on prices, school districts, transportation, demographics, and economic trends in the area (for example, whether property values are going up or down). A broker or agent should also help you find the other experts you need—such as a termite inspector, a roofer, or a soil engineer—and help arrange financing and assist with the closing.

Real estate agents work usually on commission, not salary, and get paid only after you find a home, negotiate the contract, and complete the transaction. An agent's commission is a percentage of the price of the home (typically 5–6%), and is usually paid by the seller.

Because most real estate transactions involve two brokers—one who helps the buyer and one who helps the seller—the commission is divided, usually 50-50, between the two brokerage offices. Then, within each office, the agent who handled the transaction gets a share, usually 50% of the office's share.

In most states, brokers are allowed to represent both the buyer and the seller in the same real estate transaction, unless there is a written agreement to the contrary. (In some states, like California, the broker must inform both the buyer and seller of this dual agency in writing.) Sometimes this means that the individual broker represents both buyer and seller. Sometimes it means that different agents from the same brokerage office represent the buyer and seller. The latter situation is common, especially if a few big brokerage offices handle most of the real estate deals in the area. Either way, be aware that in this type of dual-agency relationship, your broker may be looking out for interests other than just your own.

Even if your real estate broker represents only you and not the seller, the broker's interests may conflict with your own. Your broker won't get a commission until you purchase a property. And when you do, the commission depends on the sale price. So, the broker may have an interest in (1) pushing you to buy a property very quickly, to limit the amount of work the agent must do to make the commission, (2) encouraging you to buy an expensive property to increase the commission, and (3) making sure you offer enough money on a particular property to close the deal. You, on the other hand, will be (1) looking to buy a home within your financial means and (2) trying to get

Buying a House Without a Broker

For a variety of reasons, you may be tempted to proceed on your own, without a broker. But bear in mind that buying real estate takes a lot of work and patience, and involves understanding a fair amount of strange jargon. And since it's almost always the seller who pays the entire real estate commission, it's often easier to let someone knowledgeable do at least some of the work for you. If you do decide to enter the transaction without an agent, it's only to your benefit if the seller will agree to reduce the price or give you some other concession in return, because it's the seller who normally covers this expense. So, unless the seller is willing to reduce the price a bit, we encourage you to have your own agent.

But just as you (the buyers) don't have to hire a broker, neither does the seller. A small but significant number of people sell their own homes in an effort to avoid paying the hefty real estate commission. You can find homes sold by owners—and sometimes negotiate to share some of the seller's savings—by checking newspaper and online ads or driving around and looking for "for sale by owner" or "FSBO" (so-called "fizzbo") signs. Be careful, however, if you've already started working with an agent who will represent you in the transaction. Some FSBO owners won't pay any agent commissions, which means you'll have to pay your agent's fee yourself. Of course, you can reduce the amount of your purchase offer to cover this additional cost. If neither party is using an agent, you might want to have your documents reviewed by an attorney or a consulting agent, just to be sure that everything is in order.

the lowest price possible. Of course, a good agent knows that if you offer more than you can afford it makes very little difference (for example, if you spend an extra $10,000, the agent will probably only see about $150 more in commission) and may even jeopardize the deal if you don't qualify for the financing you need. The best agents also realize there's little to be gained from a dissatisfied customer, since customer referrals are an important part of their business. Still, if you feel the agent is showing you homes outside of your price range or is pushing you to buy before you're ready, be sure to speak up.

To find a good agent, get recommendations from friends, family, coworkers, and others you trust. The best referrals come from those who have recently bought a home in the area where you're looking. Be sure to check an agent's reputation and references before agreeing to work with him or her. If you find your agent at an open house, in the yellow pages, or on the Internet, make sure you thoroughly check the agent's credentials and experience before you sign a contract.

Househunting Online

A good real estate broker will be sensitive to your interests and show you properties that meet your needs and budget. But there's a lot that you can do on your own. Scanning listings to see which homes are available and worth a visit, how much they cost, and what they offer is now as easy as turning on your computer. Thanks to the Internet, homebuyers no longer have to rely solely on real estate agents or newspaper ads for information about homes for sale. Now you can access the Multiple Listings Service (MLS) online through sites such as Realtor.com (sponsored by the National Association of Realtors), Microsoft's HomeAdvisor.com, and Homes.com. Your state or regional realty association may also offer a website of homes for sale. These sites may include details such as location, price, size, amenities, and other criteria. Many also include pictures.

For listings of new homes and developments in major metropolitan areas, see Homebuilder.com, operated by the National Association of Home-builders.

To check out FSBOs (homes sold without a broker), see www.forsalebyowner.com or www.salebyowner.com. Some FSBOs also appear on the MLS.

Finally, check out online editions of newspapers; many have online MLS access or similar classified sections.

Home Financing and Mortgages

It's essential to determine how much you can afford to pay before you look for a house. Many people don't understand how institutional lenders (banks, savings and loans, and credit unions) decide how much money they'll lend to you. If you don't do the calculations ahead of time, or talk to a loan broker, you may enter into a home purchase contract and then not qualify for the necessary financing.

To determine how much a bank will lend you, compare your anticipated monthly housing payments (including principal, interest, taxes, and insurance), plus your monthly payments on other long-term debts, to your gross (total) monthly income from employment and other sources. This is called the "debt-to-income ratio." Lenders normally want you to make all monthly debt payments with around 36% of your gross monthly income. You can qualify at a lower or higher percentage depending on the amount of your down payment, the interest rate on the type of mortgage you want, your credit history, the number of other long-term debts you have, your employment stability and prospects, the lender's philosophy, and whether money is tight or fairly easily available in the U.S. economy as a whole.

Your Credit Score Is Important When Applying for a Home Loan

When deciding whether to approve your home loan application, most lenders will consider your credit score. Credit scores are numerical calculations between 300 and 850 that are supposed to indicate the risk that you will default on your payments. High credit scores indicate less risk and low scores indicate potential problems.

Factors that many companies use when generating credit scores include:

- your payment history
- amounts you owe on credit accounts
- length of your credit history—in general, a longer credit history increases the score
- your new credit. It helps to have an established credit history without too many new accounts. Opening several accounts in a short period of time can represent greater risk, and
- types of credit—credit scorers look for a "healthy mix" of different types of credit.

You can now get a free credit report every year, but in most cases, it won't include your score. You should be able to purchase a report including the score for less than $20. See Chapter 4 for information on how to get a copy of your credit report and correct errors, if necessary.

To keep up on credit scoring developments, visit www.creditscoring.com, a private website devoted to credit scoring.

Usually, lenders assume you can spend around 28% of your gross monthly income on a mortgage payment and the rest of the overall 36% on other debts. But the greater your other debts, the lower the percentage of your income lenders will assume you have available to spend each month on housing. Conversely, if you have no long-term debt and a good credit history, and are able to make a larger-than-normal down payment, a lender may approve monthly housing costs that exceed 36% of your monthly income—perhaps as high as 40%.

RESOURCE

Dozens of websites offer free calculators to help you quickly determine monthly payments on different size mortgages so you can learn how much house you can afford. You can find easy-to-use real estate calculators at www.nolo.com, www.homepath.com, www.quickenloans.quicken.com, or Yahoo! Real Estate, http://realestate.yahoo.com, as well as on the sites of individual mortgage lenders.

The following sections provide some background information on home financing.

How Much Down Payment Will You Make?

Unless you're eligible for a government-subsidized mortgage under a program offered by the Federal Housing Authority (FHA) or Department of Veterans Affairs (VA), which requires either no, or a very low, down payment, or you are willing to pay a high interest rate, you'll probably need to put down 5%–20% of the cost of the house to qualify for a loan. Also, you'll have to pay the closing costs, an additional 2%–5% of the cost of the home.

Generally speaking, the larger the percentage of the total price of a house you can put down, the easier it will be for you to qualify for a mortgage. This is because a big down payment means less money will be due each month to pay off your mortgage. And because the amount of your monthly mortgage payment (plus taxes and insurance) is the major factor in qualifying for a loan, it's easy to see that the lower this is, the more likely a lender is to say yes. It also assures a lender that if you default on your loan, there will be enough equity in the property for the lender to recover what it's owed. And of course, the lender is less worried about you defaulting,

because you stand to lose more if you do. A bigger down payment often means lower interest rates, too. Finally, if your loan is for more than 80% of the home's value, your lender will require you to buy private mortgage insurance (PMI). Though you pay PMI, it protects the lender in case you default. If you put 20% down, you won't have this additional expense.

CAUTION

Feeling shaky about your relationship? If you are insecure about your romance, it makes sense to consider a house that one of you could afford on your own or one that readily accommodates a roommate. That way you won't be forced to sell the place if the relationship dissolves.

If you don't have a lot of money for a down payment, you may be tempted to ask your parents or grandparents for a gift or a loan. Whether this is wise, given your family situation, and how best to structure the transaction, are topics beyond the scope of this book. But we will note one thing: This approach will usually only help you to qualify for a mortgage loan if you do not have to pay the money back promptly. Otherwise, the amount you'll need to repay to your friends or relatives for this extra down payment money may increase your debt level so much that you won't be able to qualify for the loan. Your lender may ask your "donor" to sign a letter affirming that this is a gift, so remember, legally this won't be a loan—even if you voluntarily pay it back later on. If you do receive a down payment gift, be clear about whether this is a gift to both you and your partner or just one of you.

What Are the Different Types of Mortgages?

The two basic types are fixed and adjustable rate mortgages. Here's how they differ.

Fixed Rate Mortgages

With a fixed rate mortgage, the interest rate and the amount you pay each month remain the same over the entire mortgage term, traditionally 15, 20, 30, or even 40 years.

Adjustable Rate Mortgages

With an adjustable rate mortgage (ARM), the interest rate fluctuates according to current market interest rates. Initial interest rates on ARMs are typically offered at a discounted ("teaser") rate lower than that for a fixed rate mortgage. Over time, when the initial discount ends—sometimes after only one month—the interest rate adjusts according to current market rates plus an extra amount, called a margin. ARMs can be tied to different market-sensitive financial indexes, such as one-year U.S. Treasury bills. Some indexes fluctuate up or down more quickly than others. To avoid constant and drastic changes, ARMS typically regulate (cap) how much and how often the interest rate and payments can change in a year and over the life of the loan.

Which Is Better—a Fixed or Adjustable Rate Mortgage?

It depends. Because interest rates and mortgage options change often, your choice of a fixed or adjustable rate mortgage should depend on:

- the interest rates and mortgage options available when you're buying a house
- your view of the future (generally, high inflation will mean ARM rates will go up and lower inflation means that they will fall), and
- how willing you are to take a risk.

When mortgage rates are low, a fixed rate mortgage is the best bet for long-term buyers. In the long run, ARMs are likely to go up, meaning most buyers will be better off to lock in a favorable fixed rate now and not take the risk of much higher rates later.

However, not all buyers must choose one or the other—there are other options that combine both. For example, some buyers choose hybrid adjustable rate mortgages. These mortgages start out with a fixed rate for the first few years of the loan—often five or seven years—and become adjustable after that. Usually, the interest rate offered for the fixed period is lower than what's available for other fixed rate mortgages. If you're buying a home and don't expect to stay in it longer than about seven years, or you expect to refinance the mortgage, this type of loan may work best.

What Are the Best Sources of Home Loans or Mortgages?

Many entities make home loans, including banks, credit unions, savings and loans, insurance companies, and mortgage bankers. To get the best deal, compare loans and fees with at least a half a dozen lenders. Because many types of home loans are standardized to comply with rules established by the Federal National Mortgage Association (Fannie Mae) and other quasi-governmental corporations that purchase loans from lenders, comparison shopping is not difficult. Be sure to ask for the same size, type, and length of mortgage—such as a 30-year fixed rate mortgage for $300,000—so you're comparing apples to apples.

Current mortgage rates and fees are usually published in the real estate sections of metropolitan newspapers, and are widely available on online mortgage websites. However, keep in mind that these advertised rates usually only apply to borrowers with the best credit history, and you may not be offered the same great rates. You can also work with a mortgage broker, someone who specializes in matching house buyers to appropriate mortgage lenders. A broker will be able to compile many different options from various lenders. If your income arrangements are atypical or if either buyer has credit problems, working with a skilled mortgage broker may be the only way you can obtain a decent loan.

Be sure to check out government-subsidized mortgages, which have no down payment and low down payment plans (see "Government Loans Available to Home Buyers," below). Also, ask banks and other private lenders about any "first-time buyer" programs that offer low down payment plans and flexible qualifying guidelines to low- and moderate-income buyers with good credit.

Online Mortgage Information

Dozens of websites provide a wide range of mortgage information and loans.

No-loan sites don't broker or lend mortgage money, but typically provide mortgage rate information—just what most mortgage shoppers want and need. Two of the best no-loan sites are www.hsh.com and www.bankrate.com. Offering vast libraries of mortgage information for consumers, no-loan sites are a great place to examine mortgage programs, keep daily tabs on mortgage rates, indexes, and market events that push costs up or down, learn mortgage lingo, get questions answered about the loan qualification process, and crunch numbers with online mortgage calculators.

There are also many mortgage loan sites that offer direct access to mortgage loans. You can search for a specific bank or lender or check out one of the many mortgage shopping sites that let you shop for loans among dozens of lenders. Some multilender shopping sites are E-Loan.com, QuickenLoans.com, and iOwn.com.

TIP

If you have unconventional sources of income or if your purchase is complicated, we recommend that you use a local lender or mortgage broker, rather than an online source.

Government Loans Available to Home Buyers

Several federal, state, and local government financing programs are available to home buyers. The two main federal loan programs are administered by the Federal Housing Administration (FHA) and the U.S. Department of Veterans Affairs (VA). State and local programs may also be available.

FHA Loans

The Federal Housing Administration (FHA), an agency of the Department of Housing and Urban Development (HUD), insures loans to all U.S. citizens and permanent residents who meet financial qualification rules. Under its most popular program, if the buyer defaults and the lender forecloses, the FHA pays 100% of the amount insured. This loan insurance lets qualified people buy affordable houses. The major attraction of an FHA-insured loan is that it requires a low down payment, usually about 2% to 5%. A drawback of FHA loans is that they usually have low loan limits, meaning you'll either have to make up the difference with a large down payment or another mortgage, or you'll have to buy an inexpensive property.

At one time, it was difficult for unmarried couples to qualify for FHA loans—the FHA would make the loan but count only the man's income in determining whether the couple qualified. The FHA no longer does this and now considers the income of both partners in both married and unmarried couples when determining financial ability.

RESOURCE

For more information on FHA loan programs, contact a regional office of HUD or check the FHA website at www.hud.gov/mortprog.cfm.

Veterans Affairs (VA) Loans

The U.S. Department of Veterans Affairs (VA), like the FHA, guarantees loans. VA loans are available to most veterans who served a minimum time. If you default, the VA pays the lender the amount guaranteed. This guarantee makes it easier for veterans to get favorable loan terms with a low down payment. The loans are an excellent value—one of the best for moderately priced housing.

If one member of an unmarried couple is a qualifying veteran and the other isn't, the VA will guarantee only the veteran's share, which probably means the nonveteran will have to make a larger down payment. VA loans discriminate against unmarried couples—a married veteran whose spouse does not qualify can have the entire loan guaranteed.

RESOURCE

For more information, check the VA's website at www.homeloans.va.gov, or contact a regional VA office for advice.

How to Find the Least Costly Mortgage

You can save money if you shop carefully for a mortgage. Everything else being equal, even a one-quarter percentage point difference in interest rates can mean saving thousands of dollars over the life of a mortgage.

However, don't just look at the advertised interest rate. In addition to comparing interest rates, there are a variety of fees—and fee amounts—associated with getting a mortgage. Mortgage-related costs include things like application fees, credit check fees, and points (explained below). Lenders are required to advertise the annual percentage rate (APR), which factors in the cost of these other fees. A loan that looks like it has a very low rate may in fact be quite expensive when these other costs are factored in. The downside of the APR is that it is calculated by spreading theses costs of these fees over the life of loan, and many people don't keep

their loans that long because they refinance or sell their homes before the mortgage is paid off.

There are sometimes benefits to taking out loans with higher fees, however. This is particularly true of a loan with points. Points make up the largest part of lender fees: One point is 1% of the loan principal. Thus, your fee for borrowing $250,000 at two points is $5,000. The benefit of paying points is that the more points you pay, the lower your rate of interest.

To decide whether to get a loan with points, factor in how long you plan to own your house. The longer you live in your house (or pay on the mortgage), the better off you'll be paying more points up front in return for a lower interest rate. On the other hand, if you think you'll sell or refinance your house within two or three years, you're probably better off obtaining a loan with no points.

A good loan officer or loan broker can walk you through all options and trade-offs such as higher fees or points for a lower interest rate. Or you can check online mortgage and financial calculators, such as www.homepath.com, to quickly compare various combinations of interest rates and points. This website, operated by Fannie Mae, includes a wide range of consumer information on mortgages and is especially useful to new home buyers.

Loan Preapproval vs. Loan Prequalification

Once you've done the basic calculations and completed a financial statement, you can ask a lender or loan broker for a preapproval letter. This is the lender's agreement to loan you a specific amount, based on your credit history and financial situation and subject to certain conditions like a satisfactory appraisal of the property, title report, and purchase contract. Having a lender preapprove you for a loan is crucial in a competitive market; it shows that you're in the financial position to follow through on your offer.

Don't get loan preapproval confused with loan prequalification, however. With prequalification, a lender just speculates what you're likely to be able to borrow based on the financial information you provide. The lender doesn't check your credit history or promise to loan you the money. While prequalification can help you ballpark how much you can afford, it won't give you any assurance or impress any sellers.

Proceeding With Your Purchase: Offers, Inspections, Escrow, and Closing

Finding a house you want and can afford to buy is just the first step. You must still reach a firm agreement on price and terms with the owner, arrange inspections, and go through escrow before you actually own the house.

Real Estate Offers

A legal offer to buy a house must be in writing, delivered to the seller or the seller's agent, and contain specific financial and other terms so that if the seller says "yes," the deal can go through. The seller's acceptance, too, must be in writing.

Real estate offers often contain contingencies—events that must happen within a certain period of time (such as 30 days) before the deal becomes final. For example, you may want to make your offer contingent on qualifying for financing, the house passing certain inspections, or even your ability to sell your existing house first. Be aware, however, that the more contingencies you place in an offer, the less likely the seller is to accept it. In a competitive market, the seller is more likely to take the offer that doesn't have contingencies.

If your bid is far too low, the seller is likely to reject the offer on the spot. But even very attractive offers are rarely accepted as written. Typically, the seller will respond with a written counteroffer

accepting some of the offer terms, but proposing certain changes. Most counteroffers correspond to these provisions of an offer:

- price—the seller wants more money
- occupancy—the seller needs more time to move out
- buyer's sale of current house—the seller doesn't want to wait for this to occur, and
- inspections—the seller wants you to schedule them more quickly.

You may accept the seller's counteroffer, reject it, or present a counteroffer of your own. Then, the negotiations will continue until either a deal or an impasse is reached.

A contract is formed when either the seller or the buyer accepts all of the terms of the other's offer or counteroffer in writing within the time allowed. In some states, the parties will sign a more detailed contract prepared by lawyers; in other states the broker-prepared contract remains *the* contract governing the sale.

House Inspections

Inspecting the condition of a house is an important part of the homebuying process. In some states, such as California, the law requires sellers to disclose considerable information about the house, as well as potential hazards from floods, earthquakes, fires, and environmental hazards. But whether or not the seller provides disclosures, you should have the property inspected for defects or malfunctions in the building's structure such as the roof or plumbing.

Your purchase offer and any resulting contract should be contingent upon experts inspecting the house and reporting that it is in good condition or can be repaired for a reasonable price. The contract should also allow you a reasonable time to arrange for all required inspections. A buyer often pays for inspections, but it is possible to negotiate with the seller to pay a portion. Inspections routinely include termite, electrical and plumbing, and roof. In addition, you may want a soil engineer to check the foundation, or a general contractor to do a full inspection. Depending on the property, you may want to arrange specialized inspections for hazards from floods, earthquakes, and other natural disasters, as well as environmental hazards like asbestos and lead.

If the house is in good shape, you can proceed, knowing that you're getting what you paid for. If inspections reveal problems—such as an antiquated plumbing system or major termite problems—you can negotiate with the seller about who will pay for necessary repairs, or you can back out of the deal, assuming your contract is properly written to allow you to do so.

RESOURCE
For local referrals to inspectors and useful FAQs about home inspections, visit the American Society of Home Inspectors (ASHI) at www.ashi.com.

Escrow and Closing Costs

The final transfer of the house to the buyer is called the "closing." It occurs after both the seller and the buyer have met all the terms of the contract. (See "What Is a Deed?" below.) In buying and selling a house, paperwork and money must eventually change hands. The practice is for the buyers to deliver their money and the sellers to deliver the house deed to a third person, called an escrow holder. As a matter of custom, in some areas, the buyer pays for this service, but in others, the seller pays or the cost is shared. Oftentimes you (the buyers) will also be paying some expenses, like insurance and taxes, at closing. The escrow holder hangs on to everything until all inspections are complete, the papers are signed, and financing is arranged. Then, "escrow closes," which means the seller gets his or her money and the buyer becomes the official owner, subject to the lender's "security interest" in the property.

In some states, a lawyer must handle the real estate closing, unless you handle the transaction without professional help from a broker or agaent.

In many other states, attorneys typically are not involved in residential property sales, and a title or escrow company handles the entire closing process.

Check with your real estate broker or with your state department of real estate for advice on house closings.

What Is a Deed?

Before escrow closes on a new house, you'll need to choose how to take "title" (documented legal ownership). Title is evidenced by a deed recorded at the County Recorder's office or other land records office. A deed is the document that transfers ownership of real estate. It contains the names of the old and new owners and a legal description of the property, and is signed by the person transferring the property.

Taking Title to Your New Home

When you buy a house with your partner, you must decide how you will own the property, or, as they say in the real estate business, how you will "take title." Since in this context "title" is a synonym for "ownership," your decision has huge and lasting consequences, particularly on estate planning issues. Assuming you are buying the house for personal and not business use, you have three basic choices:

- one person holds title as sole owner
- both of you hold title as "joint tenants," or
- both of you hold title as "tenants in common."

This section explains what each of these legal arrangements means and when each of them is appropriate. Later sections in this chapter provide contracts for different types of ownership (equal or unequal), and cover such basic issues as what happens to the house if you break up.

Home Buying and the Marriage Question

Buying property will likely be an occasion for the two of you to talk about "the marriage question." We don't offer any relationship advice, but we do recommend that if marriage is on the horizon, this would be the right time to make that decision. Title and taxation issues both are profoundly different if you are married, and changing your marital status after you buy the house can invite some complicated tax and ownership issues. And by the way, don't be tempted to tell the title officer you're married if you're not—it will only create confusion and possible problems down the road.

SEE AN EXPERT

If you have any questions about taking title, be sure to consult with an experienced real estate attorney.

One Person's Name: Sole Owner

If a recorded deed contains only one name, that person is the legal owner and has full legal power to sell or will away the house or other real property, even if someone else has contributed to its purchase and holds a nonrecorded interest.

Sometimes, a couple that jointly owns a house is tempted to put only one name on the deed to save on taxes, avoid creditors, or for some other reason. The tax savings can be attractive if one of your incomes is very high and the other's is very low, because it allows the high-income person to take all the house-related tax deductions. Or, if one person's credit is terrible, it may seem like a good idea not to mention his or her interest in the property in order to get a loan to buy the house.

However, in most cases the risks inherent in putting a jointly owned house in one person's name far outweigh the benefits. If your partner is the only one named on the deed (and is therefore presumed to be sole owner), you may be out of luck if your partner sells the house and pockets the money, or dies and leaves it to someone else. Sure, you can sue your ex-partner in an attempt to recover the amount of your financial interest in the property, but this type of lawsuit is often difficult to win, as most states have a strong legal presumption that the person whose name appears on the deed is the owner. In any case, a lawsuit designed to prove that a person whose name does not appear on the deed is a co-owner is likely to be expensive, stressful, and time-consuming.

If one person's credit will absolutely doom a loan application, it may be possible to take out the loan and purchase the property in one partner's name alone, and then add the second partner's name to title immediately thereafter. But be very careful here: Make sure you actually follow through and add the partner's name officially, and be aware that in some places transfer taxes and fees may apply to the transfer. In some instances the lender may be entitled to "call in the loan" if you add someone to title like this, but in our experience this rarely happens as long as you stay current on the loan payments.

TIP

What if you decide not to name both owners on the deed? If you decide to list only one name on the deed, you may want to sign a separate contract that spells out the actual property interests of both parties. Before you do this, be sure to see a lawyer. Being an "off-title" owner can create a myriad of problems, especially with the tax authorities. You may not be able to deduct your mortgage contributions or any profits earned if you later sell the property. Or, creditors may claim that you are trying to conceal assets from them, which could lead to other problems. You should also talk with a lawyer about whether to record such an agreement with the County Recorder's office if you do make it. In some places it can be very expensive to add someone to title later on, especially if that person is not your legal spouse, so make sure you investigate before making a final decision.

Joint Tenancy

If you take title as joint tenants, you share equal ownership of the property and each of you has the right to use the entire property. If one joint tenant dies, the other automatically becomes the owner of the deceased person's share, even if there's a will to the contrary. This is called the right of survivorship. In fact, some states require that after the words "joint tenants," you add the words "with right of survivorship" (hence the common abbreviations JTWROS or Jt Ten WROS).

> **CAUTION**
>
> **Check your state's required language.** If in doubt about the specific language you must use when taking title to a house, ask a title company, real estate broker, or attorney for the exact terminology required in your state.

An advantage of joint tenancy is that at the death of the first joint tenant, the property passes to the surviving joint tenant without the expense and trouble of probate proceedings.

Keep in mind, however, that just because you establish a joint tenancy does not mean it will last forever. If one joint tenant sells her share, the joint tenancy ends (in most states this is true even if the other joint tenant is unaware of the sale). The new owner and the other original owner become tenants in common (see "Tenants in Common," below). And in most states a joint tenant may end the joint tenancy at any time, again with the result that the owners become tenants in common with no right of survivorship.

Domestic Partnership and Title

In some cities, counties, and states, unmarried couples can register as domestic partners; some employers also provide benefits to registered domestic partners. Certain registries are only open to same-sex couples, based upon the philosophy that if you can marry legally, you don't need the domestic partner benefits. In any event, domestic partner registration won't have any impact on who holds title, nor on any claim a non-owner might have, based on contributions to a partner's property. The only effect it might have is on transfer taxes in some cities or counties. Check with your local County Recorder if this is an issue for you.

Before taking title as joint tenants, be sure to consider the following issues.

Joint Tenancy Means Equal Shares

Joint tenancy is appropriate only when each joint tenant (in theory, there can be any number) owns the same percentage of the property. Thus, you and your partner can each own 50% of the house, or three people can each own one-third. But if you own 60% of a house and your partner owns 40%, joint tenancy won't work. In that case, you'll be tenants in common.

However, having one person provide most or even all of the down payment doesn't mean you can't be joint tenants. As long as you agree to own the house equally, joint tenancy will work fine. This can be accomplished if the person making the down payment gifts a half interest to the other or, more typically, if the more affluent partner agrees to lend the other his or her half of the down payment. If this is your plan, make sure that the loan is documented in a promissory note or a written agreement, as in some states a joint tenant has no right to a reimbursement unless the owners have a written agreement.

Joint Tenancy Is Often a Poor Substitute for a Will

Taking title to a house in joint tenancy is an effective way to pass it on to the survivor without going through probate (and with no need to include it in a will). However, if you own a home by yourself, and want your partner to get it when you die, it's rarely a good idea to change the title to a joint tenancy just to achieve this result. Here's why.

First, by putting the house in joint tenancy, you immediately gift one-half of it to your partner. (This may have tax consequences—see "Check Out Legal and Tax Issues Before Transferring a Share of Your House," below.) If you later split up, in most states you have no right to get that half back. Second, if your partner incurs debts, creditors can attempt to collect from his or her share of the equity—something that wouldn't be possible if the house were still in your name alone.

If you want your partner to get the house when you die, it is far better to make a will or living trust stating that desire. Then, if circumstances change, you can simply change the will or trust. See Chapter 9 for details on joint tenancy as it relates to wills and estate planning.

Sometimes, the partner who owns the home is worried that, upon the owner-partner's death, the other partner will have no place to live. But the owner-partner would eventually like the home to go to another heir, perhaps a child. In this case, the owner-partner could retain sole ownership of the property but grant a life estate to the other partner— which would give the nonowner-partner full use of the property until his or her death. Then, when the nonowner-partner dies, the home passes to the heir. Joint tenancy also can create estate tax problems if only one person in the couple has contributed to the purchase. If this is your situation, talk to an estate planning lawyer familiar with legal issues facing unmarried couples.

Tenants in Common

Perhaps the most common way for unmarried couples to take title to real property is as "tenants in common." Unlike a joint tenancy, a tenant in common has no automatic right to inherit the property when the other partner dies. When one tenant in common dies, his or her share of the jointly owned property is left to whomever is specified in a will or living trust. This might well be his or her living together partner, but it could also be someone else. If there's no will, the person's intestate heirs will inherit his or her share–and that does not include a living together partner.

If you choose to own the home as tenants in common but agree that if one partner dies, the other will get the entire home, be careful. Your partner could change his or her will at any time to leave his or her share of the property to someone other than you. And there's no rule that says your partner must notify you of the change.

TIP

Living trusts are a way for tenants in common to avoid the cost and trouble of probate. See Chapter 9 for advice on transferring property through a living trust.

Tenants in common can legally own property in unequal shares—for example, one person could own 80%, and the other 20%. When ownership is unequal, both names are still listed on the deed as tenants in common. In most states, you can specify your ownership percentages on the deed or in a separate written agreement that you sign, and in some instances may wish to record the document along with the deed at your County Recorder's office. You can also use a written agreement to provide for reimbursement of a down payment.

If you'd like your share of the home to go to someone other than your partner when you die, but want to make sure your partner has a place to live, you can own the home as tenants in common and include a life estate provision in the deed.

This means that upon your death, your partner can remain in the home until he or she dies. Then, your share of the home passes to your chosen heir.

CAUTION

If ownership shares are unequal, put it in writing. The law will normally presume 50-50 ownership when the deed to a piece of property says it is held by tenants in common or as joint tenants. If your ownership interests are unequal, put it in writing in the form of a contract, such as the one set out in "Contract for Unequal Ownership of a Home," below.

Changing Title

What happens if you take title in one legal format and later jointly agree you want to change it to another? For instance, because one of you makes a larger down payment, you decide to take title as tenants in common. Several years later, after the birth of your child, you both decide it makes sense to change to joint tenants so as to avoid probate if one of you dies. This can be accomplished by purchasing a blank deed form and then making and recording a new deed granting the property "from Andrew West and Joanne Yu as Tenants in Common, to Andrew West and Joanne Yu as Joint Tenants With Right of Survivorship." You will also need to prepare and record a new deed if one partner is sole owner of a house and the other partner will become a co-owner (discussed below). Check with someone knowledgeable about real estate law to make sure you're using the proper deed and language and to determine whether this will trigger any tax liabilities.

RESOURCE

Californians who want to transfer title to California real estate should see *Deeds for California Real Estate*, **by Mary Randolph (Nolo).**

Contracts for Couples Owning a Home Together

A house is a major economic asset—usually a couple's biggest. It follows that it's important to define your expectations and obligations promptly and clearly in writing. (This is in addition to taking title via a deed.) The rest of this chapter provides several different contracts for unmarried couples owning a home together. These contracts cover basic issues such as how you're sharing costs and ownership, what happens to the house if you break up or one of you dies, and how you intend to deal with disputes.

CD-ROM

The forms CD includes copies of the contracts for couples owning a house together, and Appendix B includes blank tear-out copies of these forms:

- Contract for Equal Ownership of a House
- Contract for Unequal Ownership of a House
- Agreement for One Person to Move Into the Other's House and Become an Immediate Co-Owner, and
- Agreement for One Person to Move Into the Other's House and Become a Co-Owner Gradually.

CAUTION

Get it in writing. Any unmarried couple that plans to jointly own a house or other real property should prepare a written contract. When it comes to an investment of this size, it's just plain nuts to try and wing it with pillow talk. If, later, your relationship becomes rocky, your memories of the details of a spoken agreement may differ. The unhappy result may be a lawsuit. As emphasized throughout this book, especially in Chapter 2, a written contract, particularly over something so expensive and important as a house, is the only way to protect yourself should you separate from your partner. Even if you are equal owners, having an agreement in place can make a dissolution far easier to manage.

Editing Contracts

One of our contracts for ownership of a house may be exactly what you need, but it's possible you may want to edit, add, or delete clauses. See "How to Edit or Modify a Living Together Agreement," in Chapter 3 for advice on editing contracts and agreements.

SEE AN EXPERT

Some situations need a lawyer. If your circumstances require something more complicated than the house ownership contracts included here, or if you want to make extensive changes on your own, get advice from a lawyer with experience in real estate.

Notarizing and Recording a House Ownership Contract

After your contract is written, the safest legal approach is to record it at your County Recorder's office along with the deed. To do this in most states, you'll need to get your signatures notarized. Notarization means that a person authorized as a notary public certifies in writing that you're the person you claim to be. If you want to have your contract notarized, you and your partner must appear in front of the notary and show proof of your identity. The notary will watch each of you sign the document and then will complete an acknowledgment, including a notarial seal. You can often find a notary at a bank, lawyer's office, real estate office, or title insurance office, or at private post office businesses. Most charge under $20 to notarize a document.

Some couples, however, shouldn't or don't want to record their agreement—either for privacy reasons or because they don't want to bother recording every amendment they make in the future. And, some counties won't allow such documents to be recorded, though they may allow you to record a one-page "Memorandum" or "Abstract" of your agreement, summarizing the basic terms.

There's no clear right or wrong here. Recordation isn't necessary to make the agreement legally valid. Just make sure you have a safe place to keep the agreement, like a safe deposit box or other secure location.

CROSS REFERENCE

What happens to your house ownership contract if you get married? Basically, an agreement between unmarried couples will not be enforceable after marriage unless it was created shortly before the marriage in the anticipation of marriage. Instead, your state's marital property laws will apply. If marriage is in your future, be sure to read Chapter 2, which covers the impact of marriage on written living together agreements.

Contract for Equal Ownership of a House

This section includes a contract for unmarried couples who want to share equal ownership of a house. The Contract for Equal Ownership of a House form is designed for two people who intend to share equally all house-related costs, including the down payment, purchase price, closing costs, insurance, taxes, repair and maintenance costs, and the like. Recognizing, however, that many unmarried couples want to share ownership equally even when they don't share equally in down payment and housing costs, this section also explains how to prepare a contract that reflects your particular situation.

Equal Ownership of a House— Each Partner Contributes One-Half of the Down Payment

This section describes choices you'll have to make when completing the Contract for Equal Ownership of a House, such as how to split housing costs, and explains standard language you'll see in the contract.

Clauses You Need to Complete

Clause 2 (Title). Here you specify how you are taking title (ownership)—as tenants in common or as joint tenants.

Clause 3 (Splitting Costs). This clause states that you will share equally in the down payment, purchase price, and all other housing costs, including maintenance and repair bills. To avoid disputes over money spent on home improvements, we recommend that improvements over a set dollar amount (such as $500—the amount is up to you) require mutual consent, with each partner paying half.

If you won't be sharing costs equally—for example, you're splitting the mortgage and other monthly housing costs two-thirds/one-third—simply edit the contract accordingly. If you're not sharing equally in the down payment or costs, and one person is lending the other money, see "Equal Ownership of a House—One Person Lends the Other Some or All of the Down Payment," below.

CAUTION

Keep track of all expenses. Even if your contract clearly spells out the costs that each partner will bear, you should keep records of your respective contributions as you make mortgage payments, repairs, and the like. That way, if you stray a bit from the original agreement (or even if you don't), you'll have written proof of who covered which expenses. This could be valuable if you later split up and disagree about who paid for what. And if worse comes to worst and you end up in court, these documents will also provide proof as to the exact amount of funds you poured into the home. Judges in these types of cases typically look to the contributions each partner made in determining how the proceeds of the home sale will be divided. A joint checking account ledger can often serve the same purpose.

Clause 4 (Effect of Breakup on Home Ownership). The most complex clause in the Contract for Equal Ownership of a House deals with what happens if the two of you break up. This contract recognizes three possibilities:

- One of you wants to keep the house and the other doesn't.
- Both of you want the house.
- Neither of you wants the house.

Most likely, only one of you will want to stay or both of you will choose to move on. But if both of you want the house, problems are likely to develop. Clause 4 anticipates this possibility by providing several choices for deciding who gets the house should you split up and both partners want it:

4 (b) (1). Right of First Offer. You may want your contract to automatically give one of you the first right to buy out the other partner's share in the house at fair market value within 90 days. (This is different from a right of first refusal, where you get to match a third-party offer.)

4 (b) (2). Coin Toss Method. You may opt for a coin toss to decide who gets to buy out the other. (The winner of a coin toss is entitled to buy out the loser's share at fair market value within 90 days.)

4 (b) (3). Other. You may come up with your own approach to decide the question of who owns the house if you both want it. For example, you could provide for the decision to be made with the help of a mediator, rather than the caprice of a coin toss, relying on a coin flip only if mediation fails.

If one partner does buy out the other, it is extremely important to change title to the home to reflect the new ownership arrangement. Clause 4 specifies that the buying partner must execute the appropriate documents to do this. In addition, the partner selling a share of the home should ensure that his or her name is taken off the home loan. Otherwise, the selling partner will have no interest in the home, but will still be on the hook for the mortgage. Even if you and your partner agree in writing that the selling partner is not responsible for the mortgage, the original agreement with the lender remains unchanged. If the buying partner

Contract for Equal Ownership of a House

_____Michael Angelo_____ and _____Helen Rifkin_____
make the following agreement to jointly purchase and own the house at ___423 Bliss Street, Rockford, Illinois___
(hereafter house).

1. We will purchase the house for $_____380,000_____ (including closing costs).

2. We will take title as [*choose one*]:

    ☐   tenants in common, or

    ☒   joint tenants with right of survivorship.

3. We will each contribute one-half of the down payment and closing costs and pay one-half of the required payments for the mortgage, homeowners' insurance, property taxes, costs for needed repairs and routine maintenance, and [*fill in any additional costs or fees such as any fees required by a homeowners' association*] . Any improvements to the house costing more than $__500__ will be made by mutual consent with each of us agreeing to pay for half of all such improvements.

4. Should either of us decide to end the relationship and cease living together, one of the following will occur:

    (a) If one person wants to stay and the other wants to move on, the person staying will pay the person leaving fair market value (see Clause 5) for his or her share within 90 days. When payment is made, the person selling his or her share will deed the house to the person buying the house. The person buying the house will ensure that the selling partner's name is taken off the mortgage. If the lender refuses to remove the selling partner's name from the mortgage, the buying partner will obtain a new loan in his or her name only. If the buying partner cannot obtain a new loan in his or her name only, the house shall be sold.

    (b) If both of us want to keep the house, we will try to reach a mutually satisfactory agreement for one to buy out the other. If by the end of two weeks we can't, the decision will be made as follows [*choose one*]:

    ☒   (1) Right of First Offer. __Helen__ shall have the right of first offer. This means that __Helen__ may purchase __Michael's__ share of the house within 90 days for its fair market value (see Clause 5). If __Helen__ does not make full payment during this 90-day period, __Michael__ shall have an additional 90 days in which to buy out __Helen's__ share for its fair market value. When payment is made, the person leaving will deed the house to the person retaining it in his or her name alone. The person buying the house will ensure that the selling partner's name is taken off the mortgage. If the lender refuses to remove the selling partner's name from the mortgage, the buying partner will obtain a new loan in his or her name only. If neither person exercises his or her buyout right, or if the buying partner cannot obtain a new loan in his or her name only, the house shall be sold.

    ☐   (2) Coin Toss Method. A friend will be asked to flip a coin within 60 days of our decision to separate. The winner of the coin toss is entitled to buy out the loser's share, provided the winner pays the loser fair market value (see Clause 5) within 90 days. If full payment isn't made during this period, the loser of the coin toss will have an additional 90 days in which to buy out the winner's share of the property at fair market value (see Clause 5). When payment is made, the person leaving will deed the house to the person retaining it in his or her name alone. The person buying the house will ensure that the selling partner's name is taken off the mortgage. If the lender refuses to remove the selling partner's name from the mortgage, the buying partner will obtain a new loan in his or her name only. If the buying partner cannot obtain a new loan in his or her name only, the house shall be sold.

    ☐   (3) Other. _____
    _____ .

Contract for Equal Ownership of a House (continued)

(c) If neither of us wants to own the house or payment isn't made within 90 days, the house will be sold and the profits divided as follows: ___equally___ .

(d) We are both responsible for our share of the mortgage, insurance, and taxes until the house is sold or it changes ownership. If one of us moves out of the house before it is sold, the remaining person will make a good faith effort to find a tenant who will pay a fair market rent. Assuming a tenant is found, the rental amount will be credited against the departing partner's payment for shared housing costs.

5. Should either of us decide to end the relationship, we will do our best to agree on the fair market value of our house. However, if we can't agree, we will jointly choose and pay for the services of a licensed real estate appraiser to conduct an appraisal, and abide by the result. If we can't agree on an appraiser in the first place, each of us will independently retain and pay for the services of a licensed real estate appraiser. The fair market value of the house will be the average of the two appraisals. "Fair market value" for one person's share of the property is defined as an amount equal to the fair market value of the entire property, less the then-current mortgage amount, multiplied by that person's percentage ownership interest in the property.

6. Should either of us die, the survivor, if he or she has not become the owner of 100% of the deceased person's share through joint tenancy or a will, has the right to purchase the portion of the property given or left to someone else at the fair market value of that share (to be arrived at under the terms of Clause 5) within 200 days of the date of death.

7. If either of us is unable or unwilling to pay his or her share of the mortgage, taxes, or insurance payments in a timely manner, the other may make those payments. The extra payments will be treated as a personal loan to be paid back by the person on whose behalf they are made within six months, including _____% interest per annum. If the loan isn't repaid in six months, the debtor must vacate the house and either sell his or her interest to the other party (in which case the buying partner must ensure that the selling partner's name is removed from the mortgage, as set forth in Clause 4) or agree to sell the entire property at fair market value which will be established by appraisal as set out in Clause 5.

8. This contract is binding on our heirs and our estates.

9. Any dispute arising out of this agreement will be mediated by a third person mutually acceptable to both of us. The mediator's role will be to help us arrive at a solution, not to impose one on us. If good faith efforts to arrive at our own solution with the help of a mediator prove to be fruitless, either of us may make a written request to the other that the dispute be arbitrated. If such a request is made, our dispute will be submitted to arbitration under the rules of the American Arbitration Association, and one arbitrator will hear our dispute. The decision of the arbitrator will be binding on us and will be enforceable in any court that has jurisdiction over the controversy. By agreeing to arbitration, we each agree to give up the right to a jury trial.

Michael Angelo   _December 15, 20xx_
Michael Angelo   Date

Helen Rifkin   _December 15, 20xx_
Helen Rifkin   Date

fails to make the mortgage payments, in some states the lender can seek payment from the selling partner. If this happens, the selling partner's only remedy is to sue the buying partner to force him or her to make the payments (or to reimburse the selling partner for any payments she has made). Such lawsuits are costly and time intensive. In addition, if the buying partner fails to make payments, the selling partner's credit rating will likely be damaged.

Unfortunately, most lenders will not agree to simply remove one partner's name from the loan documents. Usually, in order to get the selling partner's name off the loan, the buying partner must obtain a new loan (refinance the home) in his or her name only. Clause 4 requires this of the partner buying the home. If the buying partner cannot qualify for a new loan, Clause 4 states that the home must be sold to a third party.

TIP

Remember to pay attention to allocating any costs of transfer or taxes that might be triggered by a buyout.

Boilerplate Language

The Contract for Equal Ownership of a House provides standard "boilerplate" language for joint home ownership, including:

- how to determine the market value of the house should one of you need to buy out the other (Clause 5), and
- what happens to the property if one of you dies (Clause 6), or one of you is unable to pay your share of the expenses, such as monthly mortgage payments (Clause 7).

The contract also specifies that your agreement is binding on your heirs and estates (Clause 8) and provides for mediation should a dispute arise (Clause 9).

CROSS REFERENCE

For a detailed discussion of mediation and arbitration, see Chapter 10.

TIP

You can choose the interest rate for the partner paying the other partner's share. Paragraph 7 of the Contract for Equal Ownership of a House (which also shows up in some of the other contracts) provides that if one partner isn't able to make payments on the mortgage or expenses, the other partner can make those payments and the extra payments will be considered a loan from the paying partner to the nonpaying partner. The sample agreement shows that the loan comes with an interest rate of 3%, but you can choose whatever interest rate seems appropriate to you, as long as it's not usurious (completely unreasonable). We recommend using a rate that is close to the interest rate that a bank would pay on a savings account if the paying partner had kept his or her money in the bank, but you can use a higher one if you want it to serve as a deterrent to nonpayment. You also could provide that no interest will accrue at all, if you don't want your partner to have to pay interest just because he or she couldn't make the payment for a time.

Equal Ownership of a House—One Person Lends the Other Some or All of the Down Payment

You may wish to edit the Contract for Equal Ownership of a House agreement to deal with the common situation in which both members of a couple wish to own a house equally, but only one can come up with all the cash needed for the down payment. Assume Andrew, a successful artist, is able to sell a few paintings to come up with the full $50,000 down payment and closing costs for a little cottage with a mansard roof. Unfortunately, Alice, his partner, has no savings and can't contribute more than a few thousand dollars. However, Alice does have a good job, meaning she can afford to pay Andrew for a half interest in the house over time.

In this situation, a common approach is for Alice and Andrew to take title to the house as equal owners (either as joint tenants or tenants in common) with Andrew lending Alice her one-half of the down payment and Alice agreeing to repay him in affordable monthly installments. To accomplish this, Andrew and Alice should do two things:

a) rewrite Clauses 3 and 4 of the Contract for Equal Ownership of a House to reflect the unequal sharing of down payment costs, and

b) prepare a separate promissory note setting out the exact terms of the loan.

This section shows how to do these two things.

Substitute Language for Clauses 3 (Splitting Costs) and 4 (Effect of Breakup on Home Ownership)

Clause 3 of the Contract for Equal Ownership of a House specifies that you will share equally in the down payment costs. If you will not be paying equal amounts of the down payment, simply substitute the following for Clauses 3 and 4:

3. _Andrew Dobbs_ [*name of person making the down payment*] will contribute all the down payment and closing costs for the house, amounting to _$50,000_, with _Alice Parker_ [*name of person borrowing money*] signing a promissory note to pay _Andrew Dobbs_ $25,000, plus simple interest of _6%_ over the next two years in equal monthly installments. Other than the down payment and closing costs, we will each pay one-half of the required payments for the mortgage, homeowners' insurance, property taxes, the costs for needed repairs and routine maintenance, and _[fill in any additional costs or fees such as any fees required by a homeowners' association]_ . Any improvements to the house costing more than _$500_ will be made by mutual consent with each of us agreeing to pay half for all such improvements.

Clause 4 of the Contract for Equal Ownership of a House form lets you specify who gets the house should you split up. You may want to choose Clause 4(b)(1) and give the person making the down payment (in this case, Andrew) the right of first offer—at least until the time that the down payment loan has been repaid. It's a good idea (especially if you're the person borrowing the down payment money) to clarify what happens once the down payment loan has been repaid. Simply add language such as the following to Clause 4:

> If our relationship ends after _Alice Parker_ has fully repaid the loan as provided in the promissory note called for in Clause 3 of this agreement, the following will occur: _[specify 4(b)(1), 4(b)(2), or 4(b)(3)]_ .

How to Prepare a Promissory Note

A promissory note is nothing more than legal jargon for a written promise to pay money to someone else. As with all legal documents, promissory notes often contain loads of needless hyped-up legalese. The note here is designed primarily to be used between family and friends, such as a close unmarried couple. You can use the Promissory Note included here for a down payment loan or any other loan between you and your partner.

The primary function of a promissory note is to serve as written evidence of the amount of a debt and the terms under which it will be repaid, including the repayment schedule (installments versus one lump sum payment) and interest rate (if any). To avoid disputes down the line, you should clearly spell out the terms of your agreement.

The Promissory Note shown below allows for repayment of the down payment in installments, rather than all at once, and it charges interest. Simply plug in the following information:

- names of the borrower and lender

- loan amount

Promissory Note
(Loan Repayable in Installments With Interest)

Name of Borrower: _____ Alice Parker _____

Name of Lender: _____ Andrew Dobbs _____

1. For value received, Borrower promises to pay to Lender the amount of $_____ 25,000 _____ at
   _____ 10 Rose Street, Oakland, California, _____ at the rate of __3__% per year
   from the date this note was signed until the date it is paid in full, no later than __October 1, 2017__.
   Borrower will receive credits for prepayments, reducing the total amount of interest to be repaid.

2. Borrower agrees that this note shall be paid in installments, which include principal and interest, of not less
   than $__277.55__ per month, due on the first day of each month, until such time as the principal and
   interest are paid in full.

3. If any installment payment due under this note is not received by Lender within __60__ days of its due
   date, the entire amount of unpaid principal shall become immediately due and payable at the option of
   Lender without prior notice to Borrower.

4. In the event Lender prevails in a lawsuit to collect on it, Borrower agrees to pay Lender's attorney fees in an
   amount the court finds to be just and reasonable.

_____ Alice Parker _____   _____ November 1, 2008 _____
Borrower's signature   Date

_____ Alice Parker _____
Print name

- address where payment is to be made (such as your home address)

- interest rate (this should be between 3% and 7%, or somewhat less than the market rate for a bank certificate of deposit for the same time period)

- monthly installment payment (you'll need to figure this out based on the loan amount, interest rate, and the number of months the borrower will take to repay the loan—see "Amortization Calculators: How to Get the Math Right," below), and

- the number of days (such as 30 or 60) that the borrower has to pay each installment before the lender may require immediate and full payment of the loan balance. (Without this "acceleration" provision, a lender can't sue

for loan installments not yet due, even if a borrower has missed many payments and has no intention to repay.)

The borrower must sign and date the promissory note. The lender gets the signed original and the borrower gets a copy.

What if you sell the house before the loan is repaid? Under the terms of the Promissory Note shown here, the borrower would still have the full amount of time (in our Alice-Andrew example, ten years from the start of the loan) to repay the loan. This may be years after the house is sold. In this situation, you may want to require that the complete balance of the loan be repaid before the borrower receives any proceeds from the house sale. If so, add this type of language to the end of Clause 2 in your promissory note:

If our house at 10 Rose Street, Oakland, California
is sold before this loan and all interest due has
been repaid, the Borrower will pay the Lender
the remaining balance owed before receiving any
proceeds from the house sale.

TIP

**There are many alternative ways to structure
loan payments.** You can prepare a promissory note
with different terms (for example, installment payments
without interest, or a lump sum payment with interest).
More versions are available in *101 Law Forms for Personal
Use*, by Robin Leonard and Ralph Warner (Nolo). The
Nolo website (www.nolo.com) also has a variety of
promissory notes for sale in the Web Forms section.

Amortization Calculators: How to Get the Math Right

To compute the exact amount of monthly loan
payments that include interest, all you need to
know is the amount of the loan, the interest rate,
and the repayment period. Then simply plug
this information into an amortization calculator.
Check out Nolo's free mortgage calculator at
www.nolo.com.

CD-ROM

The forms CD includes a copy of the Promissory Note, and Appendix B includes a blank tear-out
copy of the form.

Equal Ownership of a House— One Person Buys the House and the Other Fixes It Up

It's not uncommon for one person to contribute a
greater portion, or even all, of the down payment,
while the other agrees to contribute labor and/or
materials to fix the place up, in exchange for equal
ownership in the house.

EXAMPLE:

Bob and Evie plan to purchase a graceful but
dilapidated Victorian. Evie has the cash for the
down payment. Bob has no savings but used to
work as a carpenter and has the expertise and
time to renovate the house. Bob and Evie can
each afford to make half the monthly mortgage,
taxes, and upkeep expenses, and they want to
own the place equally. After discussing different
possibilities, they agree that Evie will contribute
the entire $60,000 for the down payment and
closing costs. Bob will match this amount by
contributing $60,000 worth of materials and
labor (at $25 an hour) to pay for his share. If
Bob fails to do so or the couple separates in the
next two years, Bob owes Evie the difference
between what he has contributed and $60,000.
And if the house is sold at a profit while Evie
is still owed money (she has contributed more
than Bob), she will take what she is owed off the
top, with the remainder of the proceeds divided
50-50.

If Bob and Evie want to take title to the house
as equal owners (either as joint tenants or tenants
in common), they can use the Contract for Equal
Ownership of a House. They would need to edit
this contract to reflect the fact that Evie is making
the full down payment and Bob will be paying
off his share in labor and materials to fix up the
house. To accomplish this, Bob and Evie should
substitute a new Clause 3 of the Contract for Equal
Ownership of a House to reflect their agreement.

3. Evie [*name of person making the down
payment*] will contribute all the down payment
and closing costs for the house, amounting
to $60,000 . Bob [*name of person contributing
labor and materials*] will contribute $35,000
for materials and 1,000 hours of labor (valued
at $25 per hour) over the 24 months immediately
following the closing date, for a total contribution
of $60,000 toward fixing up the house. Bob
will keep careful records of his contributions to

be reviewed and initialed by _Evie_ on a monthly basis. If _Bob_ doesn't fulfill this obligation within two years, or should we separate before the end of two years, at the time of separation, _Bob_ owes _Evie_ the difference between what he contributed and _$60,000_. Assuming money is owed, _Bob_ will sign a promissory note, agreeing to pay _Evie_ the outstanding balance plus _6%_ simple interest over a _12-month_ period in equal monthly installments. Other than the down payment and closing costs, we will each pay one-half of the required payments for the mortgage, homeowners' insurance, property taxes, and _[fill in any additional costs or fees such as any fees required by a homeowners' association]_.

Clause 4 of the Contract for Equal Ownership of a House lets you specify who gets the house if you split up. You may want to choose Clause 4(b)(1) and give the person making the down payment (in this case, Evie) the right of first offer—at least until the time that the down payment loan has been repaid. It's a good idea to clarify what happens to Clause 4 once the down payment loan has been repaid (for example, after Bob has matched Evie's share of the down payment by the time and money he spends renovating the house). Simply add language such as the following to Clause 4:

If our relationship ends after _Bob_ has fulfilled his obligation to contribute _$60,000 in labor and materials_ as provided in Clause 3 of this agreement, the following will occur: _[specify 4(b)(1), 4(b)(2), or 4(b)(3)]_.

Contract for Unequal Ownership of a House

This section includes a contract for unmarried couples who do not share equally in ownership of a house. Especially when one partner contributes substantially more to the down payment than the other, that person may want to own more than half of the property. As with the Contract for Equal Ownership of a House, you can tailor this agreement to your own particular situation when it comes to issues such as sharing monthly housing costs and what happens to the house if you break up.

To complete the Contract for Unequal Ownership of a House form, follow the directions above, with the following exceptions:

Clause 2 (Title). The Contract for Unequal Ownership of a House assumes you will take title as tenants in common, the appropriate form for taking title when you have unequal shares of ownership in the house.

Clause 3 (Splitting Costs). The clause in this contract allows you to split costs, such as down payment and monthly mortgage payments, however you want.

EXAMPLE:

Kelly and Sam contribute different amounts to the down payment on a house (Kelly one-third and Sam two-thirds) and they decide to split ownership of the house the same way. To keep things simple, Sam will pay two-thirds of the monthly mortgage, taxes, and insurance payments. Because they use the house more or less equally, Sam and Kelly agree to divide utilities and other routine monthly expenses equally.

If one person has lent the other down payment money, be sure to read the discussion of "Equal Ownership of a House," above, especially the discussion of promissory notes. It's not easy to decide whether to use the loan approach or the unequal ownership concept. If the property goes way up in value, the unequal ownership structure will favor the owner with the greater share—but if the property values go down, the one making the larger contribution would be better served by the loan model. Because you don't know which direction values are heading, there is no right or wrong answer. Instead, pick the approach that most closely matches the way you think about your co-ownership arrangement.

Contract for Unequal Ownership of a House

___Sam Rutherford___ and ___Kelly Franklin___ make the following agreement to jointly purchase and own the house at ___9 Oak Road, Austin, Texas___ (hereafter house):

1. We will purchase the house for $___400,000___ (including closing costs).

2. We will take title as tenants in common with the following shares:

   ___Sam___   ___2/3___
   ___Kelly___   ___1/3___

3. ___Sam___ will contribute ___2/3___ and ___Kelly___ will contribute ___1/3___ of the down payment and closing costs. ___Sam___ will pay ___2/3___ and ___Kelly___ will pay ___1/3___ of the required payments for the mortgage, homeowners' insurance, property taxes, and ___[fill in any additional costs or fees such as any fees required by a homeowners' association]___ . All use-related expenses (including utilities and the cost of routine repairs) and maintenance will be paid equally. Any improvements to the house costing more than $__500__ will be made by mutual consent with each of us agreeing to pay half, and each shall contribute equally to all such improvements.

4. Should either of us decide to end the relationship and cease living together, one of the following will occur:

   (a) If one person wants to stay and the other wants to move on, the person staying will pay the person leaving fair market value (see Clause 5) for his or her share within 90 days. When payment is made, the person selling his or her share will deed the house to the person buying the house. The person buying the house will ensure that the selling partner's name is taken off the mortgage. If the lender refuses to remove the selling partner's name from the mortgage, the buying partner will obtain a new loan in his or her name only. If the buying partner cannot obtain a new loan in his or her name only, the house shall be sold.

   (b) If both of us want to keep the house, we will try to reach a mutually satisfactory agreement for one to buy out the other. If by the end of two weeks we can't, the decision will be made as follows [choose one]:

   [X] (1) Right of First Offer. If both of us want to keep the house, ___Sam___ will have the right of first offer. This means that ___Sam___ may purchase ___Kelly's___ share of the house within 90 days for its fair market value (see Clause 5). If ___Sam___ does not make full payment during this 90-day period, ___Kelly___ will have an additional 90 days in which to buy out ___Sam's___ share for its fair market value. When payment is made, the person leaving will deed the house to the person retaining it in his or her name alone. The person buying the house will ensure that the selling partner's name is taken off the mortgage. If the lender refuses to remove the selling partner's name from the mortgage, the buying partner will obtain a new loan in his or her name only. If neither person exercises his or her buyout right, or if the buying partner cannot obtain a new loan in his or her name only, the house shall be sold.

   [ ] (2) Coin Toss Method. A friend will be asked to flip a coin within 60 days of our decision to separate. The winner of the coin toss is entitled to buy out the loser's share, provided the winner pays the loser fair market value (see Clause 5) within 90 days. If full payment isn't made during this period, the loser of the coin toss will have an additional 90 days in which to buy out the winner's share of the property at fair market value (see Clause 5). When payment is made, the person leaving will deed the house to the person retaining it in his or her name alone. The person buying the house will ensure that the selling partner's name is taken off the mortgage. If the lender refuses to remove the selling partner's name from the mortgage, the buying partner will obtain a new loan in his or her name only. If the buying partner cannot

Contract for Unequal Ownership of a House (continued)

obtain a new loan in his or her name only, the house will be sold.

☐ (3) Other. _____ .

(c) If neither of us wants to own the house or payment isn't made within 90 days, the house will be sold and the profits divided as follows: ___Sam: 2/3___ and ___Kelly: 1/3___ .

(d) We are both responsible for our share of the mortgage, insurance, and taxes until the house is sold or it changes ownership. If one of us moves out of the house before it is sold, the remaining person will make a good faith effort to find a tenant who will pay a fair market rent. Assuming a tenant is found, the rental amount will be credited against the departing partner's payment for shared housing costs.

5. Should either of us decide to end the relationship, we will do our best to agree on the fair market value of our house. However, if we can't agree, we will jointly choose and pay for the services of a licensed real estate appraiser to conduct an appraisal, and we will abide by the result. If we can't agree on an appraiser in the first place, each of us will independently retain and pay for the services of a licensed real estate appraiser. The fair market value of the house will be the average of the two appraisals. "Fair market value" for one person's share of the property is defined as an amount equal to the fair market value of the entire property, less the then-current mortgage amount, multiplied by that person's percentage ownership interest in the property.

6. Should either of us die, the survivor, if he or she has not become the owner of 100% of the deceased person's share through a will, has the right to purchase the portion of the property given or left to someone else at the fair market value of that share (to be arrived at under the terms of Clause 5) within 200 days of the date of death.

7. If either of us is unable or unwilling to pay his or her share of the mortgage, taxes, or insurance payments in a timely manner, the other may make those payments. These payments will be treated as a personal loan to be paid back by the person on whose behalf they are made within six months, including _____% interest per annum. If the loan isn't repaid in six months, the debtor must vacate the house and either sell his or her interest (in which case the buying partner must ensure that the selling partner's name is removed from the mortgage, as set forth in Clause 4) or agree to sell the entire property at fair market value which will be established by appraisal, as set out in Clause 5.

8. This contract is binding on our heirs and our estates.

9. Any dispute arising out of this agreement will be mediated by a third person mutually acceptable to both of us. The mediator's role will be to help us arrive at a solution, not to impose one on us. If good faith efforts to arrive at our own solution with the help of a mediator prove to be fruitless, either of us may make a written request to the other that the dispute be arbitrated. If such a request is made, our dispute will be submitted to arbitration under the rules of the American Arbitration Association, and one arbitrator will hear our dispute. The decision of the arbitrator will be binding on us and will be enforceable in any court that has jurisdiction over the controversy. By agreeing to arbitration, we each agree to give up the right to a jury trial.

___Sam Rutherford___   ___February 2, 20xx___
Signature   Date

___Kelly Franklin___   ___February 2, 20xx___
Signature   Date

Reflections on Contract Writing: Keep It Simple!

Trying to divvy up ownership of a house with 100% accuracy can be more trouble than it's worth. We can't overemphasize that the best contracts are the simplest. For example, we recommend rounding off fractional ownership interests (25% and 75%, not 24.328% and 75.672%). And if one partner puts up a little extra cash or labor, or forks out a bit more money to make an emergency roof repair, either forget it or consider the extra contribution a personal loan and record it in a separate promissory note rather than repeatedly redrafting your ownership contract to adjust your respective ownership percentages a smidgen. As long as any separate promissory notes are paid off before or when the house is sold, this approach is safe and simple.

Agreement for One Person to Move Into the Other's House and Become an Immediate Co-Owner

Sometimes one or both partners already own a house when they decide to live together. Although occasionally the couple decides to sell their existing house(s) and buy one together, it is also common for one person to move in with the other. When this happens, issues of property ownership and how to deal with expenses inevitably arise.

In some cases, the person moving in simply agrees to pay half (or some other agreed-upon portion) of monthly expenses, (mortgage payments, insurance, taxes, and the like)—putting off the decision to share ownership until both partners gain confidence that their relationship is likely to endure.

In other situations, the couple decides that the person moving in will become a co-owner by paying the original owner for half of the property's equity. This can be done in one lump sum or by paying the existing owner in monthly installments (under a separate promissory note).

The Agreement for One Person to Move Into the Other's House and Become an Immediate Co-Owner shown below can be used in either situation. To complete this contract, follow the directions in "Contract for Unequal Ownership of a House," above. It is very similar, except for the first few clauses, which spell out your agreement on the following:

Clause 2 (Fair Market Value of the House). You will need to agree upon the fair market value of the house. See Clause 9 for advice on determining this figure.

Clause 3 (Equity in the House). The current owner will need to determine how much equity he or she has in the house after you establish a fair market value of the property and adjust for the outstanding mortgage debt.

Clause 4 (Share of Ownership). The current owner can decide to sell whatever portion of ownership he or she wants.

Clause 6 (Payment for Share of Ownership). You may agree to either make full payment at the time of signing this agreement, or make monthly installments under a separate promissory note, such as the one in "How to Prepare a Promissory Note," above.

The rest of the Agreement for One Person to Move Into the Other's House and Become an Immediate Co-Owner (Clauses 7 through 13) mirrors Clauses 4 through 9 of the contracts shown above. If one person will be paying off the costs of the house in installment payments with a promissory note, be sure to read "Equal Ownership of a House—One Person Lends the Other All or Part of the Down Payment," above,

Agreement for One Person to Move Into the Other's House and Become an Immediate Co-Owner

_____ Faye Curtis _____ and ___ Fred Miller _____ agree as follows:

1. ___ Faye Curtis _____ now owns the house at
   ___ 10 Briar Cliff Drive, Atlanta, Georgia _____ (hereafter house).

2. The fair market value of the house is currently $___ 450,000 ___ .

3. Equity in the house (fair market value less mortgage and other house-related indebtedness) is $___ 150,000 ___ .

4. ___ Faye Curtis _____ hereby sells ___ ½ ___ of the equity in the house to
   ___ Fred Miller _____ for $ 75,000 _____ , retaining a ___ ½ ___ interest in the house.

5. We will take title as [*choose one*]:

   [X] tenants in common with the following shares:

   | Faye Curtis | [*name*] | ½ | [*% or fraction of ownership*] |
   | Fred Miller | [*name*] | ½ | [*% or fraction of ownership*] |

   or

   [ ] joint tenants with right of survivorship.

6. Payment is due as follows [*choose one*]:

   [X] full payment of $___ 75,000 _____ is due upon signing of this agreement.

   [ ] beginning with the first of the month after this contract is signed, payment will be made in equal monthly installments, including simple interest of _____% per year, and this agreement will be recorded in a separate promissory note.

7. All future housing costs, including payments for the mortgage, homeowners' insurance, property taxes, and
   ___*[fill in any additional costs or fees such as any fees required by a homeowners' association]*___ , will be split
   as follows: ___ equally ___ . All use-related expenses (including utilities and the cost of routine repairs) and
   maintenance will be split as follows: ___ equally ___ . Any improvements to the house costing more than
   $___ 500 ___ will be made by mutual consent with each of us agreeing to pay half, and each shall contribute
   equally to all such improvements.

8. Should either of us decide to end the relationship and cease living together, one of the following will occur:

   (a) If one person wants to stay and the other wants to move on, the person staying will pay the person leaving fair market value (see Clause 9) for his or her share within 90 days. When payment is made, the person selling his or her share will deed the house to the person buying the house. The person buying the house will ensure that the selling partner's name is taken off the mortgage. If the lender refuses to remove the selling partner's name from the mortgage, the buying partner will obtain a new loan in his or her name only. If the buying partner cannot obtain a new loan in his or her name only, the house will be sold.

   (b) If both of us want to keep the house, we will try to reach a mutually satisfactory agreement for one to buy out the other. If by the end of two weeks we can't, the decision will be made as follows [*choose one*]:

   [X] (1) Right of First Offer. If both of us want to keep the house, ___ Faye ___ shall have the right of first
   offer. This means that ___ Faye ___ may purchase ___ Fred's ___ share of the house within 90 days
   for its fair market value (see Clause 9). If ___ Faye ___ does not make full payment during this 90-
   day period, ___ Fred ___ shall have an additional 90 days in which to buy out ___ Faye's ___ share
   for its fair market value. When payment is made, the person leaving will deed the house to the person

Agreement for One Person to Move Into the Other's House and Become an Immediate Co-Owner (continued)

retaining it in his or her name alone. The person buying the house will ensure that the selling partner's name is taken off the mortgage. If the lender refuses to remove the selling partner's name from the mortgage, the buying partner will obtain a new loan in his or her name only. If neither person exercises his or her buyout right, or if the buying partner cannot obtain a new loan in his or her name only, the house shall be sold.

☐ (2) Coin Toss Method. A friend will be asked to flip a coin within 60 days of our decision to separate. The winner of the coin toss is entitled to buy out the loser's share, provided the winner pays the loser fair market value (see Clause 9) within 90 days. If full payment isn't made during this period, the loser of the coin toss will have an additional 90 days in which to buy out the winner's share of the property at fair market value (see Clause 9). When payment is made, the person leaving will deed the house to the person retaining it in his or her name alone. The person buying the house will ensure that the selling partner's name is taken off the mortgage. If the lender refuses to remove the selling partner's name from the mortgage, the buying partner will obtain a new loan in his or her name only. If the buying partner cannot obtain a new loan in his or her name only, the house shall be sold.

☐ (3) Other. _____

_____ .

(c) If neither of us wants to own the house or payment on a buyout isn't made within 90 days, the house will be sold and the profits divided as follows: _____Faye: ½ and Fred: ½_____ .

(d) We are both responsible for our share of the mortgage, insurance, and taxes until the house is sold or it changes ownership. If one of us moves out of the house before it is sold, the remaining person will make a good faith effort to find a tenant who will pay a fair market rent. Assuming a tenant is found, the rental amount will be credited against the departing partner's payment for shared housing costs.

9. Should either of us decide to end the relationship, we will do our best to agree on the fair market value of our house. However, if we can't agree, we will jointly choose and pay for the services of a licensed real estate appraiser to conduct an appraisal, and we will abide by the result. If we can't agree on an appraiser in the first place, each of us will independently retain and pay for the services of a licensed real estate appraiser. The fair market value of the house will be the average of the two appraisals. "Fair market value" for one person's share of the property is defined as an amount equal to the fair market value of the entire property, less the then-current mortgage amount, multiplied by that person's percentage ownership interest in the property.

10. Should either of us die, the survivor, if he or she has not become the owner of 100% of the deceased person's share through joint tenancy or a will, has the right to purchase the portion of the property given or left to someone else at the fair market value of that share (to be arrived at under the terms of Clause 9) within ___100___ days of the date of death.

11. If either of us is unable or unwilling to pay his or her share of the mortgage, taxes, or insurance payments in a timely manner, the other may make those payments. These payments will be treated as a personal loan to be paid back by the person on whose behalf they are made within ___six___ months, including ___3___ % interest per annum. If the loan isn't repaid in six months, the debtor must vacate the house and either sell his or her interest (in which case the buying partner must ensure that the selling partner's name is removed from the mortgage, as set forth in Clause 4) or agree to sell the entire property at fair market value, which will be established by appraisal as set out in Clause 9.

12. This contract is binding on our heirs and our estates.

Agreement for One Person to Move Into the Other's House and Become an Immediate Co-Owner (continued)

13. Any dispute arising out of this agreement will be mediated by a third person mutually acceptable to both of us. The mediator's role will be to help us arrive at a solution, not to impose one on us. If good faith efforts to arrive at our own solution with the help of a mediator prove to be fruitless, either of us may make a written request to the other that the dispute be arbitrated. If such a request is made, our dispute will be submitted to arbitration under the rules of the American Arbitration Association, and one arbitrator will hear our dispute. The decision of the arbitrator will be binding on us and will be enforceable in any court that has jurisdiction over the controversy. By agreeing to arbitration, we each agree to give up the right to a jury trial.

Faye Curtis	*March 9, 20xx*
Signature	Date
Fred Miller	*March 9, 20xx*
Signature	Date

---

for advice, including possible language changes to the contract. If a nonowner is going to contribute to his or her partner's residence and never become an owner of record, we strongly recommend having a written agreement clarifying whether or not the nonowner will receive any share of the appreciation, or will simply be considered a renter.

CAUTION

Be sure to change title. Whenever you change ownership of a house or other real property, you need to prepare and record a new deed reflecting current title.

Check Out Legal and Tax Issues Before Transferring a Share of Your House

If you decide to sell a share of your house, spend some time with a tax accountant and real estate attorney unless you are totally confident that you understand all the tax and legal issues involved. The rules for a partial buyout by an unmarried partner are a bit murky, so if a lot of equity is involved, check with an accountant or a tax attorney.

Check out the tax consequences. If you receive no money from the sale of an interest in your house in a particular year, there is normally no taxable gain or income to report from the sale; but it may be considered a gift, which can have long-term estate tax consequences for the donor. If you do receive money from the sale, you have to determine what percent is a return on your initial capital (not taxed) and what percent is interest and profit (which may be subject to a tax if the house has a great deal of value). However, federal tax law now provides that if the house has been your residence for at least two of the last five years before the sale, the first $250,000 in capital gains received by each partner is not taxed. In some states, you also may have to pay a transfer tax or increased property taxes. For information on tax laws involving real estate transactions, visit the IRS website at www.irs.gov. IRS Publication 523 specifically covers tax issues when selling your house.

Beware of the Due on Sale Clause. If you sell a share of a house already subject to a mortgage or deed of trust, you may need lender approval under the terms of a "due on sale" clause. Most real estate mortgages contain a due on sale clause that requires that the borrower pay off the entire mortgage before selling the property, unless the lender approves the sale without full payment of the mortgage. The lender may not approve for a variety of reasons, especially if your fixed rate mortgage interest rate is below the current market rate, but many lenders do not enforce this clause at all. This may mean you'll need to pay off the existing mortgage and refinance. Or it may cause you to rethink the wisdom of the entire transaction. For example, you might decide not to change ownership at all, but instead use the other partner's money to purchase other assets that would remain in his or her name, but be used to benefit both partners.

Agreement for One Person to Move Into the Other's House and Become a Co-Owner Gradually

Where one member of a couple is more affluent than the other, the most realistic approach for many couples is to draft an agreement that allows the person moving in to become a co-owner gradually. Although there are a number of ways to do this, the most common is to provide that each month the person moving in will pay a portion—or, possibly, all—of the monthly mortgage cost in exchange for receiving a tiny equity share in the house. You can use the Agreement for One Person to Move Into the Other's House and Become a Co-Owner Gradually for this purpose. A sample is shown below.

There is no correct way to determine how much the gradual co-owner must pay before he or she becomes a half-owner of the home. Many factors come into play, making the calculation tricky. For example, the value of the home probably will fluctuate during the time period when payments are made. The more the original owner has already paid, the more the gradual co-owner will have to pay. The length of the mortgage will factor in too. And finally, part of the gradual co-owner's payment will go towards interest, not principal—making the interest rate important as well.

Agreement for One Person to Move Into the Other's House and Become a Co-Owner Gradually

_____Alan Martin_____ and _____Alison Salinger_____ agree as follows:

1. _____Alison_____ owns the house at _____57 Primrose Path, Omaha, Nebraska_____ (hereafter house), subject to a mortgage with the _____Prairie National Bank_____ in the amount of $ __200,000__ .

2. The fair market value of the house is currently $__300,000__ .

3. __Alison's__ equity in the house (fair market value less mortgage or other house-related indebtedness) is $__100,000__ .

4. Beginning with the date this contract is signed, _____Alan_____ will pay all monthly expenses for the mortgage, homeowners' insurance, property taxes, utilities, and necessary repairs and maintenance, estimated to be $__2,500__ per month, and will continue to do so until his ~~or her~~ total payments equal $__100,000__ or until we separate or agree to modify this agreement, after which the payments will be split equally. Of that $__100,000__, $__50,000__ will be considered to meet __Alan's__ obligation to pay half of the expenses, while the other $__50,000__ will be considered to be repayment to _____Alison_____ of half of the equity interest.

5. __Alan's__ share of the total net equity of the house shall be figured at the rate of __1%__ for every month that he ~~or she~~ pays all of the expenses as set out in Clause 4, based on __$1,000__ of the monthly payment contribution counted as the equity buy-in amount. For example, if _____Alan_____ pays all the expenses for two years, his ~~or her~~ interest in the house equity shall be __24__ %.

6. _____Alison_____ shall deed the house to _____Alison Salinger and Alan Martin_____ as "Tenants in Common" and record the deed and this contract, upon the signing of this agreement.

7. Should we separate prior to the time that _____Alan_____ contributes $__100,000__, _____Alison_____ shall have first right to remain in the house and buy out __Alan's__ equity share as determined by Clause 5. _____Alan_____ shall leave within 30 days of the decision to separate.

8. Once _____Alan_____ contributes $__100,000__, the house shall be owned equally by both of us, and all expenses for taxes, mortgage, insurance, and repairs shall be shared equally.

9. Should we separate after the time that _____Alan_____ contributes $__100,000__, one of the following will occur:

   (a) If one person wants to stay and the other wants to move on, the person staying will pay the person leaving fair market value (see Clause 10) for his or her percentage share at the time, within 90 days. When payment is made, the person selling his or her share will deed the house to the person buying the house. The person buying the house will ensure that the selling partner's name is taken off the mortgage. If the lender refuses to remove the selling partner's name from the mortgage, the buying partner will obtain a new loan in his or her name only. If the buying partner cannot obtain a new loan in his or her name only, the house shall be sold.

   (b) If both of us want to keep the house, we will try to reach a mutually satisfactory agreement for one to buy out the other. If by the end of two weeks we can't, the decision will be made as follows [choose one]:

      ☒ (1) Right of First Offer. If both of us want to keep the house, _____Alison_____ shall have the right of first offer. This means that _____Alison_____ may purchase __Alan's__ share of the house within 90 days for its fair market value (see Clause 10). If _____Alison_____ does not make full payment during this 90-day period, _____Alan_____ shall have an additional 90 days in which to buy out

Agreement for One Person to Move Into the Other's House and Become a Co-Owner Gradually (continued)

___Alison's___ share for its fair market value. When payment is made, the person leaving will deed the house to the person retaining it in his or her name alone. The person buying the house will ensure that the selling partner's name is taken off the mortgage. If the lender refuses to remove the selling partner's name from the mortgage, the buying partner will obtain a new loan in his or her name only. If neither person exercises his or her buyout right, or if the buying partner cannot obtain a new loan in his or her name only, the house shall be sold.

☐ (2) Coin Toss Method. A friend will be asked to flip a coin within 60 days of our decision to separate. The winner of the coin toss is entitled to buy out the loser's share, provided the winner pays the loser fair market value (see Clause 10) within 90 days. If full payment isn't made during this period, the loser of the coin toss will have an additional 90 days in which to buy out the winner's share of the property at fair market value (see Clause 10). When payment is made, the person leaving will deed the house to the person retaining it in his or her name alone. The person buying the house will ensure that the selling partner's name is taken off the mortgage. If the lender refuses to remove the selling partner's name from the mortgage, the buying partner will obtain a new loan in his or her name only. If the buying partner cannot obtain a new loan in his or her name only, the house shall be sold.

☐ (3) Other

_____

_____ .

(c) If neither of us wants to own the house or payment isn't made within 90 days, the house will be sold and the profits divided as follows: ___Alison: ½ and Alan: ½___ .

(d) We are both responsible for our share of the mortgage, insurance, and taxes until the house is sold or it changes ownership. If one of us moves out of the house before it is sold, the remaining person will make a good faith effort to find a tenant who will pay a fair market rent. Assuming a tenant is found, the rental amount will be credited against the departing partner's payment for shared housing costs.

10. Should either of us decide to end the relationship, we will do our best to agree on the fair market value of our house. However, if we can't agree, we will jointly choose and pay for the services of a licensed real estate appraiser to conduct an appraisal, and abide by the result. If we can't agree on an appraiser in the first place, each of us will independently retain and pay for the services of a licensed real estate appraiser. The fair market value of the house will be the average of the two appraisals. "Fair market value" for one person's share of the property is defined as an amount equal to the fair market value of the entire property, less the then-current mortgage amount, multiplied by that person's percentage ownership interest in the property.

11. Should either of us die, the survivor, if he or she has not become the owner of 100% of the deceased person's share through joint tenancy or a will, has the right to purchase the portion of the property given or left to someone else at the fair market value of that share (to be arrived at under the terms of Clause 10) within ___200___ days of the date of death.

12. This contract is binding on our heirs and our estates.

13. Any dispute arising out of this agreement will be mediated by a third person mutually acceptable to both of

---

Agreement for One Person to Move Into the Other's House
and Become a Co-Owner Gradually (continued)

us. The mediator's role will be to help us arrive at a solution, not to impose one on us. If good faith efforts to arrive at our own solution with the help of a mediator prove to be fruitless, either of us may make a written request to the other that the dispute be arbitrated. If such a request is made, our dispute will be submitted to arbitration under the rules of the American Arbitration Association, and one arbitrator will hear our dispute. The decision of the arbitrator will be binding on us and will be enforceable in any court that has jurisdiction over the controversy. By agreeing to arbitration, we each agree to give up the right to a jury trial.

Alison Salinger   _May 7, 20xx_
Signature   Date

Alan Martin   _May 7, 20xx_
Signature   Date

There are several options to determine the amount the gradual co-owner must pay before owning a half interest in the home:

- Some couples ignore all of the above factors and decide that the new owner simply must pay an amount equal to the original owner's current equity.

- Some couples decide that the gradual co-owner must pay more than the original owner's current equity, perhaps 25% or 50% more, based on an estimate of long-term appreciation. Couples that follow this approach do so on the theory that money already invested is worth more than money to be invested in the future. And, the fair market value of the house is likely to increase over time.

- Another approach is to consult an expert in real estate finance who is familiar with the local market, and get an opinion as to what would be a reasonable amount.

Starting a Family

At some point, you and your partner may decide that even though you aren't interested in getting married, you'd like to have a child. While there are no insurmountable legal problems in raising a child without being married, there are several issues to consider. This chapter covers some of the most common questions facing unmarried couples having children, including naming the baby, naming the father (paternity), adoptions, and inheritance rights of children of unmarried parents.

Because family law varies from state to state, be sure to check your state's laws on specific rules, such as adoption, paternity, and custody, and consult a family law specialist as needed.

CROSS REFERENCE

Related topics in this book include:

- Custody, visitation, and support of children from a previous marriage: Chapter 8

- Issues involving children when an unmarried couple separates, including child support, visitation, and custody rights, and how to prepare a parenting agreement: Chapter 10

- How to research state and local laws on adoption, paternity, and unmarried couples: Chapter 11.

Having a Child: Legal Obligations of Unmarried Parents

Parents are legally responsible for their children, regardless of whether the parents are married to each other or not. Courts don't care why people have children. Whether you decide to have children after careful planning, checking the location of the planets, or just letting it happen is legally irrelevant. If a child arrives, both biological parents (married or unmarried) have a duty of support. And even if the father did not want the child, or split from

his partner before the baby was born, he remains responsible for the child's support.

CAUTION

Fathers' rights and abortions. Fathers have the legal responsibility to support their children, but have no say over a pregnant partner's decision to have an abortion.

Naming the Baby and Getting a Birth Certificate

In most states, you may give your child any first, middle, and last name you like. Whether you are married or not, you don't have to give the baby the last name of either parent if you don't want to, and the child does not have to have the father's last name to be considered "legitimate."

The procedure for naming a baby is simple. A representative of the local health department or similar agency, or a hospital social worker, meets with the new mother in the hospital immediately after the birth and asks her the child's name and some questions about the mother's health and the father's name and occupation. The mother doesn't have to name the child at this time, though she will probably be urged to do so. The information the mother gives is typed on a form that she signs. The state then issues a birth certificate, which usually doesn't reveal whether or not the parents are married.

If the baby isn't born in a medical facility, the mother or the physician, midwife, or other person assisting in the delivery must notify health officials of the birth. Again, there's no legal requirement that the baby be named at this time, but it's common to do so.

In either case, if the mother did not name the baby or did not give the father's identity, it is possible to update the birth certificate later to include that information. The state Department of Health or Bureau of Vital Statistics in every state will have procedures for adding the father's name to the child's birth certificate or amending the birth certificate to show the child's name. If you are going to be adding the father's name to a birth certificate, most states will require an unmarried father to sign an acknowledgment of paternity (see below for more detail on paternity issues).

RESOURCE

For information on your state's Department of Health (which will either handle vital statistics or refer you to the state Bureau of Vital Statistics), visit the website of the National Center for Health Statistics at www.cdc.gov/nchs.

Naming the Father: Paternity

Paternity simply means "the state of being a father." When an unmarried couple has a child, it's essential that the father's paternity be established as soon as possible after the baby is born. This protects the mother, the baby, and especially the father, by greatly reducing the possibility that a judge will deny the father custody or visitation of his child, or other rights to which fathers are legally entitled. It also helps ensure that the child will be eligible to receive benefits through the father, including health, survivors', disability, and life insurance benefits.

The best way to establish the father's paternity is by naming him on the birth certificate as described above. Under U.S. Department of Health and Human Services regulations, all states must offer unwed parents an opportunity to establish paternity by voluntarily signing an acknowledgment of paternity, either at the hospital or at a later time. In many states, as a result of political pressure to reduce the number of mothers on welfare by ensuring that there is someone else with an

obligation to support the child, hospital personnel will make every effort to get the father to sign the acknowledgment.

CAUTION

Don't acknowledge paternity if you're not the father. Although signing to acknowledge paternity is a very good idea if you are the father of the child, if you're not the father, or if you are not sure, don't sign on the dotted line. If you sign a paternity statement, you'll be liable for child support and even for reimbursing the state for welfare payments made to the mother, until you can prove that you are not actually the child's father.

In some states, including California, the only way that an unmarried father's name can be placed on a child's birth certificate is if the father signs a voluntary declaration of paternity. If the father is not present at the hospital following the birth, the mother will not be able to list him as the father on the birth certificate in his absence—the father and mother will instead have to sign the voluntary declaration of paternity at a later time, and have the father's name added to the birth certificate later. A voluntary declaration of paternity signed by both parents has the same legal effect as a court order, so once it is signed and submitted to the appropriate agency, the father's paternal rights are firmly established. If you live in a state that requires a voluntary declaration of paternity before placing an unmarried father's name on a birth certificate, and you and your partner split up before the baby is born, you may have to bring a legal action to establish paternity if your ex-partner won't sign the voluntary declaration.

Don't Lie About the Child's Father

In states where the mother can state the name of the father even if he is not present, some women are tempted to write down a name other than the actual father's on the birth information form. This is most common when the mother no longer sees the biological father and is involved with someone whom she would prefer to have raise the child or who is financially better able to do so. Identifying a man as the baby's father when that man is not actually the father is a terrible idea. An unmarried couple's current relationship may not last forever and complicated legal questions of paternity and support can grow from listing the wrong person as the father of a child. In a well-known case (*In re Clausen*, 502 N.W.2d 649 (Mich. 1993)), the mother of Baby Jessica lied on her baby's birth certificate, saying that the father was her new boyfriend, and did not tell her ex-boyfriend that she had given birth to their child. When the mother and her new boyfriend gave the baby up for adoption, the ex-boyfriend found out and wanted to step in and reclaim Baby Jessica. A long legal battle ensued between the new adoptive parents and the biological parents, with Baby Jessica caught in the middle (the baby was eventually returned to her birth parents). To avoid such potential problems, it is always best to accurately state who the biological father is.

Paternity Statements

We would be surprised if you were able to get out of the hospital without naming the father on the birth certificate or signing a voluntary declaration of paternity, if you are both present for the birth and it's clear that your partner is the child's father. However, if for some reason you do not name the father on the birth certificate or sign a voluntary acknowledgment of paternity at the hospital, then it is essential that you prepare and sign an informal "paternity statement." If you have named the father on the birth certificate or signed a voluntary acknowledgment of paternity, you can still sign a paternity statement just to make your life easier in some circumstances. For example, if you lose the child's birth certificate and haven't yet ordered a new one, you might be able to use the paternity statement at the child's school or while traveling. It also serves as additional evidence of paternity should the mother ever contest the father's relationship with the child.

If the father signs an acknowledgment of paternity or a paternity statement sometime after the child's birth, his parental rights are normally still established as long as no dispute over custody or adoption arises in the interim. However, the U.S. Supreme Court has held that if a father waits until a custody dispute arises, it may be too late to establish full parental rights—unless the father has had an ongoing relationship with the child. (*Quilloin v. Walcott*, 434 U.S. 246 (1978).) For example, the Court denied a father's right to block a child's adoption—and, by so doing, cut off his parental rights—in a situation where he had no real relationship with his children and did not try to legitimate them until the adoption proceeding began. (*Lehr v. Robertson*, 463 U.S. 248 (1983).) In some states, only a father who has established paternity by coming forward promptly and demonstrating a full commitment to his parental responsibilities must be notified of adoption proceedings. (*In re Kelsey S.*, 823 P.2d 1216 (Cal. 1992).) And if he does learn of the proceedings, he may have no legal standing to object.

In many other states, there is a trend towards giving unmarried fathers more rights, especially where the father has promptly and consistently attempted to form a paternal relationship with a young child but was prevented from doing so by the mother's actions. For example, where the mother failed to tell the father of the birth of their child, if the father later discovers the birth and promptly makes a good faith effort to assume responsibility for the child, the courts generally will protect his rights, as in the Baby Jessica case. (*In re Clausen*, 502 N.W. 2d 649 (Mich. 1993).)

Sample Paternity Statement

Assuming you haven't signed one in the hospital, or just want to do another one for the reasons described above, you can prepare a paternity statement yourself quite easily. We include a sample Acknowledgment of Parenthood, to be signed by both parents.

CD-ROM

The forms CD includes the Acknowledgment of Parenthood form, and Appendix B includes a blank tear-out copy.

CAUTION

State-issued forms are preferable to home-made paternity statements. As discussed above, all states have official forms on which a man can voluntarily acknowledge his paternity of a child. In some states, there is a time limit for signing these forms, but in others there is no time limit, and in many states, the father's signature on the forms acts as a substitute for a court order, officially establishing his parental relationship with the child. A homemade form will not accomplish the same thing, so before you create one, find out whether you can still sign a voluntary declaration of paternity with the state.

Acknowledgment of Parenthood

<u>Lazarus Sandling</u> and <u>Rebecca Conlon</u> hereby acknowledge that they are the biological parents of <u>Clementine Conlon Sandling</u>, born <u>January 1, 20xx</u>, in <u>New York City, New York</u>.

<u>Lazarus Sandling</u> and <u>Rebecca Conlon</u> further state that they have welcomed <u>Clementine Conlon Sandling</u> into their home and that it's their intention and belief that <u>Clementine</u> is fully legitimate for all purposes, including the right to inherit from and through both parents.

<u>Lazarus Sandling</u> and <u>Rebecca Conlon</u> further expressly acknowledge their duty to raise and support <u>Clementine Conlon Sandling</u>.

We declare under penalty of perjury that the information set forth in this document is true and correct.

March 2, 20xx	*Rebecca Conlon*
Date	Signature
March 2, 20xx	*Lazarus Sandling*
Date	Signature

[Notarize]

Simply fill in the father's name (and the mother's if you're using the Acknowledgment of Parenthood form), and the child's name, birth date, and place of birth in the appropriate sections.

Prepare two copies of the statement and have your signatures notarized on both copies. Notarization isn't required, but it's an excellent idea. In the event the father dies, the mother may have to present the paternity statement to various public agencies—and possibly life insurers and other private companies. Notarization proves that the father's signature wasn't forged after the father's death.

The mother and father should each keep a copy of the notarized paternity statement. Some states have set up procedures to file paternity statements with a state agency. For information on doing this, contact your state's Department of Health or Bureau of Vital Statistics. To find your state's Department of Health (which will either handle vital statistics or refer you to the state Bureau of Vital Statistics), visit the website of the National Center for Health Statistics at www.cdc.gov/nchs.

Legitimacy of Children Born to Unmarried Parents

Most states and the federal government have moved away from using the words "legitimate" and "illegitimate" in differentiating between children whose parents are married or not married. Some states have adopted the Uniform Parentage Act, which says that "the parent and child relationship extends equally to every child and to every parent, regardless of the marital status of the parents." Other states have modified versions of the Act in place, but either way, many states have now abandoned outdated notions of legitimacy.

Even in the states that have adopted this Act, however, it's still crucial to know who a child's parents are. This is because when it comes to inheritance, child support, custody, adoption, and many other areas of the law, the rights and duties of parents are clearly stated. (For an overview of these rights and duties, check out information on Nolo's website at www.nolo.com.) And don't think that a father's refusal to sign a paternity statement will get him off the hook for paying child support. If a father doesn't voluntarily sign a paternity statement, the state will go to court to establish that he is the father and collect child support.

TIP

Being named father on a birth certificate isn't always adequate proof to a court that the named man is the father. A lawsuit to have a man declared the father of a child is called a paternity or support action. It can be brought by either the mother or the father. Advances

in blood and DNA tests make it possible to determine paternity with better than 98% accuracy, and to disprove it with 100% accuracy.

In *Trimble v. Gordon,* 430 U.S. 762 (1977), the Supreme Court held that states may set up different standards of proof necessary to establish paternity, as long as the standards are not completely arbitrary.

Standards of Proof of Paternity in States Adopting the Uniform Parentage Act

In the states that have adopted the Uniform Parentage Act, a man is presumed to be the father in any of the following circumstances:

Circumstance 1: He is married to the mother at the time the child is born, or was married to her within 300 days of the birth of the child. This means that, if the man dies or the couple divorces while the mother is pregnant, he is still presumed to be the father.

Circumstance 2: He and the mother, before the birth of the child, attempted to get married (obtained a license and had a ceremony) but the marriage wasn't valid because one person was still married to someone else, the clergyperson could not perform a marriage, or a similar reason, *and* the child was born during the attempted marriage or within 300 days after the termination of the marriage, be it by court order, death, or simple separation.

Circumstance 3: After the child's birth, the father and the mother have married (or gone through a ceremony in apparent compliance with law) although the marriage could later be annulled for some reason, and the man

a) has acknowledged paternity in writing—for example, by signing a paternity statement

b) with his consent, is named the father on the child's birth certificate, or

Competing Presumptions

Some situations may present competing presumptions of fatherhood. For example, suppose a woman cohabiting with an unmarried partner is still married to another man. If a child is born during that time (while the marriage still exists), the husband is legally presumed to be the child's father. But if the unmarried partner acknowledges paternity by signing an acknowledgment of paternity and holding the child out as his child, he generally will *also* be presumed to be the child's father. When there are competing presumptions and both men want to be considered the child's father, it will be difficult to avoid a court proceeding to determine who the child's father is.

Biology is not necessarily destiny. In one California case, a man who was not the child's biological father still won a court battle of competing presumptions. (*Steven W. v. Matthew S.*, 33 Cal. App.4th 1108 (1995).) A similar result was reached in a Colorado case in which the court held that the best interests of the child must be considered in weighing competing presumptions of paternity. (*N.A.H. v. S.L.S.*, 9 P.3d 354 (2000).) In a case in Indiana, a woman was not allowed to challenge her ex-husband's paternity rights, even though genetic testing showed he was not the child's biological father, because she had been cohabiting with him when the child was conceived (before they got married) and she had consistently identified him as the father, including in court documents relating to their divorce. (*Ohning v. Driskill*, 739 N.E. 161 (2000).) On the other hand, a Maine court upheld an order declaring a man was *not* the father of a child born to his ex-wife during the marriage, because both parties knew the husband was not the biological father. (*Stitham v. Henderson*, 768 A.2d 598 (2001).)

c) pays child support under a written, voluntary promise or has been ordered to pay support by a court.

Circumstance 4: While the child is still a minor, the man (who is not married to the mother) receives the child into his home and openly holds out the child as his natural child.

These rules create presumptions. Legally, a presumption means that certain facts are presumed to produce a certain legal conclusion unless rebutted by strong evidence. For example, in Circumstance 4, if a man takes a child into his home and says he's the father—even though he never married the mother—he's presumed to be the father. This doesn't mean that he is—he or the mother might prove that though he received the child into his home and told everyone that he was the father, he wasn't. This can lead to a court fight involving blood tests to prove paternity.

Standards of Proof of Paternity in States That Have Not Adopted the Uniform Parentage Act

There are still quite a few states that haven't yet adopted the Uniform Parentage Act, and many of these still use the terms legitimate and illegitimate. But except for the use of the term illegitimate, the laws of these states relating to the rights of unmarried parents are usually similar to the provisions of the Uniform Parentage Act. This is because in a long line of court decisions, beginning with *Levy v. Louisiana*, 391 U.S. 68 (1968), the U.S. Supreme Court has struck down most state laws giving legitimate children more legal rights than illegitimate children.

In most states that still label children illegitimate, it's possible to change the label from illegitimate to legitimate if any of the following things apply:

• The parents marry each other. (Children born during a marriage that is later annulled remain legitimate.)

Abandonment of a Child

The right to be considered a full legal parent can be lost if a parent fails to exercise parental responsibilities. The law calls this "abandonment." In most states, abandonment is defined as a period of time (often two years) in which a parent who does not have physical custody fails to contact and—if the parent has the ability—to support a child. Some states have shortened this time period to one year. If you have no money and don't have the ability to support your child, you won't be considered to have abandoned your child as long as you visit regularly. The key is that if you are not the parent with custody, you must stay involved with your child to the best of your ability.

A parent who has not assumed any parental obligations for several years faces an uphill battle if there's a later abandonment action or custody fight. However, that parent is still entitled to be notified and have a hearing on a custody challenge. (*Stanley v. Illinois*, 405 U.S. 645 (1972).) It is important to note that if a parent has relinquished the opportunity to develop a relationship with the child, and has only a biological link to the child, courts may not take the claim for custody very seriously. Obviously, if a parent without custody has made repeated attempts to contact a child and has been prevented from doing so by the other parent, a court would be willing to give the case more consideration. If you have not been regularly visiting and supporting your child, you should go to court to assert your rights as soon as possible. A parent who is out of contact with a child is extremely vulnerable to having parental rights terminated in an abandonment proceeding.

- The father signs a paternity statement or voluntary declaration of paternity acknowledging in writing, under penalty of perjury, that the child is his. If the state has a registry for children born of unmarried parents, it is also a good idea to file the paternity statement with your state's Bureau of Vital Statistics.

- The father welcomes the child into his home or holds himself out as the father.

- The parents go to court and have a judge rule that the man is the father. This can usually be done by joint petition—where the parents go to court together in a nonadversary proceeding.

CROSS REFERENCE

To find your state law on legitimacy, check your state code (Chapter 11 tells you how). Look in the index under "Children," subheading "Legitimate."

Adopting a Child

In addition to, or instead of, having your own biological child, you and your partner may want to adopt a child. Adoption is a court procedure by which an adult legally becomes the parent of someone who is not his or her biological child. Adoption creates a parent-child relationship recognized for all purposes—including child support obligations, inheritance rights, and custody. The birthparents' legal relationship to the child is terminated, unless the adoption is a stepparent or a so-called "second-parent" adoption, in which case only one parent without custody loses parental rights.

Overview of Adoptions

If an unmarried couple jointly adopts a child, or if one partner legally adopts the biological child of the other, both parents are legal parents. This means both have equal legal responsibilities to raise and support the child. If the couple separates, each has the right to petition a court for custody of (or visitation with) the child, and each has an obligation to provide child support.

Adoption is primarily governed by state law. As a general rule, any adult who is found to be a "fit parent" may adopt a child as long as the child is free for adoption, meaning that appropriate consents have been given. It is legal for single people to adopt children in many states. Unmarried couples may adopt jointly, and unmarried people may adopt through a procedure known as a single-parent adoption. You'll need to check your state laws to see what rules apply in your particular situation. Some states frown on adoption by unmarried people, but most allow it.

Adoption agencies are allowed to create their own rules about who can adopt and under what circumstances, as long as they don't run afoul of state law. While there are often no specific legal prohibitions against unmarried couples adopting children, you may find that adoption agencies are biased against unmarried couples, or make it more difficult for unmarried couples to adopt. You should be prepared to explain why you haven't married and to make a good case for your fitness as a parent. In general, you should expect to do extra work to prove that your home is a stable and healthy environment for raising children. A local social service agency will conduct a home study and interview both partners and then report to the court, which must approve adoptions. You may have a longer wait for a child, or you may have to broaden your ideas about the age and type of child you want to adopt.

SEE AN EXPERT

Get a good family law attorney if you want to adopt. Social service and government agencies often discriminate against unmarried couples, and adoption proceedings can often be complex (particularly if it's a private adoption), so you'll need to get some legal advice before you and your partner try to adopt. For an overview of legal issues involving adoptions, including different options, such as agency and private adoptions, see the Parenting & Adoption topic on Nolo's website at www.nolo.com.

Stepparent and Second-Parent Adoptions

In a stepparent adoption, a parent marries someone other than his or her child's other parent, and the new spouse adopts the child. When the adopting couple is married, the adoption is usually readily approved. These adoptions usually don't cost much and may not require a home study by a social worker. The equivalent process for unmarried couples is called "second-parent adoption." When the adopting couple is unmarried, the cost may be higher and a social worker home study is almost always required. In addition, a number of states still frown upon second-parent adoptions when the couple is unmarried. If you are considering one of these adoptions, you'd be wise to consult with a local family law attorney to get an evaluation of your rights. Keep in mind that if you don't adopt your partner's biological child, you risk losing access to the child if you and your partner separate. (Separation issues are discussed in Chapter 10 of this book.)

When Can a Stepparent or Second Parent Adopt?

A child cannot be adopted without the consent of both parents, unless one parent has failed to establish a parent-child relationship with the child or has abandoned the child.

If the noncustodial parent is the father, the social service agency will determine whether his consent is needed before a stepparent or second-parent adoption can take place. A father who signs a paternity statement, provides support (if he can), and maintains a relationship with his child, can probably prevent the child from being adopted by someone else. In addition—especially if the child is a baby and the father has had little opportunity to support or visit the child—or has been prevented from doing so by the mother—he may be able to prevent the stepparent or second-parent adoption and petition the court to obtain visitation.

If the noncustodial parent is the mother, the social service agency will have to obtain her consent or recommend that her parental rights be terminated. Unmarried mothers without custody must pay support if they can and visit the child—or face losing the child to a stepparent or second-parent adoption.

Remember, once a person does formally adopt a child, that person has all the legal rights and responsibilities of a biological parent, whether the adopting parent is a partner who legally adopts the biological child of an unmarried partner or part of an unmarried couple that jointly adopts a child.

Examples of Stepparent and Second-Parent Adoptions

Here are a few examples of stepparent and second-parent adoptions. These scenarios involve an unmarried couple, Linda and Frank, who have a baby, Mollie.

EXAMPLE 1:

Frank takes off before his and Linda's baby Mollie is born. He doesn't send support or contact Linda or the baby for three years, despite having the opportunity to do so. At this point, Linda marries Herman who wants to adopt Mollie. Linda's consent is necessary for this adoption, but Frank's probably isn't. Under the laws and procedures in force in most states, the adoption agency will normally make an effort to notify Frank. If he shows up, he must be given a hearing, but his opposition to the adoption won't count for much. The fact that Frank abandoned Mollie will probably prevent him from successfully opposing the adoption by Linda's new husband.

EXAMPLE 2:

This time Linda and Frank live together for several years after Mollie is born. When they split up, Linda keeps Mollie, and later marries Herman. Frank holds Mollie out to the world as his child, visits her, and pays support to Linda. He never signs a paternity statement, however. Whether Herman can adopt Mollie without Frank's consent depends on state law. If the state has adopted the Uniform Parentage Act, Frank's consent is necessary because he has legitimated Mollie by welcoming her into his home and acknowledging that he's her father. In other states, the fact that Frank has continued to support and visit Mollie will count strongly in his favor; Frank would be in an even stronger legal position to prevent the adoption if he had signed a statement acknowledging paternity soon after Mollie was born, or even when he and Linda separated. In a state where a voluntary declaration of paternity is the equivalent of a court order, Frank's legal standing will allow him to block the adoption.

EXAMPLE 3:

Same situation as Example 2, except that when Mollie is born, Frank signs a paternity statement. Every state will require Frank's consent before allowing Herman to adopt Mollie, unless Frank later abandons Mollie.

EXAMPLE 4:

This time, before Linda and Frank split up, Frank signs a paternity statement, but never contacts Mollie again. If he refuses to consent to Herman's adopting her or can't be found, a court will decide whether Frank has forfeited his parental rights by abandoning Mollie. An effort will be made to notify Frank of the hearing.

EXAMPLE 5:

This time, Frank keeps Mollie after he and Linda split up. Frank marries Susan, who wants to adopt Mollie. Linda must consent to the adoption. If she refuses, there must be a hearing to terminate Linda's parental rights, and she must be given a chance to oppose. If Linda hasn't supported or contacted Mollie for a long time, it's likely she will lose her parental rights.

Public and Private Benefits for a Child of Unmarried Parents

If a parent becomes disabled or dies, the person's biological or legal child may be entitled to receive income, such as from Social Security, government or pension benefits, or possibly a private insurance company (life insurance). In the past, benefits derived through the father were often unavailable to or reduced for "illegitimate" children—children born "out of wedlock." For example, Social Security regulations used to grant more benefits to the legitimate child of a deceased, retired, or disabled father than to an illegitimate child.

However, the U.S. Supreme Court has long since ruled that treating children differently on this basis is unconstitutional. It no longer makes any difference whether a child is "legitimate" or "illegitimate" for purposes of receiving Social Security and similar government benefits.

When it comes to private benefits, children of unmarried couples are similarly protected in most instances. For example, if you name your children as the beneficiaries of a life insurance policy, they will receive the policy proceeds if you die while the policy is in effect, whether you're married to their other parent or not.

Even though the legal rights of children born outside of marriage have greatly improved, that's not a reason for a father to fail to take steps to further protect them. The best way to do this is to sign a paternity or parenthood statement right away when your child is born. If you die, and you have failed to sign such a statement or otherwise clearly form a parent-child relationship with your child, Social Security or other federal, state, or private benefits may be denied your child because there's no proof that you were the father.

Inheritance Rights of a Child of Unmarried Parents

You can leave your property to anyone you want in a will, trust, joint ownership device, or other estate planning device. (Chapter 9 explains how.) In short, you don't have to sign a paternity statement or raise a child to leave the child property. But to be sure your child is provided for after your death, you do need to affirmatively leave property in your will or by use of a trust. This is because if a parent of an illegitimate child dies without a will, most states do not protect the child's right of inheritance as strongly as if the child were born to married parents or otherwise legally legitimated. For example, in some states, in the absence of a will or trust, the child can fully inherit from the mother but not from an unmarried father. Even in states that allow illegitimate children to inherit from a father in the absence of a will, the time in which the child can make a claim against the father's estate may be limited.

In the case of *Trimble v. Gordon*, 430 U.S. 762 (1977), the Supreme Court made it clear that a father's signing a paternity statement will normally be adequate to fully protect the inheritance rights of children born out of wedlock if there's no will. If your state rules allow a father to acknowledge paternity for the purpose of inheritance in a way other than a paternity statement, that will also be sufficient. For example, in some states, in the absence of a will, a child can inherit if the father admitted paternity prior to his death or if paternity was determined by a court. But obviously, a child's legal right to go to court to try and claim a share of an estate is not nearly as advantageous as being left property under the terms of a will. Or to put this point bluntly, if you want a child to inherit regardless of the child's legitimacy under your state's laws, accomplish this by leaving the child property in your will or other estate planning device. Chapter 9 explains how and why unmarried couples should prepare to protect each other and their children. ●

C H A P T E R

You and Your Ex-Spouse and Children From a Prior Relationship

Getting a Divorce While Living With Someone Else 128
   Grounds for Divorce...129
   Effect of Fault on Division of Marital Property...130
   Effect of Fault on Alimony 130

Living Together and Impact on Custody of Children From a Prior Marriage........132
   Types of Custody...132
   Best Interests of the Child 133
   Anatomy of a Contested Custody Case..134
   How to Create a Custody Agreement...134

Visitation With Children From a Prior Marriage...136

Child Support for Children From a Prior Marriage..137

The Effect of Living Together on Alimony and Child Support
From a Prior Marriage...138
   Alimony...138
   Child Support...139

If you have been married in the past or are currently married to someone other than the person you live with, you may encounter special legal problems. This is especially true if you have children or receive alimony (called maintenance or spousal support in some states), and you and your ex-spouse did not part on good terms.

This chapter covers key issues you may face if you are living with someone while going through a divorce (or if you have already been divorced), including the impact of your living with someone on division of marital property, alimony, and child custody and support.

SKIP AHEAD

You can skip this chapter if neither you nor your partner has ever been married or had children outside of your current relationship.

CAUTION

If a nasty divorce threatens, think twice before living with a new partner—especially if children are involved. If you and your spouse aren't divorcing amicably, read this chapter carefully, research your state's law, and consult with a good family law attorney. If you conclude that you may lose property, alimony, or custody by living with your new partner, consider putting off living together until your divorce is final. This is especially true if cohabitation is illegal in your state. Also, remember that on a practical and emotional level, the fact that you are living with a new partner may anger a former spouse, who may look for ways to retaliate.

Finally, keep in mind that if you've already been divorced and granted alimony, living with someone may affect your right to continue receiving alimony. Because alimony laws differ from state to state and change often, it's essential to check the current legal rules of your state.

RESOURCE

For an overview of divorce and family law, see the Family Law topic on Nolo's website at www.nolo .com. Also, Nolo has several useful books on the subject of divorce, including *Nolo's Essential Guide to Divorce*, by Emily Doskow, *A Judge's Guide to Divorce*, by Roderic Duncan, *Divorce and Money*, by Violet Woodhouse, and *Divorce Without Court: A Guide to Mediation and Collaborative Law* (previously titled *Using Divorce Mediation*), by Katherine E. Stoner.

CROSS REFERENCE

Related topics covered in this book include:

- Having or adopting a child with an unmarried partner: Chapter 7
- Issues involving custody and support of children when you separate from an unmarried partner: Chapter 10
- How to find and work with a lawyer and research family law in your state: Chapter 11.

Getting a Divorce While Living With Someone Else

In every state, some type of "no-fault" divorce is available. "No fault" means that the divorce isn't based on someone being at fault for ending the marriage. The spouse suing for divorce does not need to accuse the other of wrongdoing. Instead, the person requesting the divorce must state one of two things:

- that the couple no longer gets along and want to go their separate ways (in legalese, the couple is incompatible, has irreconcilable differences, or there's been an irretrievable or irremediable breakdown of the marriage), or
- that the couple has already been living apart by mutual consent for a certain period of time.

Does this mean that if you leave your spouse and live with someone else, this can't be used against you in the divorce? Not necessarily. Although every state has no-fault divorce, over 30 states have also kept their traditional fault-based divorces (based on adultery, mental cruelty, desertion, and the like) as well. This means that in many states a spouse can, at least in some circumstances, request a fault-based divorce and show that you mistreated him or her. As explained below, this may have serious effects on how marital property is divided after divorce and whether you receive alimony (and how much). Also, no matter what type of divorce is obtained, "fault" may be raised in a property or support negotiation or in a child custody or visitation hearing.

> **TIP**
>
> **Regardless of your state's laws, you and your spouse can divide your property however you want.** Even in states where one person's fault can have a bearing on division of property or alimony, this need not make a difference to you and your spouse. Many people get civilized divorces in states where fault-based divorces are possible. They make custody, support, and property decisions in a spirit of compromise, not based on who hurt whom. If you and your spouse are separating amicably, you needn't worry about the effect of living with someone else. But in case memories grow short, consider writing down your understanding as to property, support, and custody decisions. We provide a sample cooperative custody agreement later in this chapter. This type of agreement isn't technically enforceable in court, especially as it relates to children. A court must look at all the factors when considering the "best interests of the child." But if you end up in a court fight, a judge may seriously consider the agreement if it is fair to everyone involved.

Grounds for Divorce

The "Grounds for Divorce" chart below lists the legal reasons a spouse must give to request a divorce in each state. This section explains how to read the notations on the chart.

Fault Divorce

Traditionally, in order for a couple to obtain a divorce, one spouse had to prove that the other spouse was legally at fault. The "innocent" spouse was then granted the divorce from the "guilty" spouse. The "guilty" spouse would usually have to pay a substantial amount of alimony (or receive less than he or she would otherwise be entitled to) or give up marital property to which he or she was otherwise entitled.

Today about three-fifths of the states still allow a spouse to allege fault in obtaining a divorce, on grounds such as:

- adultery—sexual relations by a married person with someone other than the person's spouse

- mental cruelty—any act of inflicting unnecessary emotional pain, and

- desertion—voluntary abandonment of someone by a spouse without the abandoned spouse's consent.

In some states, alimony and property division are not linked to fault. For example, although a fault divorce is still available in Illinois, alimony is awarded and property divided regardless of fault. Conversely, although fault divorces have been eliminated in Florida, adultery can be a factor in determining the award of alimony.

No-Fault Divorce

Any divorce where the spouse suing for divorce does not have to accuse the other of wrongdoing is a no-fault divorce. You can simply claim incompatibility, irreconcilable differences, or irretrievable or irremediable breakdown of the marriage, rather than blaming your spouse. If this is the only check on the chart, you are in a pure no-fault state.

Separation

For no-fault divorces based on the fact that the spouses have already separated, we include the time that you must be apart (Length of Separation column on the "Grounds for Divorce" chart). This may be as short as six months (Hawaii) or as long as five years (Idaho). If the separation is not by mutual consent or if there are children involved, the period of time may be different than what is shown here.

What Does All This "Fault" and "No-Fault" Language Really Mean?

If your state still has fault divorce, and your spouse is angry because you've moved in with your current love interest, your spouse may drag your living situation (which is technically adultery) into court. Also, even if your state has no-fault divorces, this doesn't mean that living with someone new won't affect your divorce in terms of the division of marital property and payment of alimony.

Covenant Marriage and Divorce

In a few states, couples can enter into a "Covenant Marriage," which is basically designed to make divorcing more difficult. Before seeking a divorce, couples must seek marital counseling, and the spouse seeking the divorce must prove fault—by proving either that the parties have been separated for a specified period of time, or that the other spouse committed adultery, committed a felony, or physically or sexually abused a child of one of the parties. Currently, Arizona, Arkansas, and Louisiana have covenant divorce.

Effect of Fault on Division of Marital Property

In most states, property acquired during marriage (except for gifts and inheritance) is divided more or less equally between husband and wife at divorce.

In some states with fault divorces, living with someone new (adultery) may result in your being awarded less of the marital property (real estate, furniture, cars, stocks, etc.) than you would have otherwise received. And even in a few states that have no-fault divorces, adultery can still be considered when it comes to dividing your marital property, with a judge empowered to award more to the spouse who is not living with someone. On the other hand, some states allow divorces based on one spouse's adultery, but adultery cannot be used to keep that spouse from getting his or her share of the marital property.

Effect of Fault on Alimony

Alimony (sometimes called spousal support or maintenance) is the money paid by one ex-spouse to the other for support under the terms of a court order or settlement agreement following a divorce. Alimony is not the same thing as child support (discussed in "Child Support for Children From a Prior Marriage," below).

Alimony was necessary in most divorces a generation or two ago—when men typically went off to work, leaving mother and children at home. Today, with so many women working, alimony is granted less frequently (or for shorter periods) and isn't even requested in some cases. Typically, if no alimony is awarded at the time of divorce, a spouse can't seek alimony at a later time.

When couples have been married for many years, alimony is still commonly granted, especially if the woman has had primary responsibility for raising the children and has been out of the workplace or working only part-time. Alimony may also be granted in a situation in which both spouses work, but one enjoys a significantly higher income than the other.

Living with an unmarried partner may affect your right to receive alimony in some states. In many states, a spouse who is considered guilty of adultery may either be barred from receiving

Grounds for Divorce

Here is a state-by-state listing of the legal reasons a spouse must give to request a divorce. For an explanation of the headings (Fault, No-Fault, etc.), see "Grounds for Divorce," above.

	Fault Grounds	No-Fault Grounds	Separation	Length of Separation
Alabama	✓	✓	✓	2 years
Alaska	✓	✓		
Arizona		✓		
Arkansas	✓		✓	18 months
California		✓		
Colorado		✓		
Connecticut	✓	✓	✓	18 months
Delaware	✓	✓		
District of Columbia			✓	6 months[1]
Florida		✓		
Georgia	✓	✓		
Hawaii		✓	✓	6 months[2]
Idaho	✓	✓	✓	5 years
Illinois	✓	✓	✓	2 years
Indiana		✓		
Iowa		✓		
Kansas	✓	✓		
Kentucky		✓		
Louisiana	✓		✓	6 months
Maine	✓	✓		
Maryland	✓		✓	1 year[3]
Massachusetts	✓	✓		
Michigan		✓		
Minnesota		✓		
Mississippi	✓	v		
Missouri	✓		✓	1 year[1]
Montana		✓	✓	180 days
Nebraska		✓		
Nevada		✓	✓	1 year
New Hampshire	✓	✓		
New Jersey	✓		✓	18 months
New Mexico	✓	✓		
New York	✓	✓	✓	1 year
North Carolina	✓		✓	1 year
North Dakota	✓	✓		
Ohio	✓	✓	✓	1 year
Oklahoma	✓	✓		
Oregon		✓		
Pennsylvania	✓	✓	✓	2 years
Rhode Island	✓	✓	✓	3 years
South Carolina	✓		✓	1 year
South Dakota	✓	✓		
Tennessee	✓	✓	✓	2 years
Texas	✓	✓	✓	3 years
Utah	✓	✓	✓	3 years
Vermont	✓		✓	6 months
Virginia	✓		✓	1 year[4]
Washington		✓		
West Virginia	✓	✓	✓	1 year
Wisconsin		✓	✓	12 months
Wyoming		✓		

[1] if both parties agree in writing; otherwise 1 year

[2] if both parties agree in writing; otherwise 2 years

[3] if both parties agree and there's a finding of "no reasonable expectation of reconciliation"; otherwise 2 years

[4] or 6 months if there are no children of the marriage

alimony altogether or receive less than a full share of alimony. Ironically, some of these states have done away with adultery as a basis for divorce. Also, this is not a universal rule. Some states with fault divorces don't allow adultery to influence property division. Some states do not reduce or terminate alimony on the basis of adultery. But almost all states may reduce alimony payments if the recipient cohabits—especially if this reduces that person's need for support. Finally, several states are silent on the issue of fault consideration and alimony.

Living Together and Impact on Custody of Children From a Prior Marriage

If you and your former spouse agree on custody, the court will normally ratify your agreement without considering the details of how you lead your life. For instance, a judge won't know (or necessarily ask) whether one of you is living with another person unless your ex brings it to the judge's attention.

If you and your spouse are battling over custody, however, the traditional advice is to not live with a new partner and to be discreet in your sexual activity, at least until the court makes a decision. This advice applies to both fault and no-fault divorces, as a parent's living arrangement is always admissible in a custody dispute on the theory that a court needs as much information as possible to determine "the best interests of the child."

As you'll notice, we use the word "traditional" to describe the "no sex, no living with anyone" advice. This is because many states now have more relaxed legal attitudes toward living together. While we can't say that most judges are enthusiastic about granting custody to a parent who is part of an unmarried couple, judges will not necessarily deny custody to a parent solely because the parent

lives with someone else, especially when the new relationship is stable and nurturing. Therefore, the decision to live or not live with someone (other than a platonic roommate) while fighting over custody should be decided situation by situation, state by state. Especially if your former spouse is likely to make an issue of it, you should consult with a family law attorney to find out about local practices and prejudices.

Types of Custody

There are two types of custody in most states—physical and legal. Physical custody is the right to have the child live with you. Legal custody is the right to make important decisions about the child's upbringing—for example, regarding schooling and medical care.

Custody should not be confused with child support. Every parent has an obligation to support his or her children. When one parent has physical custody and the other has visitation rights, the parent with visitation rights is usually ordered to pay some child support to the other parent, who is usually deemed to be meeting his or her obligations through the custody itself.

Custody may also be sole or joint. Joint legal custody means that the parents plan jointly for their children's future, as they did before the divorce. Joint physical custody is typically worked out by the parents, taking into consideration things like the parents' and children's schedules and desires, the quality of schools, relationships with friends, and so on. Joint custody doesn't mean that the children must spend six months of each year or half of every week with each parent. In fact, in many states, a judge may award joint legal custody at the same time one parent is named as the primary caretaker of the child and one house as the primary home for the child.

For parents who communicate well and are equally dedicated to raising their children, joint custody can be an ideal situation. In fact, in some states, courts are required to order joint custody unless there is some unusual circumstance. By balancing the power and decision making, both parents are more likely to provide financial support for and maintain close relationships with their children. A potential drawback to joint custody is the possibility that arguments will drag on forever because neither parent has final say. However, family counseling (sometimes called "divorce" or "separation" counseling) can go a long way towards avoiding or working through such problems.

Best Interests of the Child

In all states, child custody and visitation issues are decided according to "the best interests of the child." This means that the judge who hears the case will consider all evidence before deciding who will provide the better home. Although mothers are more often granted physical custody than are fathers, particularly for young children, there is no longer an automatic preference in favor of women. Today, many men win physical custody of their children.

Frequently asked questions about custody and visitation include:

- *If I live with a man, can my children be taken from me?*

- *If my husband is an alcoholic (or a recently recovering alcoholic), will he be able to get custody of (or visitation with) the children?*

- *I was once arrested for possession of marijuana; does this mean I can't get custody?*

- *My income comes from Social Security disability and other public programs, while my husband has a well-paying job. Does this mean he'll get custody of the kids?*

- *My son is nine years old and wants to live with me; will the court let him?*

- *Is it possible for a father to get custody of young children?*

The answer to all of those questions is, "It depends." No matter what your next-door neighbor, best friend, or brother-in-law tells you, the law doesn't say that adultery, smoking marijuana, or even being involved in antisocial conduct means you can't win, or will lose, custody. In addition, the fact that one parent's income is much larger than the other's isn't necessarily a reason the court will use to award the more affluent parent custody.

The point is that many factors—not just whether or not you're living with someone else—are related to what is in a child's best interest. The court's decision will normally favor the parent who will best maintain stability in the child's life. The way each parent lives can be an important factor when a court decides custody issues. In any given case, the judge may consider one person's lifestyle to be more in the best interest of the child than the other's.

In a few states, a judge can use a parent's cohabitation to deny custody. For example, an Arkansas court stated "a mother's ongoing relationship was immoral, failed to set a proper example for the children, and resulted in harm to the children." (*Nix v. Nix*, 706 S.W. 2d 403 (Ark. 1986).) Courts in a few other states have similarly disapproved of cohabitation and have forced a change in custody, especially where the children were aware of their custodial parents' intimate conduct.

In general, however, the bottom line is that the judge, as a human being, will apply his or her own standards and prejudices when deciding which parent gets custody. Some judges don't like unmarried persons living together, even though society no longer considers living together the "no-no" it was 30 years ago.

Custody Issues If You Have Been Divorced for Some Time

Now suppose you have been divorced for some time and have custody of your children. You want to move in with a new partner, but want to be sure this won't give your former spouse legal grounds to challenge your custody of your children.

The question of child custody can always be reexamined by the court. If a judge finds that it's in the best interest of your children to change the custody of your kids to the other parent, then the judge can order this. State law varies as to whether a judge can consider your living with someone to be a negative factor in deciding whether or not custody arrangements should be modified.

Anatomy of a Contested Custody Case

In many places, fighting over custody is no longer as simple as going into court with your arguments at the ready. Now, parents with custody disputes usually must attend court-ordered mediation sessions to try to work out a parenting plan, before they'll be allowed to see a judge. In some places, the mediator will make a report to the judge with a recommendation of how custody should be decided. In others, the mediator simply works with the parents, but doesn't report to the court afterwards.

Some courts may also order an evaluation of the family, which might be performed by a social worker employed by the county or by a private social worker or therapist with training in child custody evaluation. A child custody evaluation will include interviews with both parents and the children, background checks, and sometimes psychological testing.

Once all the mediation and evaluations are completed, you'll then have your day in court. The judge isn't compelled to follow the recommendations of the mediator or evaluator, but as a practical matter most do. If the social worker or mediator recommends that you get custody, you've won more than half the battle. If not, you're at a serious disadvantage, but you can still proceed to the trial, and you may ask the social worker or mediator to come to court to be cross-examined about the report. This is especially important if the report contains factual inaccuracies.

At the trial, the judge may ask your children where they want to live. Some judges ask only older children; other judges never ask any children. Most judges will pay little—if any—attention to the opinion of a child under seven, but will probably respect the wishes of a teenager if the chosen parent is otherwise suitable. Judges also tend to keep brothers and sisters together unless there is a strong reason not to.

> **CAUTION**
>
> **A judge has the power to deny custody to both parents.** During a divorce proceeding, a judge need not award custody of the children to either the mother or the father if he or she finds them unfit. Instead, the judge can award custody to a relative, a friend, or even the local juvenile court.

How to Create a Custody Agreement

Even though you may never want to speak to your former spouse or partner again, it is vital for you both to sit down and decide how you will continue to raise your children. Because the two of you know your children best, forming a parenting agreement together makes the most sense. Also, it will save you from the risk of a drawn-out court battle.

A very basic custody agreement, Sample Cooperative Custody Agreement, is shown below. It is common for custody agreements to be much more detailed, covering when parents will spend time with the children, how to handle holidays, vacations, and birthdays, the role of each parent in the children's education, health care and more. This

---

Sample Cooperative Custody Agreement

Sean and Barbara Washington agree to the following:

1. We have decided to go our separate ways and no longer plan to live together.

2. Our children John Washington, age 5, and Richard Washington, age 3, will reside with Barbara Washington, and Sean will spend as much time as possible with the children.

3. Sean will provide a reasonable amount of support to Barbara each month, taking into consideration his salary and the needs of the children. Initially, this will be $800 per month per child.

4. As neither of us plans to marry again soon, it's understood and accepted that both of us will very likely have personal friendships that may involve sex and that either or both of us may decide to live with someone of the same or opposite sex.

5. We will proceed to get a divorce as amicably as possible and neither of us will try to influence the court by raising the fact that the other is having a relationship or living with a third person.

6. Any dispute arising out of this contract will be mediated by a third person mutually acceptable to both of us. The mediator's role will be to help us arrive at a solution, not to impose one on us. If good faith efforts to arrive at our own solution to all issues in dispute with the help of a mediator prove to be fruitless, either of us may make a written request to the other that the dispute be arbitrated. If such a request is made, our dispute will be submitted to arbitration under the rules of the American Arbitration Association, and one arbitrator will hear our dispute. The decision of the arbitrator will be binding on us and will be enforceable in any court that has jurisdiction over the controversy.

Barbara Washington   _October 19, 20xx_
Signature   Date

Sean Washington   _October 19, 20xx_
Signature   Date

---

agreement may serve as a placeholder while you work out the details of a more thorough one.

While some parents can make agreements on their own without outside help, many others turn to mediators or family law counselors to help them resolve one or more problem areas.

Negotiation

Negotiating a custody agreement that is fair to both you and your former spouse makes great sense. While it may seem impossible, try to put aside your anger and hostility to create a parenting plan that puts your children's best interests first. Choose a setting that is neutral and prepare yourself by writing a list of all the important factors you want to discuss regarding the custody of your children. Obviously, this will include your children's living arrangements, education, medical care, and emotional needs. Listen to all the requests your ex makes and be willing to compromise. If you strongly disagree on a particular issue, set it aside and concentrate on the things you can work out. Often, if a spirit of compromise develops over the course of your negotiations, it will extend to solving even your most difficult problems.

Mediation

If you and the other parent can't arrive at a good agreement yourselves, your next step is to enlist the help of a neutral third party who is skilled in the area of child custody. Family mediators are trained to handle difficult custody and visitation issues. While a mediator will not make a decision for you, they are adept at guiding parents to arriving at their own plan. Many states mandate the use of a mediator to try to solve custody disputes and some even provide mediators at low cost.

CROSS REFERENCE

See Chapter 10 for more information on the subject of mediation. You'll also find an in-depth discussion of family mediation and many detailed suggestions about how to draft a child custody and visitation plan and workable parenting agreements in the book *Building a Parenting Agreement That Works: How to Put Your Kids First When Your Marriage Doesn't Last,* by Mimi Lyster (Nolo).

Visitation With Children From a Prior Marriage

If a court grants you (or your former spouse) custody of the children, the other parent (or you) will be given the right to visit, unless the court believes that the noncustodial parent's physical presence would be detrimental to the children. As with custody, decisions about visitation are also made based on the "best interests" of the children. If you and your ex-spouse can communicate enough to agree on a visitation schedule, the court will probably grant "reasonable visitation rights" and leave it to you to work out the details as to when, where, and how visitation will take place.

If, however, you and your ex-spouse cannot agree on visitation, the court will define the visitation rights for you. The court might say, for example, that "Barbara Washington shall have the right to visit with the children every Saturday from 10:00 a.m. to 5:00 p.m., plus three weeks during the summer months, the weeks to be agreed upon by the parties"; or "Sean Washington shall have the right of visitation on the first weekend of every month from 6:00 p.m. on Friday to 6:00 p.m. on Sunday provided he picks the children up from, and returns them to, Barbara Washington's home."

Sometimes, courts impose restrictions on visitation beyond times and places, such as requiring 24-hour notice of visitation; prohibiting the noncustodial parent from removing the child from the county, state, or, in rare cases, the child's own home; prohibiting the noncustodial parent from drinking alcohol while with the children; or where there's evidence of abuse, requiring another adult to be present during the visit.

In addition, courts in a few states may prohibit a parent from visiting the children in the presence of the person that parent lives with, or prohibit the children from spending the night with a parent whose new partner is present in the house. If the custodial parent has a new relationship, most courts will continue to allow visitation as long as the living together situation doesn't have an adverse effect on the child. Louisiana is one state that still prohibits visitation when the parent's live-in lover is present in their home, even when the couple is discreet, because such visits might undermine "the children's respect for the family institution." (*Lasseigne v. Lasseigne,* 434 So.2d 1240 (La. 1983).) Court decisions like this are far from the rule, however, and if you've been given such an order, speak to an attorney regarding your obligations, your rights, and a possible appeal. But in the meantime, understand that it's not wise to violate a court order.

Child Support for Children From a Prior Marriage

In every state, parents are required to support their children, whether or not the parents were married when the child was born. The federal Child Support Enforcement Act (42 U.S.C. § 651) requires every state to adopt a formula setting a minimum amount of child support depending on the financial resources of the parents, the needs of the children, and other factors, such as the amount of time the child spends with each parent. The effect of this law is that child support—or at least a minimum amount of child support—is set more or less automatically by plugging parents' income and expense information into a computer program. The law has resulted in higher child support awards than in the past, and has decreased litigation, because there's less to fight about. Your state's formula may be available from court clerks' offices or the local support division of the district attorney's office (which enforces child support orders). In some states there are also support calculation programs available online for a moderate fee.

RESOURCE

For more information on child support and links to state agencies that administer and enforce child support programs, see the website of the federal Office of Child Support Enforcement at www.acf.dhhs.gov/programs/cse.

CAUTION

Failure to support is a crime. If you have custody of your children and live with someone else, your ex-spouse is still required to support the children. Your ex may be angry at your new living arrangement and tempted to try to get out of paying by quitting his or her job or refusing to look for work. However, the court will probably structure payments based on the other parent's ability, not inclination, to work. Refusing to support your children when you have the ability to do so is a crime in all states. People who repeatedly fail to take their child support obligations seriously may spend a short time behind bars and may be denied professional licenses or passports.

If the person you live with is not your children's parent, then that person has no obligation to support your children. The amount of child support your ex-spouse is ordered to pay usually isn't affected by the fact that you live with someone else. However, if your new partner provides shelter or buys food, clothing, or other items for you, your ex-spouse may petition the court to reduce his or her child support obligation. It will be your ex-spouse's responsibility to show that your new partner pays many of the children's expenses, freeing up most of your income. If your ex-spouse can prove this, a court may rule that you have more income available to support your children, and reduce your child support.

In most states, judges have at least some discretion to deviate from the support formula if the amount is unjust or inappropriate, based on factors such as the financial resources of the custodial parent and child-related expenses.

TIP

If you receive child support and live with your partner or new spouse, consider signing an agreement to keep all of your earnings and property separate. That way, you stand a better chance of not losing your support payments. Courts in some states have held that joint income could not be considered in making a child support award when the custodial parent and new partner had such an agreement.

Be aware that states are buckling down in collecting child support. All states have laws to grab the wages of a parent who falls behind in child support. A wage attachment means that an amount to cover the child support is taken out of a paycheck and paid directly to the custodial parent or a government agency. With the help of the federal government, states are cooperating to collect child support from parents who move to another part of the country. In short, paying child support is not only morally good, but it can also keep you out of jail.

The Effect of Living Together on Alimony and Child Support From a Prior Marriage

Once your divorce is final and alimony and child support decisions are made, either by the court or through your own agreement with your ex, can they be changed? Once again, it depends.

Alimony

If alimony is granted for an extended period, it normally terminates if the receiving spouse remarries, unless there's an agreement or court order to the contrary entered at the time of the divorce. However, judges in some states, in some circumstances, have the discretion to continue alimony even after the spouse receiving it remarries—unless your written settlement agreement specifies that payment will stop if one of you remarries.

What happens if the alimony recipient starts living with a partner, rather than remarrying? Alimony may still be terminated or reduced, depending on where you live and the circumstances:

- Most states will authorize reduction or termination of alimony upon cohabitation only if the cohabitation significantly decreases the recipient's need for support.

- Other states will terminate alimony regardless of whether the recipient's economic need is diminished by cohabiting.

- In still other states, alimony will not be affected should the spouse who receives it begin living with someone.

The definition of "cohabitation" may vary widely:

- A court in Illinois recently held that a former spouse could be deemed as cohabiting with another person on a "resident, continuing conjugal basis" although her boyfriend lived in a separate residence. What this jargon amounts to is that even though her boyfriend always spent the night at his own apartment, the court felt that the fact that he spent most of his time in her apartment and ate meals there was enough to qualify him as cohabiting with her and, as a result, terminated her alimony. (*In re Marriage of Herrin*, 262 Ill. App. 3d 573 (1994).)

- Some states, like New York, require that the alimony recipient must not only live with someone (cohabit), but also "hold herself out as the wife" of the man she lives with before alimony is terminated (alimony recipients rarely do this, so alimony is seldom cut off).

- Arkansas has taken a different tack, and requires that the alimony recipient not only live with, but also have children with, the new partner, before alimony will be terminated.

- California and Tennessee both presume that the recipient's need for support has been reduced once he or she starts cohabiting. In other words, if you move in with a new partner, unless you can prove to a judge that you still need the same amount of alimony, it will be reduced or terminated.

In those states that do not have laws or court decisions that specifically address the impact cohabitation might have on alimony, it is difficult to predict how a judge will rule. Regardless of state law, if you and your ex-spouse have made an agreement that support or alimony won't be affected by the person who receives it living together with someone new, your agreement will stand. And bear in mind that the person requesting a change in alimony or support payments is the one who must prove that an ex-spouse's economic situation has changed significantly.

Child Support

Child support may only be changed by court approval following a formal request for modification of child support. If you're a noncustodial parent and you live with someone—perhaps even support that person and his or her children—will the amount of child support you pay be reduced?

Because you have no legal duty to support your new partner and new partner's children, a judge won't reduce your support obligation. Your primary duty is to your own children, not your friend's. At the same time, if your living expenses are reduced because you share them with another person, a judge may deviate from the child support formula because a greater amount of your income has been freed up. ●

Wills and Estate Planning

Many of us avoid the subject of death whenever possible. We don't plan for what will happen to our property, who will care for our minor children, or even whether we'll be buried or cremated.

Unfortunately, this invites disaster for unmarried couples. If you die without making legally binding arrangements for your partner to inherit your property, it will usually go to your closest relatives—not your partner. State laws dealing with inheritance are designed to pass property only to spouses and blood relatives.

This chapter explains what you need to do now to ensure that your property goes to the people you want to inherit it. It also explains how you can structure these arrangements with an eye toward sparing your survivors the hassle and expense of probate.

TIP

Planning for incapacity. In addition to planning for your death, you should also take steps to protect yourself, your partner, and your assets in the event that you ever become unable to make your own medical or financial decisions because of injury or serious illness. The best way to ensure that your affairs will be managed as you wish is to prepare a health care directive and a durable power of attorney for finances. (See "Making Medical and Financial Decisions for Your Partner" in Chapter 4.)

What Happens If You Don't Do Any Estate Planning?

Without a will or other legal means for transferring property (for example, a living trust), the survivor will inherit nothing unless the couple has a legally recognized common law marriage (discussed in Chapter 2), a registered domestic partnership in the states that allow it, or a valid contract (discussed below). Instead, close blood relatives will inherit everything. (See "Who Inherits If There's No Will? An Overview," below, for details.)

Who Inherits If There's No Will? An Overview

The following is a summary of who inherits under a typical state law, called an "intestate succession" law, if you die without a will and are not married at your death. The exact rules vary from state to state, but an unmarried partner is not included on any state's list.

- If you have children, your property is divided equally among them. The only exception is if you have a deceased child who had children (your grandchildren). These grandchildren divide the deceased child's share.

- If you leave no children or grandchildren, all of your property goes to your parents equally if they're alive.

- Next in line are your brothers and sisters, who share equally unless any have died leaving children, in which case the nieces and nephews split your deceased sibling's share.

- If you leave no children, grandchildren, parents, or siblings, your nephews and nieces share your estate equally unless you have grandnephews and grandnieces whose parents have died, who receive their deceased parents' share.

- If you have none of the relatives listed above, your estate passes half to your paternal grandparents and half to your maternal grandparents. If they're not alive, their children (your parents' siblings and your uncles and aunts) take equally. If any of these relatives have died, their share goes to their children.

- If you have none of these relatives, your property goes to the state.

To learn more about your state's intestate succession laws, visit www.mystate.will.com.

The Effect of Living Together Contracts

If partners have a written agreement about ownership of their property, most states will recognize and enforce it. (These contracts are discussed in Chapters 2 and 3.) For example, if you have a written contract stating that you're the half-owner of specific property, your partner has no power to dispose of your share, either during your life or at your death. And if the contract says that you become the sole owner at the other's death, this provision can be enforced through a probate court proceeding, as long as a will doesn't contradict the contract. However, if a will leaves the deceased partner's share of the property to someone else, it's likely there will be a legal fight over who gets that portion of the property. This is something you and your partner can avoid through good joint estate planning.

What if you and your partner had an agreement, but it wasn't in writing? In some situations, you might be able to get a portion of your deceased partner's property. But that isn't easy. You would have to bring a lawsuit against the people who would otherwise inherit the property and prove that you and your partner had an oral or implied contract to share property ownership.

The outcome of a lawsuit based on an oral or implied contract is uncertain at best. But a court might rule in your favor if:

- You worked in the home and your partner earned the money, but you agreed orally to share everything.
- You worked in the home and your partner earned the money and there was an implied contract between you, under which you expected to share in the fruits of your labor but never did.
- You and your partner bought items jointly and agreed that all property belonged to both of

you, with the survivor taking 100% if the other died. You may succeed, especially if friends and relatives step forward and testify that they knew about your understanding. It will also depend, to some extent, on the attitude of your deceased partner's relatives who would otherwise inherit. If they support you or will work out a compromise (through direct negotiation or mediation), a probate court will likely go along.

Another Possible Claim

As a surviving partner left without any inheritance from a deceased partner, you might also prevail in court by proving that basic fairness demands that you be treated as a partial owner of the property. In other words, you worked hard to buy or create the property, so you should get at least part of it. For example, you might show that you and your partner jointly contributed to the purchase of a piece of real estate, but for some reason the property was put only in your deceased partner's name. If you could show why you did it that way, and that you made significant contributions, a court might rule that you are entitled to a share of the property.

Figuring Out What You Own: Taking Inventory

We hope we've convinced you to plan ahead to deal with the inevitability of your death. Before making a will or doing other estate planning, however, you need to know what property is yours. If you've lived with a partner for a long time, your property may be so mixed up with your partner's that you can't tell who owns what. If you and your partner want to leave all of your property to the survivor, who owns what doesn't matter as much. But if

Sample Property Ownership Agreement

Tomas Finnegan and Keija Adams agree as follows:

1. We have been living together for ten years, and during that time much of our property has been mixed together so that it isn't completely clear who owns what.

2. The purpose of this agreement is to divide all of our real and personal property owned on January 10, 20xx, into three categories as set out below. Property purchased after that date will be owned by the person who buys it, unless we decide differently as set forth in agreements made at the time of purchase or later.

3. From the date of this agreement, all property listed in Category 1 belongs solely and absolutely to Tomas, all property listed in Category 2 belongs solely and absolutely to Keija, and all property listed in Category 3 belongs to both in the shares noted. [*For real property and personal property with title documents, such as a car, make sure that ownership indicated on the deed or title slip is the same as what's in this agreement. If it isn't, change the official documents.*]

CATEGORY 1 (TOMAS)

1. 2003 Ford Mustang

2. G.E. washer & dryer

3. 100 shares of stock in Melt-in-Your-Mouth Popcorn, Inc.

CATEGORY 2 (KEIJA)

1. 2004 Yamaha Motorcycle

2. BMX Stereo & related stereo equipment

3. $12,000 deposited in the Restaurant Workers Credit Union

CATEGORY 3 (TOMAS AND KEIJA)

1. House at 2547 Jones Street owned in equal shares and held in joint tenancy under an agreement dated January 27, 1999

   [*If you already have an agreement defining ownership shares of jointly owned property, make sure this agreement says the same thing. You can incorporate the earlier agreement into this one as Keija and Tomas have done.*]

Keija Adams	*January 10, 20xx*
Signature	Date
Tomas Finnegan	*January 10, 20xx*
Signature	Date

not, sit down and make an agreement defining property ownership. A Sample Property Ownership Agreement is shown above, or you can use one of the living together agreements in Chapter 3.

An Introduction to Wills

A will is a document in which you specify who gets your property when you die. It is easy to make a will, and you can leave your property to anyone you wish, including the person you live with. You can change or revoke your will whenever you like; you're not stuck with it once you make it. Depending on your circumstances, discussing your will with your partner may be a good idea, but there is no legal requirement that you do so.

The one drawback of a will is that if you leave property through a will, probate court proceedings will probably be required before the property can be transferred to the people who inherit it after your death. If your estate is small, however, you may be able to avoid this time-consuming and sometimes costly court process. There are lots of ways to leave property but avoid probate (some of which are discussed below). But even if you do use these other methods, you still need to make a will, because it allows you to:

- Leave property that you don't think of or don't yet own when you write your will, such as a house you later inherit, lottery winnings, or a personal injury lawsuit recovery. If you have a will, its "residuary clause" passes all property not left to a specific person to your partner or whomever else you name. There's no way, other than a will, to choose who inherits such property.
- Forgive debts owed to you.
- Nominate a personal guardian for your minor children, if you have any.
- Name your executor—that is, the person who will wind up your affairs after your death. It's

wise to do this even if you establish a living trust, because the person you name to wind up your living trust (called your successor trustee) will have only the power to transfer to your beneficiaries property held in trust. An executor will still be needed to transfer property that is not in your trust.

Once you decide what property you want to transfer by will, prepare the paperwork promptly. Procrastination brings no benefit and increases the risk that your property will go to relatives chosen by your state legislature, rather than to your partner.

Who Can Make a Valid Will?

Anyone who's an adult and "of sound mind" can make a valid will. The form in this book can be used by residents of all states except Louisiana, which has a different legal system (derived from French law) from the rest of the country.

A person has to be pretty far gone to be of unsound mind. If you're reading and understanding this book, you are almost surely capable of making a valid will.

SEE AN EXPERT

Most Americans with estates worth less than $2 million can prepare a will without the help and cost of a lawyer. But if you have a large estate and want extensive planning, you'll probably want to see a lawyer, even if you read up on the subject and do much of the preliminary planning and drafting work yourself.

CAUTION

Will contests are rare, but can happen. You have the right to leave your property to anyone you choose. But if you have relatives who vehemently object to your relationship and you own valuable property, it's possible that those relatives will challenge your will on the ground that you were incompetent or under

Estate Planning Resources From Nolo

Over the last quarter century, Nolo has developed several will-drafting resources that are far more comprehensive than this chapter. All of them are easy to use, and all of them are valid in every state but Louisiana. In addition, you can find lots of free information on making a will and planning your estate on Nolo's website at www.nolo.com.

- *Quicken WillMaker Plus*, Nolo's most comprehensive will and estate planning software, lets you create a will, living trust, health care directive, durable power of attorney for finances, final arrangements letter, and more.

- Nolo's Online Will allows you to make your will quickly and easily, without using a book or buying software. Just go to Nolo's Legal Form Center at www.nolo.com and use the secure service to make your will online.

- *Nolo's Simple Will Book*, by Denis Clifford, gives line-by-line instructions for drafting wills in a number of different family and property situations. It contains more types of will clauses (including a simple child's trust and other provisions to leave property to minors) and more background information about will drafting than is contained here. It comes with a CD-ROM.

- *The Quick & Legal Will Book*, by Denis Clifford, is the procrastinator's guide to writing a basic will. This book shows how to get a basic but legal will done quickly and easily—leave property to family and friends, appoint a guardian for minor children, set up a trust for minor children, sign the will, and have it witnessed. Includes sample wills, tear-out worksheets, forms, and a CD-ROM.

- *Estate Planning Basics*, by Denis Clifford, is an overview of the estate planning process. It provides concise, easy-to-understand explanations of the major components of estate planning, including wills, living trusts and other probate-avoidance methods, estate taxes, property control trusts, and planning for someone to handle your medical and financial decisions if you are incapacitated.

- *Plan Your Estate*, by Denis Clifford and Cora Jordan, covers every significant aspect of estate planning. It is especially valuable for people with larger estates (over $2 million). *Plan Your Estate* picks up where we leave off here.

- *Make Your Own Living Trust*, by Denis Clifford, provides a thorough explanation of the most popular probate-avoidance device. All aspects of living trusts are covered, including how a living trust works and how to create one, how to transfer property to the trust, and what happens when the trust maker dies. Includes living trust forms (tear-out and on CD-ROM) with all the information and instructions necessary to make a living trust.

- *8 Ways to Avoid Probate*, by Mary Randolph, is a quick but detailed rundown of the many ways to avoid probate, including joint tenancy, pay-on-death bank accounts, and beneficiary designations for securities accounts.

Also, if your partner has died and you are the executor of his or her will, you'll want to take a look at *The Executor's Guide*, by Mary Randolph, which will lead you through the process of settling your partner's estate.

"undue influence" (unable to exert your own free will) when you made it. If there's any reasonable possibility that a relative will challenge your will, it makes sense to take steps to establish that you are of sound mind and not under undue influence when you sign it. One way is to write your will yourself, but pay a lawyer to review it and to be present at the signing. Another possibility is to have it prepared and signed in a lawyer's office, so someone can later testify that you knew what you were doing.

Typical Will Provisions

Here are some of the important matters you can take care of in a will:

- You can leave anything you own to any person or institution you choose. For example, you can leave money, book royalties, and clothes. You don't have to state your relationship to your beneficiaries—it's no one's business.
- You can forgive debts owed to you.
- You can recommend a personal guardian for your minor children.
- You can name a property guardian to manage your minor children's property.
- You can set up simple trusts to delay when a beneficiary gets the property. This is wise if you have young kids.
- You can name someone to supervise the distribution of property left by your will. This person is called your executor or, in some states, your personal representative. You can name your partner or anyone you trust to be your executor. Some states require that a bond be posted if your executor doesn't live in the state. If you have a choice, it is usually a good idea to name an executor who lives in the same state you do.
- If you are not married, you can disinherit anyone you want.

Disinheritance

In most states, it is impossible to disinherit a spouse unless you get a divorce. If you want information on that subject, see Nolo's *Simple Will Book*, by Denis Clifford, or the *Quicken WillMaker Plus* software.

You can disinherit most other people simply by not mentioning them in your will. However, if you wish to leave nothing to a child (or a child of a deceased child), you should still mention the child's name in your will. If you don't, the child might, under certain circumstances, have the right to claim a portion of your estate on the theory that he or she was inadvertently overlooked. Usually only a child born after you made your will can make such a claim. So, if you have a child after writing your will, you should write a new will that mentions the child, whether or not you wish to leave something to that child.

To head off any problem, the will form in this book asks you to name each of your children (and each child of a deceased child). If you want to disinherit a child (or child of a deceased child), just don't leave them anything. If you want to go further and use an express disinheritance clause stating that you're leaving the child nothing, you'll find samples in Nolo's *Simple Will Book*, by Denis Clifford.

Joint Wills vs. Trusts

A joint will is one document through which two people leave their property. After the first person dies, the joint will specifies what happens to the property when the second person dies. We don't recommend joint wills. They take away the freedom of the survivor to dispose of property as he or she wishes, and may not even be valid in some states.

If you wish to tie up property after your death, a better alternative is to establish a trust. One common kind of trust gives the surviving member of the couple the income from trust property for life, with the property itself going to another beneficiary (perhaps children from a former marriage) when the life beneficiary dies. This type of trust is discussed in more detail in "Balancing the Needs of Your Partner and Children," below. Keep in mind that unlike married couples, unmarried couples generally should not use a joint trust.

Handwritten Wills

Handwritten, unwitnessed wills, called "holographic" wills, are legal in about 25 states. To be valid, a holographic will must be written, dated, and signed entirely in the handwriting of the person making the will. (Sometimes, form wills that contain some machine-printed information are allowed, but all important provisions must be in the deceased person's handwriting.)

Regardless of your state's rule, it's better to type your will and have it witnessed. Courts treat holographic wills somewhat suspiciously, because they are far easier to forge than are witnessed wills. And if they contain cross-outs, additions, or machine-printed type (even a date or heading), they might be invalidated. So if you're trapped in the woods, the wolves are coming, and you don't have a will, write one out and say your prayers. Otherwise, type your will and have it witnessed.

Preparing a Basic Will

You can use the will form in this book to prepare a basic will if you have a small or moderate-size estate. This section explains some basic rules and specific instructions.

CD-ROM

Finding a form. The forms CD includes a copy of this will, and Appendix B includes a blank tear-out copy.

General Guidelines

Before we go through the will clause by clause, here are some important rules to keep in mind when you're ready to prepare your will.

- **Do it in two steps.** After reading this chapter, prepare a rough draft of your will, using or adapting the form in Appendix B or on the forms CD. Once you're satisfied you've covered everything, type the will using a computer or a typewriter. The final version must be on 8½" x 11" white paper. **You cannot just fill in the blanks and sign the document; it will not be a valid will.**

- **Complete only the clauses that pertain to you.** For example, if you don't have children, delete "II. Children." Then, renumber the remaining clauses, so that "III. Gifts" becomes "II. Gifts."

- **Use plain language and common sense.** If you write "I leave my car to my sister Sue," she will receive whatever car you own when you die. If you write, "I leave my 2004 Toyota Camry to my sister Sue," and sell it before you die and buy a Porsche, Sue gets nothing (in most states). Courts try to give effect to the intent of the will writer, but they can't contradict clear words.

- **Don't make changes before you sign your will.** If you want to change your finished will before it's signed and witnessed, don't just cross something out and initial the change. Instead, you'll need to retype it. After the will has been signed, dated, and witnessed, you can make changes only by using a "codicil" or making a brand-new will, as discussed in "Changing Your Will," below.

The sample will form below is shown as it's being prepared—that is, after the will writer has filled in the blanks and crossed out irrelevant material, but before it has been retyped into a final document that's ready to be signed and witnessed. If you prepare your own will using the form in Appendix B or on the forms CD, you'll need to

- fill in the blanks that apply to you
- eliminate clauses that don't apply to you
- renumber the remaining clauses
- remove instructional language, such as "[repeat as needed]"
- prepare a final draft
- sign it in front of witnesses, and
- have your witnesses sign the will.

How to Fill in the Will Form

Here is a look at the will, clause by clause. You'll find the blank will form in Appendix B and on the CD.

Name and Address Clause

Use your full name consistently throughout the will. If you use more than one name or if you have changed your name, use the name you now use for business and legal purposes.

The address you put down is important because if you have connections with more than one state at the time of your death, it will provide evidence about which one you considered your permanent residence. Your estate will be probated in the state where you resided, and that state will also have the right to impose estate or inheritance tax. Not all states impose these taxes, so if you have a choice, you'll probably want to establish your permanent residence in a no-tax state. Pick the state you want to be considered your permanent residence and register your securities, bank accounts, and cars there; register to vote there, and get your driver's license there. If your estate is large, see a lawyer to figure out what else you might need to do.

Clause I: Revocation

This clause revokes all prior wills, including any handwritten document that could possibly be construed as a will. Include this clause in your will.

Are You Legally Married or in a Registered Domestic Partnership?

Wills often include a clause stating the willmaker's marital status. However, we've designed this will for unmarried people, so it doesn't include a marital status clause.

- If you are married, don't use this will. Nolo offers many other do-it-yourself wills that include a marital status clause. See "Estate Planning Resources From Nolo," above.

- If you are getting divorced, but are still legally married, see a lawyer before completing your will. Until you divorce, your spouse may have a right to claim a share of your estate whether or not you include the spouse in the will.

- If you and your partner are registered in one of the handful of states that offers marriage-like benefits to same-sex couples, before your write your will, make sure you understand how your registered partnership affects your property rights. To learn about the legal rights of same-sex couples, read A Legal Guide for Lesbian & Gay Couples, by Denis Clifford, Frederick Hertz, and Emily Doskow (Nolo).

Clause II: Children

If you have children, list them all in Part A. Your children are those for whom you are a legally recognized parent—that is, children you have given birth to, biologically fathered, or legally adopted. If you are coparenting but are not legally recognized as a parent, do not include the children here. Instead, you can provide for them in Clause III.

If any of your children has died and left children of his or her own, list their names in Part B.

In Part C, name a personal guardian who will take care of your children if you can't, and name a property manager who will take charge of any property that your children own. Before you fill out this section, read "Naming a Personal Guardian and Property Manager for Your Children," below.

Sample Will

Will of _____ Samuel Troplon _____

I, _____ Samuel Troplon _____,

a resident of _____ Queens _____ County,

_____ New York _____, declare that this is my will.

I. Revocation

I revoke all wills and codicils that I have previously made.

II. Children

A. I have _____ 1 _____ children now living, whose names and dates of birth ~~are~~ is:

_____ Florette Jones-Troplon _____   _____ March 6, 1999 _____

Name   Date of Birth

[repeat name and date of birth as needed]

The terms "my children" as used in this will shall include any other children hereafter born to or adopted by me.

~~B. I have the following grandchildren who are the children of my deceased child:~~

_____   _____

~~Name~~   ~~Date of Birth~~

[repeat name and date of birth as needed]

C. If at my death any of my children are minors, and a guardian is needed, I nominate

_____ Martin Jones _____ as personal guardian of my minor children. If he/~~she~~

cannot, or declines to, serve, I nominate _____ Aaron Troplon _____ as

personal guardian. I nominate _____ Rebecca Jones _____ to be appointed

guardian of the property of my minor ~~children~~. If _____ Rebecca Jones _____

cannot, or declines to, serve, I nominate _____ Aaron Troplon _____

as guardian of the property of my minor ~~children~~.

III. Gifts

A. I make the following gifts of money or personal property:

1. I give the sum of $ _____ 15,000 _____ to _____ Alice Beckwith _____

   if ~~he/~~she/~~it~~ survives me by 30 days; if ~~he/~~she/~~it~~ doesn't, this gift shall be made to

   _____ Tim Grayson _____.

[repeat as needed]

2. I give ___my 2002 Ford Fiesta___

   to ___June Rochelle___

   if he/she/it survives me by 30 days; if he/she/it doesn't, the gift shall be made to
   ___Leo Portnoy___.

   [repeat as needed]

3. I forgive and cancel the debt of $___1,000___ owed to me by
   ___Peter Block___.

   [repeat as needed]

B. I make the following gifts of real estate:

   1. I give my interest in the real estate in ___Queens, New York___

      commonly known as ___423 75th Avenue, Forest Hills___,

      to ___Rebecca Jones___

      if he/she/it survives me for 30 days. If he/she/it doesn't survive me for 30 days, that property

      shall be given to ___Florette Jones-Troplon___.

   [repeat as needed]

IV. Residue

I give the residue of my property subject to this will as follows:

A. To ___Florette Jones-Troplon___

   if he/she/it survives me by 30 days.

B. If not, to ___Rebecca Jones___

   if he/she/it survives me by 30 days.

C. If neither ___Florette Jones-Troplon___

   nor ___Rebecca Jones___ survives

   me by 30 days, then to ___Aaron Troplon___.

V. Executor

A. I nominate ___Rebecca Jones___ as executor of

   this will, to serve without bond. If ___Rebecca Jones___ for any

   reason fails to qualify or ceases to act as executor, I nominate ___Aaron Troplon___

   to serve without bond.

B. I grant to my executor the right to place my obituary of her/his choosing in the papers she/he thinks

   appropriate.

VI. No Contest

If any person named to receive any of my property under my will, in any manner contests or attacks this will or any of its provisions, that person shall be disinherited and shall receive none of my property, and my property shall be disposed of as if that contesting beneficiary had died before me leaving no children.

VII. Simultaneous Death

If _____Rebecca Jones_____ and I should die simultaneously, or under such circumstances as to render it difficult or impossible to determine who predeceased the other, I shall be conclusively presumed to have survived _____Rebecca Jones_____ for purposes of this will.

Signature

I subscribe my name to this will this _____7th_____ day of _____March_____ , 20_08_ , at _____Queens_____ , _____New York_____ , and declare that I sign and execute this will willingly and as my free and voluntary act and that I am under no constraint or undue influence.

_____Samuel Troplon_____

Signature

Witnesses

On this _____7th_____ day of _____March_____ , 20_08_ , _____Samuel Troplon_____ declared to us, the undersigned, that this instrument, consisting of ___3___ pages was his/~~her~~ will, and requested us to act as witnesses to it. He/~~She~~ thereupon signed this will in our presence, all of us being present at the time. We now, at his/~~her~~ request, in his/~~her~~ presence and in the presence of each other, subscribe our names as witnesses and declare we understand this to be his/~~her~~ will, and that to the best of our knowledge the testator is competent to make a will, and under no constraint or undue influence.

We declare under penalty of perjury that the foregoing is true and correct.

_____

Witness's Signature

_____

Address

_____

Witness's Signature

_____

Address

_____

Witness's Signature

_____

Address

Naming a Personal Guardian and Property Manager for Your Children

Naming a personal guardian. If you have custody of minor children, you can nominate a personal guardian for them in Part C of the "Children" clause. Because state laws strongly favor granting custody to a surviving legal parent, naming a guardian normally provides for the unlikely possibility that both parents will die simultaneously, or one right after the other.

If your relationship with the other parent is strained, you may not want that person to have custody if something happens to you. You may believe that someone else—for example, your current partner—would be the best guardian for your child. You can name that person as the guardian, but if the other legal parent challenges your choice in court, he or she will almost certainly prevail unless it can be proved that the other parent:

- has never assumed—or tried to assume—the role of parent in the first place (for example, a father who never signed a statement acknowledging paternity or otherwise acted like a parent)
- has abandoned the child, or
- is unfit as a parent.

It's difficult to prove unfitness unless there are serious problems such as child abuse, substance abuse, or mental illness. The fact that you don't like or respect the other parent is never enough, by itself, to prevent a court from granting custody. If you honestly believe that the other parent is incapable of properly caring for your child or simply won't assume the responsibility, state your reasons in writing. *Nolo's Simple Will Book*, by Denis Clifford, shows you how.

You may already know who you want to name as your child's personal guardian. But remember the obvious: You can't draft someone to parent your kids. Be sure the person you name is willing and able to do the job. If your child's other parent is still alive, you should, if possible, agree on whom to nominate. And it's best not to name a couple as personal guardians, even if you expect both would act as guardians. It raises potential conflicts, especially if the couple splits up.

The person you nominate formally takes the position after being approved by a court. If there are no conflicts about who should be guardian, the process is usually straightforward. A judge who is convinced that it is in the child's best interest does have the authority to name someone other than your choice. In practice, however, guardianship nominations are rarely contested, and a court will almost certainly confirm the person you nominate.

Naming a property manager. If you have property to leave to your children, you must think about who will manage that property if you die while your children are young. Most states prohibit minors from owning more than a few thousand dollars in their own names. If they have more than that, an adult must manage it for them. If you don't designate a property manager in your estate plan, a court will appoint one for you. These court procedures are time-consuming and costly and may produce a result you wouldn't approve of. Here are several ways to appoint the manager you prefer:

- **Leave property directly to your children's other parent.** This is an excellent approach if you have a close-knit family and the other parent is a competent financial manager. Especially if moderate amounts are involved, it often doesn't make sense to create a more elaborate plan. You can use the will in this book to do this.
- **Use the provisions of the Uniform Transfers to Minors Act (UTMA).** In all states except South Carolina and Vermont, you can very simply and easily use a law called the UTMA to name a custodian to manage property you leave to your minor children for the child's benefit until the children are either 18 or 21 (up to 25 in several states). The UTMA works

Naming a Personal Guardian and Property Manager for Your Children (continued)

particularly well if you're leaving $100,000 or less, as the chances are good that this amount of money will be spent for the child's education and living expenses by age 21. To use the UTMA, you will need a specialized will-drafting product (see "Estate Planning Resources From Nolo," above).

- **Appoint a property guardian in your will.** This normally is not the best solution—except as a backup device for property not covered by the UTMA or a child's trust (discussed below). That's because under a guardianship, children must receive property when they turn 18, and in the meantime court supervision is required.

- **Create a child's trust.** For large estates, consider establishing a simple child's trust in your will or living trust. The person you name as trustee of the trust manages the money for your child and doles it out for education, health, and other needs under the terms of the trust. The child's trust ends at whatever age you designate, and any remaining money is turned over to your child outright at that time. This allows parents with large estates to provide for property management until their children are in their mid or late 20s, or sometimes even older.

TIP

Consider buying term life insurance. Before you can worry about leaving money or property to minor children you must have something to leave. If you have little beyond a big mortgage and car payments, consider buying a moderate amount of term life insurance to cover your children until they're on their own. Because term life insurance pays benefits only if you die during the covered period, it's far cheaper than other types of life insurance. Remember, too, that the dependent children of a wage earner who dies are eligible for Social Security survivor's benefits.

Because all this information may seem over-whelming at first, let's look at two examples.

EXAMPLE 1:

John and Liz have two minor children, Tommy and William. Also, John's 12-year-old son from an earlier relationship, Paul, lives with them. Paul's mother hasn't been heard from in many years. John's will names Liz as personal guardian for all three children; Liz's will names John as personal guardian for Tommy and William. In the event they die simultaneously, they

name John's brother Peter as alternate personal guardian for all three kids, after getting his approval.

John and Liz each have a few thousand dollars saved up and a little equity in their jointly owned house, but it doesn't amount to much. To provide a fund to take care of their children if they should die while the children are still minors, they each buy a ten-year term life insurance policy to pay $100,000 if one of them dies ($200,000 if they both do). Each names the other as primary beneficiary and names the children as alternate beneficiaries. In their wills, they leave all their property to each other, with the children as alternate beneficiaries under the Uniform Transfers to Minors Act and Peter as custodian.

EXAMPLE 2:

Now assume John and Liz have a larger estate, which they own jointly under the terms of a written contract. This time, they forgo the term life insurance because the children will inherit enough without it. They decide that given the value of their property, it makes sense to plan to avoid probate. To accomplish this, they use a living trust to leave their property to each other (or the children if they die simultaneously).

In the trust document, they establish a separate child's trust for each child. They name John's brother Peter as trustee of each, with the power to manage and dole out the money until each son is 25, at which time each son gets what is left in his trust. Because a living trust will not work to name a personal guardian for the children, John and Liz also write wills taking care of this important matter. (See "An Introduction to Wills," above, for other reasons why it's important to prepare a backup will even if you have a living trust.)

TIP

Name the same person to care for your child and any property you leave that child. It's usually wise to name the same person as both personal guardian and manager of your children's money (as the property guardian in your will, under the UTMA, or in a child's trust). But if that person doesn't have good financial sense, you are better off naming two different people to care for your children and manage their finances. Make sure your choices are compatible with each other—they will have to work together.

Clause III: Gifts of Money or Personal Property

Here you decide who gets what pieces of your property. Use the clauses in Part A to leave gifts of money or personal property or to forgive debts owed to you. Use Part B to leave gifts of real estate.

If you want to leave everything you own to one person, you can skip these specific bequests. Just eliminate the entire "Gifts" clause and leave your entire estate through the "Residue" clause, described below.

Clause III, Part A: Gifts of Personal Property, Money, and Debt Forgiveness

Part A lets you make direct, unconditional gifts to a single beneficiary, either a person or organization.

If you want to leave a certain item of property to be shared by two or more people, you'll need to use one of Nolo's other will-making books or software or a lawyer. If you want to place conditions on a gift—for example, "I leave my boat to Ronald, but only if he graduates from culinary school"—you'll need to see a lawyer.

You can also name an alternate beneficiary for any property in case your first choice doesn't survive you. If you don't name an alternate, and the primary beneficiary dies before you, your property becomes part of your estate's "residue" and goes to your residuary beneficiary. (See "Clause IV: Residue," below.)

Because many people sensibly don't want to leave property to anyone who will never benefit from it, they require that each beneficiary survive them by some specified period of time. The will in this book requires the beneficiary to survive you by 30 days in order to receive the property. If the beneficiary doesn't survive you by 30 days, the property goes to the alternate beneficiary, if you named one. Otherwise it goes to your residuary beneficiary. When you create the final version of your will, you can substitute any other reasonable period you want, such as five days (two years isn't reasonable).

If you plan to leave specific items of property to a beneficiary, describe them in enough detail so there is no question as to what items you mean. If you want to leave many small items to someone, however, and you don't want to list them all, you can state that you give "all my furniture [or my tools or my books] to ____ [name] ____ ."

Using Part A.3, you can also forgive debts owed you. Forgiving a debt is, in reality, making a gift to the debtor, who would otherwise owe the money to your estate.

Clause III, Part B: Gifts of Real Estate

In Part B, you name beneficiaries for your real estate. As with personal property, it's wise to include a survivorship period and to name an alternate beneficiary in case the primary beneficiary doesn't survive you. If the beneficiary (and alternate beneficiary, if you name one) doesn't survive the required time, the real estate becomes a part of your estate's residue.

When you make a gift of real estate, all mortgages and other debts (such as tax liens) on the property go with it. When describing real estate in your will, you can simply provide the street address or, for unimproved property, the name by which it is commonly known: "my condominium at 123 45th Avenue," "my summer home at 84 Memory Lane in Oakville," "the vacant lot next to the McHenry Place on Old Farm Road." You need not provide the legal description from the deed.

Clause IV: Residue

The "residue" of your estate is pretty much what it sounds like—all property subject to your will remaining after the specific gifts (in Clause III) have been made. You can select any people or organizations you want to receive the residue of your estate. It's prudent to name an alternate beneficiary for your residue. If you want to be really careful, you can name a second alternate beneficiary to receive the residue if the first two don't survive you.

If you plan to leave all or most of your property to your partner, there is another way to use the residuary clause. Rather than list items of property and designate a beneficiary for each in Clause III, you can skip Clause III and name your partner as residuary beneficiary to receive all of your property.

EXAMPLE:

Keija decides she wants all of her property to go to Tomas. She names Tomas as her residuary beneficiary and makes no other bequests. When she dies, Tomas, as residuary beneficiary, receives everything not left to someone else, which in this case is all property subject to Keija's will.

Clause V: Executor

Your executor is responsible for handling your property after you die. Your executor should be someone you trust and can rely on, and who will likely be available at the time of your death. You should name at least one successor executor in case your first choice dies before you, declines to serve, or is unable to serve when you die. (If your will names no executor or no alternate when an alternate is needed, the probate court appoints one.) Your executor can be a person who inherits under your will. So if you plan to leave your partner the bulk of your estate, it's also fine (and common) to name him or her as executor.

If you don't state that the executor is to serve without bond, the probate court will probably require the executor to post a sum of money. This acts as a kind of insurance policy that protects your beneficiaries in the event that the executor misuses your estate's property. In most situations however, a bond is unnecessary, and it either ties up a large amount of cash from the estate or costs the estate a bondsman's fee (usually 10% of the amount of the bond).

If you name an out-of-state executor, the court may require a bond (even if you stated that no bond was required) or impose other requirements. If you want to name an out-of-state executor, check your state's laws at www.nolo.com or contact an attorney to see whether your state places any restrictions on your choice.

Clause VI: No Contest

This clause is designed to discourage beneficiaries from challenging your will in court. If someone does challenge it, and loses, that person will receive nothing.

Clause VII: Simultaneous Death

This clause covers the unusual situation in which you die at the same time as your partner or other primary beneficiary. Under a law called the

Uniform Simultaneous Death Act, which most states have adopted, it's presumed that when two people die together and it's impossible to know who died first, the beneficiary is presumed to have died first. This way, the will writer's property passes to the alternate beneficiaries, and not to the deceased beneficiary and then to that person's beneficiaries. If you name alternate beneficiaries and impose a survivorship period (they need to survive you by 30 days to inherit), simultaneous deaths shouldn't be a problem. Even so, it doesn't hurt to include this provision in your will.

Similarly, if you own property in joint tenancy, and you and the other joint tenant die simultaneously, you're presumed to have died last. Thus your share passes through your will (through your residuary clause), and the other joint tenant's share passes in his or her will (see "Joint Tenancy," below).

Finally, if you own insurance, and you and the beneficiary die simultaneously, the proceeds of the policy are also distributed as if the beneficiary had died before you—that is, to any alternate beneficiary named in the policy or under the residuary clause of your will.

Signing and Witnessing Your Will

Sign and date your will in front of at least two adult witnesses. You should tell the witnesses that the document is your will, but they don't need to read it.

Have the witnesses sign and date the will after watching you sign and date it. The witnesses must be people who aren't beneficiaries under the will. It's best to use younger witnesses who will likely outlive you and will be available to authenticate your signature, if necessary.

In almost all states, witnesses can sign a docu-ment called a "self-proving affidavit," which can simplify or even eliminate witnesses' need to go to court after the will writer dies. You can find self-proving affidavits and instructions for using them

in *Nolo's Simple Will Book*, in *Quicken WillMaker Plus*, and in Nolo's Online Will that you can find at http://nolonow.nolo.com.

Storing and Copying Your Will

Store your will in a safe place, one that your executor has ready access to. A house safe or locked metal box is usually a good place. A safe deposit box is often a poor choice, because your executor may not be able to immediately gain access to it after you die.

You can make photocopies of your signed will for any person you choose, but you should have only one will with your original signature. If you have more than one document with an original signature, you may run into trouble if you decide to revoke or amend your will.

Changing Your Will

At some point, you may want to change your will. For example, say your friend Mary dies, and the book collection you were going to leave her you now want to leave to Martha.

When you should change your will is a matter of common sense. It's usually time to do it when your family undergoes a significant change, such as the birth of a child or the ending of your partnership. You will also want to change your will if your property ownership situation changes in a major way, as would be the case if you buy a house or receive a good-sized inheritance. When you do wish to make a change, you can't just cross out a provision in your will or handwrite a change in the margin. Changes must be made formally.

It usually makes good sense to make a new will, rather than changing the old one. But if you have just a small change to make—say, swapping one beneficiary for another—then you can add a "codicil" to your current will. A codicil is a sort of legal "P.S." to a will. It must be signed, dated, and witnessed just like a will. If possible, it should be typed on the last page of the will itself. The witnesses don't have to be the same ones who witnessed the will, but try to use them if they're available.

> **CAUTION**
>
> **Codicils should be used only for relatively minor matters.** A will that has been substantially rewritten by a codicil is often confusing and awkward to read, and may not clearly show the relationship of the codicil to the original will. For major revisions, draft a new will; the first provision in your will—"I revoke all wills and codicils that I have previously made"—will revoke your earlier will and any codicils to it.

Below is a sample codicil shown in the draft stage, like the sample will above.

> **CD-ROM**
>
> **Finding a codicil.** The forms CD includes a copy of this codicil and a blank tear-out copy is in Appendix B.

Revoking Your Will

It's also possible you might need to revoke your will entirely—say, if you and your partner split up. It's easy to revoke a will. You can do so by:

- writing a new will, expressly stating that you are revoking all previous wills, or
- destroying the old will.

If you destroy your will, do it in front of witnesses. Otherwise, after you die, it may be difficult to determine whether you really intended to destroy it, or whether you did, in fact, destroy it. For example, someone with a copy of the original will may claim that it was unintentionally lost, and not destroyed, creating a legal battle between those who inherit under the terms of the will and those who would inherit if it didn't exist. And, unlike married partners, unmarried partners generally are not automatically disinherited from their partner's will if the relationship ends.

Avoiding Probate

Probate is a court proceeding where your will is filed, assets gathered, debts and taxes paid, and property distributed to your beneficiaries. The process is time-consuming and expensive. Although the cost of probate (attorney fees, court filing fees, and often, appraisal fees) varies, depending on your state and the type of property you own, it can amount to up to 5% of your estate. These fees are taken out of your property and reduce the amount received by your beneficiaries. In contrast, if property is transferred outside of probate, you eliminate fees. And beneficiaries get their property as much as nine months to a year sooner than they would if your estate were probated.

> **When to Worry About Probate**
>
> If your property is of modest value (less than $100,000), planning to avoid probate probably won't result in enough savings to be worth the trouble. Even if you own considerable property, if you are reasonably young and in good health it still often makes sense to limit estate planning to writing a simple will. Later, when you're older or seriously ill, you can engage in more sophisticated planning. After all, estate planning results in no savings until your death and, if done too soon, must be redone.

If you wish to avoid probate, there are several well-established methods of transferring property that do so. These include:

- revocable living trusts
- payable-on-death bank accounts
- U.S. government securities, retirement accounts, and, in most states, stocks and bonds, for which a beneficiary can be named
- joint tenancy
- life insurance, and
- gifts.

Sample Codicil

__First__ Codicil to the Will of __Samuel Troplon__

dated __March 7__ , 20 _08_ .

I, __Samuel Troplon__ ,

a resident of __Queens__ County, __New York__ ,

declare this to be the first codicil to my will dated __March 7__ , 20 _08_ .

First. I revoke Item __2__ of Clause __III, Part A__ , and substitute the following:
__I give the sum of $5,000 to Alice Beckwith, if she survives me by 60 days;__
__if she doesn't, this gift shall be made to June Rochelle.__

Second. I add the following new Item __5__ to Clause __III, Part A__ :
__5. I give the sum of $5,000 to the Save the Harbor Fund.__

Third. In all other respects I confirm and republish my will dated __March 7, 2008__ . I subscribe my
name to this codicil this __18th__ day of __October__ , 20 _08_
at __Queens,__ , __New York__ ,

and declare that I sign and execute this codicil willingly and as my free and voluntary act and that I am
under no constraint or undue influence.

_____Samuel Troplon_____
Signature

On the date written below, _Samuel Troplon_

declared to us, the undersigned, that this instrument, consisting of ___2___ pages, including this page

signed by us as witnesses, was the __first__ codicil to his/~~her~~ will and requested us to act as witnesses

to it. He/~~she~~ thereupon signed this codicil in our presence, all of us being present at the same time. We

now, at his/~~her~~ request, in his/~~her~~ presence and in the presence of each other, subscribe our names as

witnesses, and declare we understand this to be his/~~her~~ codicil, and that to the best of our knowledge

the testator is competent to make a will, and under no constraint or undue influence.

Executed on _____October 18_____ , 20 _08_ at ___Queens_____ ,

_____New York_____ .

We declare under penalty of perjury that the foregoing is true and correct.

_____
Witness's Signature

_____
Address

_____
Witness's Signature

_____
Address

_____
Witness's Signature

_____
Address

Each method has advantages and drawbacks, which we briefly discuss below.

CROSS REFERENCE

More information. See "Estate Planning Resources From Nolo," above, for books and software on living trusts, probate, and other aspects of estate planning.

Revocable Living Trusts

A basic revocable living trust does essentially the same job as a will—that is, leaving your property to the beneficiaries you name—with the major plus of avoiding probate. Living trusts are the most comprehensive way for members of an unmarried couple to avoid probate. They are very flexible. You can transfer all your property by living trust, or if appropriate, use one to transfer only some assets, leaving the rest by other methods.

The document that creates the trust is normally just a few pages long; in it, you name yourself as trustee (the person in charge of trust property) and say who is to inherit what. You also name a successor trustee—the person who will distribute the trust property to your beneficiaries after you die. The successor trustee (who can be a trust beneficiary) can also be empowered to manage the trust if you become incapacitated.

Then—and this step is crucial—you must legally transfer property to yourself in your capacity as trustee. The trust document can control property only if it is owned in the trustee's name.

These trusts are called "living" because they're created while you are alive (sometimes they're called "inter vivos" trusts by folks who can't give up Latin). And they're called "revocable" because you can revoke or change them at any time, for any reason, before you die. While you live, you still effectively own all the property you hold in your living trust and you can do whatever you want with it: sell it, spend it, or give it away.

Aside from some paperwork necessary to establish a living trust and transfer property to it, there are no serious drawbacks or risks involved in creating or maintaining it. Unlike other trusts, you don't need to obtain a taxpayer ID number for the trust or maintain separate trust tax records. All transactions that are technically made by the living trust are reported on your personal income tax return. After you die, your successor trustee simply obtains the property from whoever holds it, and transfers it to your beneficiaries. No probate or other court proceeding is required.

EXAMPLE:

Robert creates a living trust and names his partner, Kate, as successor trustee. In the trust, Robert leaves several small items to friends and names Kate as the beneficiary of his main assets, a house and an apartment building. Robert executes and records deeds transferring title to those buildings to himself in his capacity as trustee. When Robert dies, Kate, as successor trustee, distributes the small gifts to Robert's friends and executes deeds transferring the house and apartment building to herself. No probate is needed.

CAUTION

Even with a living trust, you still need a will. If you establish a living trust, you should also have a will to deal with property acquired shortly before death or not otherwise covered by the trust, and to name a personal guardian for any minor children.

Payable-on-Death Bank Accounts

A payable-on-death bank account (P.O.D.), sometimes called an "informal trust," is a bank account that avoids probate. On a simple form provided by the bank, you name the person or people you want to receive the money when you die. During your life, you retain full and exclusive control over the account—you can remove any funds in the account for any reason, make deposits, or close the account. At your death, the account passes to the beneficiary without probate.

There are no drawbacks to a payable-on-death bank account, except that most financial institutions will not allow you to name a backup beneficiary in case your first choice predeceases you (something you can do with a living trust). Most banks have standard forms allowing you to create a P.O.D. account by either opening a new account or placing a beneficiary designation on an existing account. Bank fees for P.O.D. accounts are normally no higher than the fees for other types of bank accounts.

Naming a Beneficiary for Securities, Retirement Accounts, and Other Investments

You are allowed to name a pay-on-death beneficiary for several other types of investments. Your beneficiary will inherit the property after you die, with no need for probate. These investments include:

- U.S. government securities (bonds, notes, and bills)
- money in IRAs, Keoghs, and 401(k) retirement plans
- stocks, bonds, and other marketable securities in states that have adopted the Uniform Transfers on Death Security Registration Act (all states except New York, North Carolina, and Texas)
- vehicles (currently allowed only in California, Connecticut, Kansas, Missouri, and Ohio), and
- real estate, with a transfer-on-death deed (available only in Arizona, Colorado, Kansas, Missouri, New Mexico, and Ohio).

Joint Tenancy

Joint tenancy is a form of shared property ownership that can be used for both real estate and personal property. What sets joint tenancy apart from most other forms of joint ownership is its "right of survivorship" feature—when one joint tenant dies, his or her share automatically passes to the surviving joint tenant. If there is more than one survivor, each acquires an equal share of the deceased's interest. Indeed, you can't leave a share of joint tenancy property to anyone except the other joint tenant. Any attempt to do so by using a will or living trust is invalid.

Joint tenancy is an excellent probate-avoidance device for property you and your partner acquire equally together, assuming you each want your share to pass to the other at your death. Because in almost all states joint tenants must own equal shares, it usually won't work if one person owns a larger share than the other. Joint tenancy ownership can be created in property owned solely by one person if the owner transfers title to both partners "as joint tenants with right of survivorship" (or similar language required in some states).

But establishing a joint tenancy by transferring one partner's separately owned property simply to avoid probate is often a poor idea. Here's why:

- **You're giving away property.** If you make someone else a joint tenant of property that you now own yourself, you give up half ownership of the property. The new owner has rights that you can't take back. For example, the new owner can sell or mortgage his or her share—or lose it to creditors.
- **You may have to file a gift tax return.** If the value of the interest you give to a new co-owner (except your spouse) exceeds $12,000 in one year, you must file a gift tax return with the IRS. No tax is actually due, however, until you give away a large amount (currently, more than $1 million) in taxable gifts. There's one big exception: If two or more people open a bank account in joint tenancy, but one person puts all or most of the money in, no gift tax is assessed against that person. But when a joint tenant who has contributed little or nothing to

the account withdraws money from it, this may be considered a taxable gift.

- **The IRS often treats the first partner to die as the owner of 100% of the property (until the surviving partner can prove otherwise).** This can create significant tax problems for a high-asset estate.

Life Insurance

Life insurance proceeds are paid directly to the policy beneficiary without going through probate. The only exception is if the proceeds are payable to the deceased's estate, as opposed to a specific beneficiary, in which case they are subject to probate and are included in the value of the probate estate. For this reason, it's usually a poor idea to name your estate as beneficiary, unless the estate will have large obligations for debts or taxes and there are no other liquid assets available to pay them. See "Avoiding or Reducing Estate Taxes," below, for information on how giving away life insurance while you're alive can save on estate taxes.

Gifts

Obviously, any property given away before death, even immediately before, isn't in your estate when you die and doesn't have to be probated. (But see "Federal Gift Taxes," below, for a caveat about gifts and estate taxes.)

Simplified Probate Procedures for Small Estates

Almost every state now offers shortcuts through probate—or a way around it completely—for "small estates." Each state defines that term differently. Many large estates, worth hundreds of thousands of dollars, also benefit from these laws by qualifying for special transfer procedures that speed property to inheritors.

There are two basic kinds of probate shortcuts for small estates:

- **Claiming property with affidavits—no court required.** If the total value of all the assets you leave behind is less than a certain amount, the people who inherit your personal property—that's anything except real estate—may be able to skip probate entirely. The exact amount depends on state law, and varies hugely. Some states allow up to $100,000 or $150,000. If the estate qualifies, an inheritor can prepare a short document stating that he or she is entitled to certain items of property under a will or state law. This paper, signed under oath, is called an affidavit. When the person or institution holding the property—for example, a bank where the deceased person had an account—receives the affidavit and a copy of the death certificate, it releases the money or other property.
- **Simplified court procedures.** Another option for small estates (again, as defined by state law) is a quicker, simpler version of probate. The probate court is still involved, but it exerts far less control over the settling of the estate. In many states, these procedures are straightforward enough to handle without a lawyer, so they save money as well as time.

You can find the details of these procedures in *8 Ways to Avoid Probate*, by Mary Randolph (Nolo).

Estate and Gift Taxes

Traditionally, the federal government has levied a tax on property you leave at death (the estate tax) or give away while you are alive (the gift tax). In addition to federal taxes, a number of states also impose their own estate tax or inheritance tax at your death. Due to several major exemptions, however, only the wealthy pay estate or gift tax.

Both federal and state taxes are imposed whether property is transferred by will (through probate) or another device (outside of probate, such as a trust). If your estate is large enough to be subject to estate taxes (discussed in "Will Your Estate Pay Federal Taxes," below), you'll find that although estate taxes are difficult to reduce or avoid, there are, nevertheless, some ways to achieve savings.

Repeal of the Federal Estate Tax

In 2001, after years of debate, Congress passed and President George W. Bush signed a law that repeals the federal estate tax over a period of ten years and increases the exemption amount for the gift tax. But the repeal, if not renewed by Congress, will expire in 2011, which means estate taxes will again come into play unless Congress extends the law.

Estimating the Value of Your Property

Federal estate taxes are assessed against the net worth of your estate (called the "taxable estate") when you die. Thus, to determine whether your estate will pay taxes, you must first estimate your net worth.

In estimating the value of your estate for tax purposes, keep in mind these rules:

- All property you legally own will be included in your federal taxable estate.

- For tax purposes, your net worth is what you own, less what you owe.

- Only the value of your share of jointly owned property is included in your estate. (See "Estate Tax Valuation of Joint Tenancy Property," below.)

- Property that you have transferred but still control (perhaps because you are the trustee of a trust and have power to revoke the trust) is included in your estate.

Remember that you're making only a very rough estimate. Your assets will surely change by the time of your death, so the only point now is to see whether or not you should even think about estate tax.

It often helps to make a written list of your assets and debts when you are valuing your net worth. See the "Net Assets [or Worth] of Betty Adams," below, as an example.

Estate Tax Valuation of Joint Tenancy Property

The total value of property held in joint tenancy is included in your taxable estate, less the portion the surviving joint tenant can prove she contributed. The government presumes that the deceased contributed 100% of any joint tenancy property, and the survivor contributed nothing. If the survivor can prove otherwise, the taxable portion will be reduced accordingly.

EXAMPLE: Years ago, Edmund and Eva bought a lemon-yellow Jaguar XKE together, and have preserved it in mint condition. It's always been owned in joint tenancy, but the records proving each person's one-half contribution to the purchase price have long since been lost. Edmund dies. The government will include the current market value of the entire car in Edmund's taxable estate unless Eva can somehow prove that she contributed half the cost.

Net Assets [or Worth] of Betty Adams

PERSONAL PROPERTY	VALUE	LOCATION OR DESCRIPTION
Cash	$ 500	Safe Deposit Box
Savings accounts	2,500	Tyson Bank
Checking accounts	1,500	Tyson Bank
Government bonds	0	
Listed (private corporation) stocks and bonds	5,000	Matco Corporation
	2,000	Break-Monopoly Company
Unlisted stocks and bonds	0	
Money owed to me, including promissory notes and accounts		
receivable (including mortgages owed, leases, etc.)	5,000	Jason Michaels (sold him my car)
Vested interests in profit-sharing plan, pension rights,	7,000	Death benefit from Invento
stock options, etc.		Corporation Pension
Automobiles and other vehicles [include boats and	3,000	Honda motorcycle
recreation vehicles; deduct any amounts you owe]	7,000	Toyota
Household goods, net total	10,000	In my house
Art works and jewelry	1,000	3 lithographs in my bedroom
Miscellaneous	3,000	Silver set
REAL ESTATE [separately list each piece owned]		
Current market value	275,000	1807 Saturn Drive, Newkirk, DE
Mortgages and other liens that I owe on the property	(185,000)	
Equity (current market value less money owed)	90,000	
My share of that equity [if you have less than sole ownership]	45,000	
BUSINESS/PROPERTY INTERESTS		
(including patents & copyrights)		
Name and type of business		Invento Corporation; patentor of
		telephone-related inventions
My share	33%	
When acquired	1980	
Estimated present market value of my interest	250,000	
LIFE INSURANCE [list each policy separately]		
Company and type (or number) of policy		AETCO
Name of insured		Betty Adams
Owner of policy		Betty Adams
Beneficiary of policy		Tomas Finnegan
Amount collectible	50,000	
Cash surrender value, if any	1,000	
TOTAL VALUE OF ASSETS	$492,500	
Debts (excluding mortgage on real estate)	3,000	
Taxes (excluding anticipated estate taxes)	12,000	
Total (other) liabilities	15,000	
TOTAL NET WORTH	$477,500	

Will Your Estate Pay Federal Taxes?

Whether your estate will pay federal or state estate taxes depends on the size of your estate at your death (valuing your net worth is discussed immediately above), whether any of your property is exempt, and the value of any large gifts you made during your lifetime.

Federal Estate Taxes

For 2007 and 2008, estates worth up to $2 million can be transferred free of federal estate tax, assuming the deceased person didn't made any large gifts during life. In 2009, the exemption then increases to $3.5 million and the tax disappears entirely in 2010. (For details, see "How the Estate Tax Will Fade Away," below.)

Unfortunately, for estate planning purposes, you can't rely on the complete elimination of estate taxes after 2009. If Congress doesn't extend the repeal, the estate tax will reappear again in 2011 with a $1 million exemption. And Congress may change the law before then. In fact, most estate planning experts believe that Congress will have to revisit and revise the law sometime before 2010. This makes estate planning tricky for those with potentially taxable estates, because no one can be certain what the law will be when he or she dies. For purposes of this discussion, we take the safe approach, and assume that the estate tax will be around for some time.

CAUTION

Tax laws will probably be changing significantly. If you have a large estate, you should consult one of Nolo's more comprehensive estate planning products. (See "Estate Planning Resources From Nolo," above). Keep up with estate tax changes at www.nolo.com. Also, consider consulting an estate planning expert, especially as 2010 approaches.

In addition to the general exemptions listed above, there are other specific items that are exempt from federal estate taxes, such as:

- the expenses of your last illness, burial costs, and probate fees and expenses
- certain debts, such as any state death taxes
- all bequests to tax-exempt charities
- all property left to a surviving spouse, but not a living together partner (see "The Marital Deduction," below, for more on this), and
- money left to directly pay another person's medical or educational expenses.

The Marital Deduction

One of the biggest estate tax exemptions is the marital deduction. All property left to a surviving spouse, as long as that spouse is a U.S. citizen, is exempt from federal estate tax. Because estate tax rates are so high, this can be a powerful reason for people living together who have a lot of property to consider marriage. Wealthy couples should also consider using a bypass or life estate trust, discussed in "Avoiding or Reducing Estate Taxes," below.

EXAMPLE: Toshiro and Yuko have lived happily together for 13 years. During that time, their small electrical supply business has grown into a medium-sized regional supplier with 50 employees and a value of about $8 million. Both Toshiro and Yuko have made a probate-avoiding living trust naming the other as sole beneficiary. The problem is that if either partner dies (at least, before 2010), his or her one-half share will be subject to a hefty estate tax. To pay a huge tax bill, the survivor might even have to sell the business. Contrast this to what happens if Toshiro and Yuko marry. Now, because all property transferred to a surviving spouse is exempt from estate tax, the survivor won't owe any estate tax.

How the Estate Tax Will Fade Away			
Year	Estate tax exemption	Gift tax exemption	Highest estate and gift tax rate
2007	$2 million	$1 million	45%
2008	$2 million	$1 million	45%
2009	$3.5 million	$1 million	45%
2010	Estate tax repealed	$1 million	35%
2011	$1 million unless Congress extends the repeal or otherwise acts	$1 million	55% unless Congress extends the repeal or otherwise acts

Federal Gift Taxes

Federal gift taxes are assessed if the deceased person gave away more than $1 million of taxable gifts before death. However, most lifetime gifts aren't taxable. You can give away $12,000 per person, per year, without the amount counting towards your lifetime limit. (See "Avoiding or Reducing Estate Taxes," below, for an example of how this exception works.) In addition, gifts to spouses, donations to tax-exempt charities, and direct payments for someone's medical or educational expenses also don't count towards the lifetime limit.

The maximum gift tax rate for 2007 through 2009 is 45%. The rate will drop to 35% in 2010, and is scheduled to rise to 55% in 2011.

There are different exemption amounts for gifts made during life and for property left at death. In 2007 and 2008, you could have a taxable estate of $2 million at your death and not owe estate tax—if you left all of that property at your death. But the gift tax exemption for those years is only $1 million. So if you made more than $1 million worth of taxable gifts (very rare), then you would owe gift tax on the taxable gifts in excess of $1 million.

EXAMPLE 1:

While Tamar is alive, she makes taxable gifts totaling $900,000. At her death, she leaves an additional $1 million. In 2007, the year of her death, the gift tax exemption is $1 million, and the estate tax exemption is $2 million.

Her estate does not owe any gift tax, because she didn't make more than $1 million in gifts. And she doesn't owe any estate tax, because her total estate (including the taxable gifts) is $1.9 million, just under the $2 million exemption amount.

EXAMPLE 2:

Kenneth gives away $1.2 million in taxable gifts during his life and leaves another $700,000 worth of property at his death. Like Tamar, he dies in 2007, and like Tamar, he leaves and gives away a total of $1.9 million. But because his taxable gifts exceed the $1 million gift tax exemption, his estate will owe gift tax on the $200,000 excess. The estate will not owe additional estate tax.

State Inheritance or Estate Tax

Some states impose an estate tax (on the estate, before property is distributed to inheritors) or an inheritance tax (on people who inherit).

State estate tax. Until recently, most states didn't impose a separate estate tax; instead, they took a share of the federal estate tax paid by large estates. (This was called a "pick-up" or "sop" tax.) But the federal government put an end to that, and states no longer get a share of federal estate tax. To get back some of what they're losing, almost half the states have started collecting their own estate tax. These taxes don't normally take a large bite out of

State	Inheritance tax	Estate tax	State	Inheritance tax	Estate tax
Alabama			Montana		
Alaska			Nebraska	X	X
Arizona			Nevada		
Arkansas		X	New Hampshire		
California			New Jersey	X	X
Colorado			New Mexico		
Connecticut		X	New York		X
Delaware			North Carolina		X
Dist. of Columbia		X	North Dakota		
Florida			Ohio		X
Georgia			Oklahoma		X
Hawaii			Oregon		X
Idaho			Pennsylvania	X	X
Illinois		X	Rhode Island		
Indiana	X		South Carolina		
Iowa	X		South Dakota		
Kansas		X	Tennessee	X	
Kentucky	X		Texas		
Louisiana			Utah		
Maine		X	Vermont		X
Maryland	X	X	Virginia		X
Massachusetts		X	Washington		X
Michigan			West Virginia		
Minnesota		X	Wisconsin		X
Mississippi			Wyoming		
Missouri					

an estate, but you may want to research your state's law to see what your estate may owe at your death.

Inheritance tax. This tax is paid by the people who inherit property and is based on the value of what they inherit. In many states with inheritance taxes, your partner will pay more inheritance tax than if you left the same property to a spouse or blood relative. This is because the inheritance tax rate, or the amount of property that is exempt from inheritance tax, is often based on the relationship of the deceased to the beneficiary. Commonly, property left to a spouse is exempt from tax. Minor children get a big exemption, too, and pay a low rate. Unrelated individuals (called "strangers" by some statutes) who inherit from you get the lowest exemption and pay the highest rate.

You can get a copy of your state rules from your state tax office. Also, there is a summary of state inheritance tax rules in *Plan Your Estate*, by Denis Clifford (Nolo).

TIP

Locate in a no-tax state if you have a choice. As noted in the discussion on wills, figuring out where you legally reside isn't always simple. If your voting records, driver's license, car registration, bank accounts, and other key documents all contain one address, that's the state of your residence. If you divide your time between more than one state, it may not be clear where you reside. Pick the state with no, or a lower, estate or inheritance tax and make sure all key records support your choice. If you're very wealthy, get some legal advice on this issue.

Avoiding or Reducing Estate Taxes

Estate tax planning is often thought to be a form of lawyer's magic or chicanery. And certainly there's some gimmickry in many schemes the rich use to escape or reduce estate taxes, although tax law changes have reduced this considerably from former years. The truth, however, is that for most folks with estates over the federal estate tax exemption amount, the tax isn't easy to escape. However, there are a few legal ways to reduce death taxes.

Make Gifts of $12,000 or Less

Currently, gifts of up to $12,000 per person per year are not subject to gift tax. So, in order to avoid reaching the $1 million lifetime limit, structure your gifts to fit within this $12,000 exclusion.

EXAMPLE:

If Max gives $15,000 to Luna, $3,000 is subject to gift tax, which must eventually be paid if Max's estate is subject to gift tax at his death. If Max gives $12,000 to Luna and $12,000 to Blair, no gift tax is assessed. Similarly, if Max gives $12,000 each year to Luna for three years, no gift tax is assessed.

In addition, the $12,000 annual gift tax exemption can be used to greatly lower the eventual value of your estate if each year you give a gift of $12,000 to more than one person.

If you're very wealthy, other gift options—including giving money to a charity in trust—are available. If your estate is worth well over the estate tax exempt amount, see *Plan Your Estate*, by Denis Clifford (Nolo); once you know the basics, consult an experienced tax attorney or tax accountant.

Make a Gift of Life Insurance

Making a gift of a life insurance policy while you're alive can significantly reduce federal estate taxes. The reason is that when you give away a policy before death, it is valued, for federal estate and gift tax purposes, at a far lower dollar value than the amount it will pay off at death. By contrast, if you own the policy on your life when you die, all proceeds paid to your beneficiaries are included in your taxable estate.

In order to take advantage of this favorable rule, you must transfer ownership of the policy more than three years before your death. Or put another way, if you die within three years of making the gift, the proceeds of the policy will still be counted as part of your estate.

EXAMPLE:

Norm's total estate, including life insurance policies that will pay $400,000 at his death, amounts to $2.2 million. His plan is to leave all his property to his partner Trudy. If he keeps ownership of his life insurance policy and dies in 2008, $200,000 of his estate will be subject to estate taxes. But if Norm gives the policy to Trudy a number of years before his death, the policy is valued at far less for gift tax purposes, with the result that Norm's estate is likely reduced to an amount below the taxable level.

The main risk in transferring ownership of a life insurance policy is obvious—once the policy is given, it's gone. You can't get it back, cancel it, or change the beneficiary. The new owner has total power over the policy. In the above example, Norm can't pay the premiums himself or make Trudy pay them because if he did, the IRS would consider him the owner of the policy. He also can't prevent Trudy from cashing in the policy if she chooses. In short, make a gift of a life insurance policy only to someone you fully trust.

Making a gift of a life insurance policy is easy. But simply naming a beneficiary won't do it. You must sign a document available from the insurance company (called a "Notice of Assignment") transferring ownership to the new owner.

Create a Bypass Trust

Older couples (married or not) with large estates should consider leaving property to each other in a bypass or life estate trust (commonly called an AB trust), rather than leaving it outright to each other. With such a trust, the property of the first partner to die goes into an irrevocable trust. The survivor receives the income produced by the trust property, and can even spend principal under certain conditions, but doesn't own it outright. When the second partner dies, the trust principal goes to a named beneficiary—perhaps the couple's children, if they have any. This allows each partner to take full advantage of his or her personal estate tax exemption, which in turn means that the couple can transfer twice the amount of the exemption ($2 million in 2007 and 2008) free from estate tax.

RESOURCE

More information. To learn more about this type of trust and other estate planning devices for people with large estates, see *Plan Your Estate*, by Denis Clifford (Nolo).

Balancing the Needs of Your Partner and Your Children

If you or your partner has children from prior marriages or relationships, special issues may emerge when it comes to estate planning. You may feel conflicted about how to leave your property in a way that's fair to all your loved ones. On one hand, if you die first, your surviving partner may need additional income or the use of your property to live comfortably. On the other hand, you probably want to leave something to your children from a former relationship. Things get even more complicated if the children themselves feel entitled to inherit your property and become resentful if they believe they will lose it to your partner. If your current partner and your children don't get along, the situation gets even dicier.

Fortunately, there is an estate planning solution to deal (at least partially) with the problem of possible conflicts over property: a property control trust. You'll need a lawyer to draw up this kind of trust.

How a Property Control Trust Works

A property control trust lets the surviving partner use all or just some of the trust property (or income from that property) for the rest of his or her life. When the survivor dies, the property goes to the children.

A property control trust restricts the rights of the surviving partner to use the property placed in the trust. The surviving partner is usually called the "life beneficiary" of the trust. His or her rights to use trust property, receive trust income, or spend trust principal are as limited as the person who establishes the trust (the grantor) determines they should be. Restricting the surviving partner's rights protects the trust principal, so that much of it remains when the surviving partner dies. Then, the trust property goes outright to the grantor's children from a prior marriage or to other beneficiaries the grantor named.

EXAMPLE 1:

Grant and Helga, each in their late 60s, decide to live together. Grant has two children, ages 36 and 24, one from each of his two marriages. Helga has one child, age 39. Grant has an estate worth roughly $375,000; Helga's is worth $230,000. Both partners receive Social Security income and, in addition, Helga has a small pension. Neither has enough saved to be truly financially independent should the other die first. Each creates a property control trust and puts most of his or her property in it. Each trust provides that the surviving partner will have income from the trust for life, but absolutely no right to spend the trust principal. This way, they've each ensured that their estate will remain intact, to be received by their child or children after the surviving partner dies.

EXAMPLE 2:

Lisi and Greg begin living together in their late 50s. Lisi has a child from an earlier marriage; Greg has two children from prior marriages. Lisi owns property worth $400,000. Greg owns property worth $310,000. They decide to buy a condo that costs $320,000. Each contributes half the down payment, and they share the mortgage payment equally.

Each partner decides to create a property control trust. Under the terms of each trust, the other partner, as life beneficiary, has the rights to:

- remain in the condo for life
- receive the income from other property placed in the trust, and
- spend trust principal only for medical costs that can't be paid from other resources.

Each partner names the final beneficiaries for his or her trust. Lisi decides that her final beneficiary will be her daughter. Greg, who is on good terms with his children and is also close to Lisi's daughter, names all three as his final beneficiaries, to share trust property.

Property control trusts are no guarantee that family conflicts and tensions will be eliminated or even reduced. But they can achieve at least some sensible control over a surviving partner's assets, and give you the comfort that you've done your best to provide for both your partner and your children.

Imposing Restrictions on How Trust Property Is Used

With a property control trust, you can impose a wide variety of restrictions on your partner's rights to use the trust property. For instance, you may give your partner the right to receive income from the trust, with no right to spend the trust principal. Or, although it's common to name the life beneficiary as the person to manage the trust (called the successor trustee), you could name someone else as the successor trustee. By doing this, presumably there's less chance that your partner will take too much of the trust principal.

Here are some of the controls that can be placed on a surviving partner's right to control trust property:

- The survivor can live in a house owned, or partially owned, by the trust, but has no right to sell it.
- The survivor can live in a house owned, or partially owned, by the trust, and can sell it only for the purpose of buying another residence, and then only with the approval of all trust beneficiaries.
- The survivor can live in a house owned, or partially owned, by the trust, but cannot sell it or rent it. If the survivor moves into a nursing home and stays there for more than 90 consecutive days, the house must be turned over to the trust's final beneficiaries.
- The survivor is not the trustee, and will be paid trust income only as the trustee determines it is necessary for medical care or basic needs.

- The survivor is cotrustee with one of the final beneficiaries. Any decision regarding trust income or property, including distribution of income to the surviving partner, requires approval of both trustees. (Clearly, if you include this kind of provision, there must be good will between the cotrustees.)

- The survivor may drive a valuable car owned by the trust (as long as it's adequately insured), but can sell it only with consent of at least one final beneficiary.

- The survivor must follow specific directions set out in the trust document, down to how he or she can use many items of trust property and how to care for valuable antiques.

- All rights of the surviving partner to the trust property end if he or she marries or moves in with another living together partner.

EXAMPLE:

Leticia, in her 70s, lives with Ben, also in his 70s. Leticia has been married twice, and has one grown child from each marriage. Her estate consists of her house worth $275,000 (all equity) and investments of $580,000. Ben owns much less, about $40,000 in savings and a modest pension plus Social Security.

Leticia wants her property to eventually go equally to her two children—but if she predeceases Ben, she doesn't want him thrown out on the street. To be sure this doesn't happen, she creates a trust to control her property, appointing the older of her two children as trustee. She arranges for her house and savings to go into the trust.

Ben is given the right to remain in the house for his life. However, if he leaves it for more than four consecutive months, whether to move to some tropical paradise or a nursing home, the house can be sold or rented if the trustee decides that's desirable.

Ben also has lifetime use of all furnishings and possessions in the house, with the same stipulation as above, and is to receive income of $5,000 per year from the investments in the trust. If the income from these investments is lower than $5,000, Ben receives that lesser amount. If the income exceeds $5,000, the trustee has the power to give Ben more if he determines Ben needs it for basic needs, such as health care.

SEE AN EXPERT

If you are interested in seeing whether a property control trust fits your needs, talk to a lawyer. But before you do, we recommend that you read *Plan Your Estate*, by Denis Clifford (Nolo). It contains excellent material on how to use trusts in subsequent relationships.

Funerals and Other Final Arrangements

Many people make burial or cremation plans informally, trusting their loved ones to take care of the details after death. This works fine if you're confident your plans will be carried out. Sometimes, however, families ignore the deceased person's wishes and substitute their own, especially if they dislike the person you live with. This is possible because, in some states, only blood relatives have a say in making funeral plans.

If you're concerned about that possibility—or you just want to help your survivors by giving them some guidance during what is sure to be a hard time—you can:

- **Make the practical arrangements yourself.** Get a burial plot or arrange for cremation, and plan your funeral or memorial ceremony.

- **Leave a letter of instruction in a place where it will be available immediately at your death.** This is better than putting your instructions in your will, which may not be read for several days. Readily available instructions will be a great aid to family and friends.

EXAMPLE:

"Upon my death I wish to be buried in the Green Meadow Cemetery in Lancastershire, Massachusetts, in plot number 4321B, which is reserved and paid for [or which will be paid for by my burial insurance through Carpenters Union 18]. I wish no elaborate ceremony and wish my remains to be prepared for burial by the Fraternal Brothers Burial Society under the contract that I have signed with them. Any decisions not already made, or necessitated by circumstances that I cannot now foresee, I entrust to my friend of many years, Lucinda Whitehorse."

RESOURCE

Help with final arrangements. Nolo offers two excellent resources to help you decide on final arrangements—from burial or cremation to memorial ceremonies—and leave instructions for loved ones. Nolo's *Quicken WillMaker Plus* software lets you use your computer to prepare a final arrangements letter that makes your wishes clear. Or, if you prefer to use a workbook, *Get It Together,* by Melanie Cullen and Shae Irving (Nolo), provides a complete system to help you organize all your important paperwork and personal information, including instructions for final arrangements, for your survivors.

Moving On—When Unmarried Couples Separate

Despite your best intentions—just as is true for your married counterparts—statistics suggest that your relationship may not last forever. The anger and sense of loss that so often accompany a separation cannot be overcome by any law or counsel; emotional crises are best addressed through the help of friends, family, and therapists. On the legal front, however, breaking up can be a lot easier for unmarried couples than going through a divorce. As long as you and your ex can agree on how to divide up your assets, there is no need to involve lawyers or the court system. Even if children are involved, in most states you have the opportunity to separate in private, according to whatever arrangements the two of you agree on. But, if you and your ex are unable to resolve your disputes in an amicable fashion, you may end up in court. This can often be very difficult, because the codified divorce procedures that apply to married couples do not apply to unmarried folks.

This chapter will help you tackle the business of breaking up and minimize the likelihood of an ugly court battle. It covers:

- the laws that affect your separation
- the various stages of a breakup and the procedures and tasks involved with separating, such as dividing joint assets
- alternative dispute resolution methods, such as mediation, collaboration, and arbitration, and how these methods can help resolve conflicts, such as property disputes, faster, less expensively, and usually more fairly than a court fight
- basic guidelines for litigating your dispute in court, if it comes to that
- legal rules that cover property-related disputes
- how to prepare a settlement agreement, and
- important issues, such as custody, that face separating couples who have children.

SEE AN EXPERT

Expert advice may be necessary. When substantial assets or children are involved, consult an experienced attorney or financial adviser before agreeing about major issues of custody, property settlement, or support.

Why Living Together Agreements Are So Important If You Separate

Repeatedly throughout this book, we urge unmarried couples to prepare written agreements covering your property, your home, and other important issues. Properly written living together agreements are legally enforceable in court. Most important, a written living together agreement can minimize the potential of even going to court. The agreements in this book provide the basic framework for dividing property, deciding who lives where, and handling disputes out of court through mediation and arbitration.

Without a written agreement, separation will be more difficult, particularly if you have lived together a long time, or a lot of money or property is involved and your split is not amicable. In this case, you'll definitely want to consult an attorney or financial adviser.

Rules of the Unmarried Dissolution

While the specific rules differ slightly from state to state, the basic legal principles that regulate the property rights of unmarried couples can be summed up as follows:

- Laws governing married couples who divorce (generally labeled marital or family law) do not apply to unmarried couples who separate—

with the exception of unmarried couples living in a state that recognizes common law marriage (see Chapter 2) who qualify under their state rules, or those who qualify as domestic partners in a few states.

- Each unmarried partner is presumed to own his or her own property and debts unless you've deliberately combined your assets (such as opening a joint account or putting both names on a deed to your home). This differs from married couples, for whom any debt or asset acquired by either spouse during marriage will usually be considered jointly owned in the event of a dissolution—unless the parties signed a prenuptial agreement modifying these rules.

- The legal presumption of independent property ownership of unmarried partners can generally be overcome by a written agreement to share assets; in many states a proven oral or implied-from-the-circumstances agreement to share assets can also be enforced by the courts (although this can be extremely difficult to do if there is no written contract).

- Where it's established that an unmarried couple's assets are jointly owned (for example, when both names are on a deed), the assets are considered to be owned in equal 50-50 shares unless there is proof of a different agreement or, in some instances, where one partner clearly made a greater contribution and can prove it.

- The property aspects of your dispute will generally be handled by the ordinary business section of your state's civil courts, just as though you were going through a business dissolution. This means in most places you aren't entitled to any special mediation services or expedited hearings, which are common in divorce court, unless you have child custody or child support conflicts (these will most often be handled by the family law division of your local court).

- In most states, neither unmarried partner is entitled to receive any alimony-type support after a breakup unless there is proof of a clear agreement to provide post-separation support; in some states this must be a written agreement. The fact that one of you supported the other one during your relationship or that you signed wills providing for each other upon death generally is irrelevant to a claim for support unless you can prove that a contract to provide support after separation existed. For married couples, on the other hand, if either party has been financially dependent on the other, or if one person earns significantly more than the other, the judge can order the higher earner to pay alimony (spousal support or maintenance). Interestingly, a recent report by the American Law Institute, an influential organization of lawyers, judges, and legal scholars, recommended sweeping changes in family law, including extending alimony-like payments to unmarried couples living together who split up after a long time. Some states are considering instituting some of these proposals, and one county in Arizona has already adopted support guidelines based on the report. In California, registered domestic partners will be entitled to sue for alimony from their partners—but the law covers only same-sex couples and opposite-sex couples in which one partner is over 62.

- If you are jointly raising children and you are both legal parents, you normally have the opportunity to work out a joint agreement without court intervention. But if you end up in court, the issues of custody, visitation, and child support will be handled just as they are for married couples. If only one of you is the legal parent (because the other parent did not adopt the child), in most states the nonlegal parent will have no right to future custody or visitation of the child, and will have no duty to support the child.

The Process of Separation

Now that you know the basic rules, you are ready to navigate the potentially troubled waters of dissolving your relationship. This section covers the chronological steps most unmarried couples follow after their decision to separate. Keep in mind that the more you are able to divide the emotional from the practical aspects of separation, the more likely you are to reach a fair and amicable settlement (easier said than done, we know).

> **TIP**
>
> **Consider the children.** If you have children, bend over backwards to reach amicable and realistic decisions about their custody and care. Remember, children are the truly needy members of your family, and they should come first. Getting the help of an experienced family mediator is often essential. There's more about kids below.

Pre-Breakup Tasks

If you are the one initiating the dissolution or you sense that the sky is about to fall, it is highly sensible to take pre-separation precautions— especially if the breakup is not mutual. Here is a list of the tasks that may apply to your situation:

Review any living together, house ownership, or property agreements you have. In the best case scenario, you already have a written agreement that covers division of property and separation issues. If so, read it carefully, and determine what must be done in accordance with that agreement.

Organize financial documents and records. Locate the critical documents of your joint financial lives, make copies, and store them in a safe place. This includes joint bank and brokerage accounts, property deeds, business records, insurance policies, credit card information, tax returns, title certificates for cars, investment records, promissory notes, and wills.

Protect physical assets. Secure valuable items of personal property, such as precious art or irreplaceable family heirlooms, if you believe your partner may try to sell or take them.

EXAMPLE:

Jon and Marie are constantly fighting. Marie is worried that Jon, who has lost his job, may simply leave, taking with him all their valuables. To prevent this, she asks a trusted mutual friend to hold their artwork and her family silver. Then, she sends the oriental rugs out for cleaning and arranges to have them stored temporarily at the cleaners. Finally, she locks other valuables in a storage locker and gives the only set of keys to a neighbor she trusts completely.

Make an exit plan. Start thinking about who is going to live where. If you have a friend or close relative you can easily stay with for a while, make some tentative arrangements. Be careful, however, that you don't vacate your residence to such an extent that your partner could claim you've abandoned all rights of possession of your property. Continue to pay your share of the expenses, even if you aren't living there, until you and your partner agree otherwise in writing. And continue to pick up your mail and check on the condition of the property.

Research the law. Find out how the law in your state handles the key elements of unmarried dissolutions. Start by reading "Rules of the Unmarried Dissolution," above, if you haven't already. If you have children or significant assets (especially if you have not signed written agreements), you may need to do more research or consult a lawyer. Chapter 11 shows how.

Stop spending. Avoid any new financial ventures with your partner, such as putting large sums of money into his or her business or into a joint bank ccount, agreeing to jointly incur a big debt such as a major renovation, or taking out a new line of credit on your house. If you have a significant amount of money in a joint account or a high limit on a joint credit card, consider closing these accounts or reducing their size. But in doing so, be sure you act fairly, in a manner that assures your partner that you are not trying to take anything that may belong to him or her.

If you are concerned about domestic violence, take steps to protect yourself. (See "If Your Partner Turns Violent," below.)

Immediate Breakup Issues

Once the bad news has been declared, or if you are undergoing an interim "trial" separation, each of you will face a series of practical, as well as emotional, challenges. While every dissolution presents its own list of property-related issues, here are a few simple guidelines that should help you manage the separation:

If Your Partner Turns Violent

If your partner has been physically abusive in the past or you suspect your partner may become violent as you're separating, take steps to protect yourself.

While you're still living together, have a departure plan and place to go on short notice. Alert a friend or neighbor of the possibility that you may show up without warning. To facilitate a quick exit (if necessary), keep a set of keys and some cash either on your person or with a friend.

If your partner has moved out, change all the locks and consider buying an alarm system; get a new (unlisted) phone number.

Call the police if you feel threatened or have been a victim of violence. This is important for your physical safety, but will also be useful evidence if you want to obtain a temporary restraining order (TRO)—a decree issued by a court that requires the perpetrator to stop abusing you. The TRO may require, for example, that your ex stay away from your home and place of work. The order will also prohibit further acts of violence. Make sure your neighbors and coworkers know about the restraining order (and what your ex looks like) so they can call the police if he shows up at your home or office.

It's often a simple process to obtain a TRO. You can pick up the necessary forms at any police department, crisis intervention center, domestic violence organization, or, often, at the courthouse. While a TRO isn't a guarantee of safety, in most instances it can be very effective.

Once a court issues a temporary restraining order, a copy will be delivered to the batterer ordering him (or her) to stay away from you. A date will be set for the batterer to appear in court at which time a judge will decide whether to issue a permanent restraining order.

For more information, see Domestic Violence in the Family Law section of Nolo's website at www.nolo.com. For referrals to local domestic violence resources, contact a local police department, crisis intervention center, social service organization, or battered women's shelter. Other useful resources are the National Domestic Violence Hotline (800-799-7233) and the National Coalition Against Domestic Violence (303-839-1852 or www.ncadv.org).

Immediately close all joint credit cards and bank accounts. If you have joint financial assets (for example, a joint brokerage account) you don't want to risk losing, immediately put them in a blocked account that requires both signatures for a withdrawal. If you haven't done so already, go back and read Chapter 4, which covers basic debt and credit issues involving unmarried couples. Also, "Solutions for Property Division Problems," below, discusses how to deal with joint bank accounts, joint credit accounts, and other assets and liabilities.

Pay the bills. Make a list of the bills it is essential to pay, such as home insurance, utilities, and the car and mortgage payments. Create arrangements (together if possible) to keep these bills current. If money is tight, decide jointly which bills can be postponed.

TIP

A friend can help keep essential bills current. If communication between you and your ex has completely broken down, ask a trusted friend to collect the necessary money from both of you and pay the most important bills. By following this approach you may still lose your mate, but you won't lose your house, find yourself uninsured, or end up (literally) in the dark.

TIP

Figure out who is going to live where in the short term and write up an agreement on how you are going to handle the costs and logistics of your decision. If you jointly own a house and one of you has agreed to move out, make it clear that a temporary departure is not a permanent abandonment of the residence. Also, decide whether the temporarily absent partner should pay any portion of the mortgage or insurance costs. If you are renters, you may need to decide whose name is going to stay on the lease and who is entitled to a return of the security deposit. You may have already addressed issues, such as who gets to keep the house or apartment, when you moved in together, using one of the agreements in Chapter 5 (renters) or Chapter 6 (homeowners). If not, go back and reread these chapters.

Also, see "Solutions for Property Division Problems," below, which covers housing issues for tenants and homeowners when separating.

You can use the Short-Term Agreement Regarding Separation and Housing shown below as a template for preparing an agreement to handle your interim housing affairs. If you wish, you can add or substitute other clauses, such as a more detailed mediation and arbitration clause, from the agreements in Chapters 5 and 6.

CD-ROM

The forms CD includes a copy of the Short-Term Agreement Regarding Separation and Housing, and Appendix B includes a blank tear-out copy of the form.

Make some reasonable, practical decisions about the furniture and personal possessions. You may have already addressed these issues (what property is separate, what is jointly owned, who gets to keep what if you break up) in one of the property agreements included in Chapter 3. Whether or not you have a written agreement, don't feel compelled to sort everything out the moment you break up. Unless an object was clearly purchased by one person alone and was never gifted to the other partner, deciding who gets what may not be so simple. Valuable items, such as precious art or irreplaceable family heirlooms, should be handled with some thought. If one of you fears that the other may take or sell your personal belongings, it may be a good idea to put your possessions into a limited-entry storage locker for a few months or have a friend store them for you. (If you're really concerned, you might do this as one of your pre-breakup tasks.) If you want to be a real stickler, prepare an Agreement to Protect Property During a Breakup, such as the sample shown below.

Short-Term Agreement Regarding Separation and Housing

_____Sally Herendeen_____ and _____Scott Spencer_____ agree as follows:

1. We have agreed to live apart, effective _____July 1, 20xx_____ .

2. _____Sally_____ will remain in our apartment at _____145 Spruce Street, Cleveland, Ohio_____ and _____Scott_____ agrees to move out no later than _____July 14, 20xx_____ . If _____Scott_____ elects to leave any of his ~~or her~~ personal belongings behind, he ~~or she~~ will remove them no later than _____August 1, 20xx_____ , at his ~~or her~~ expense, giving _____Sally_____ _____three days_____ prior notice of time of pickup. Any of _____Scott's_____ personal belongings that he ~~or she~~ does not remove prior to _____August 1_____ may be retained or disposed of by _____Sally_____ , unless we jointly agree in writing to another plan.

3. Any household expenses incurred prior to _____July 1, 20xx_____ will be split between us, following our usual allocation. Any household expenses incurred after _____July 1, 20xx_____ will be the sole responsibility of _____Sally_____ , even if _____Scott_____ remains until _____July 15_____ .

4. Housing costs will be split as follows [complete (a) or (b) depending on whether you rent or own your home together]:

   ☒ (a) Renters

   _____Sally_____ will be solely responsible for any and all rent due on or after _____July 1, 20xx_____ . The security deposit in the sum of $_____1,000_____ will be retained by _____Sally_____ , in exchange for the agreement to pay the utility bills, telephone bills, and insurance incurred on or after _____July 1, 20xx_____ .

   ☐ (b) Homeowners

   Bills and expenses. Effective _____[date]_____ , since _____[name]_____ will be living in the residence, he or she will pay all monthly bills, including mortgage payments, insurance, utilities, and day-to-day maintenance costs (to unplug a toilet, for example). Property taxes and all necessary major repairs (to fix a leak in the roof or replace the furnace, for example) will be split by us equally. So long as we both continue to pay our share of these major expenses, we both shall be entitled to half of any increase in property values between _____[date]_____ and the time the house is sold.

   House ownership. We both agree to make a good faith effort to promptly resolve the issue of which of us will own the residence long-term (or whether it will be sold). _____[name]_____ agreement to vacate the residence at this time shall not be interpreted as a waiver of his or her claim to an equal share of the equity, either through a buyout or a market sale. Unless an agreement is reached by _____[date]_____ or we agree jointly in writing to extend this agreement, the property shall be listed for sale on _____[date]_____ and, after paying off the mortgage and other house-related debts, the proceeds of sale shall be split equally between us.

5. Any disputes arising out of this agreement will be submitted first to mediation. We both agree to meet in good faith with a mediator for no fewer than _____ meetings in a month's time, with expenses to be shared equally. If any disputes remain unresolved after the mediation, the disputes will be submitted to binding arbitration, with the costs of the arbitration split equally between us. By agreeing to arbitration, we each agree to give up the right to a jury trial.

_____Sally Herendeen_____   _____July 1, 20xx_____
Signature   Date

_____Scott Spencer_____   _____July 1, 20xx_____
Signature   Date

Agreement to Protect Property During a Breakup

_____Sally Herendeen_____ and _____Scott Spencer_____ agree as follows:

1. We disagree over who has the right to retain the following items of personal property: __three oriental rugs,__ __two Peggy Hopper serigraphs, and china set.__

2. In order to resolve this dispute, we have agreed to place these items in storage at the __AAA Storage Locker in__ __Cleveland, Ohio__ . __Scott__ will pay the monthly cost of storage, and our friend __Suzanna Freed__ will retain the only key. Neither of us will attempt to gain access to this locker or remove any items from it until we have resolved this dispute.

3. If we are unable to resolve this dispute within __three months__ of today, we will attempt to resolve the dispute in mediation, meeting with a mediator chosen by __Suzanna__ and approved by both of us. If mediation does not result in a settlement, we will submit the dispute to binding arbitration, with the arbitrator chosen by __Suzanna__ and approved by both of us.

4. Upon settlement of the dispute or receipt of the arbitrator's decision, __Suzanna__ will open the locker and we will each take the items awarded to us or as agreed upon by us.

_____Scott Spencer_____ _____July 1, 20xx_____
Signature   Date
_____Sally Herendeen_____ _____July 1, 20xx_____
Signature   Date

CD-ROM

The forms CD includes a copy of the Agreement to Protect Property During a Breakup, and Appendix B includes a blank tear-out copy of the form.

Deal with pets. Don't let your own emotional turmoil put your pets' well-being at risk. Unless your dog or cat clearly belongs to one person, follow a "best interests of the pet" approach, and attempt to agree on a living arrangement that is really in the animal's best interests. If one of you is getting custody of your pet, you should either make a financial adjustment (to allow the other party to buy an equivalent new pet) or agree on regular visitation. Be sensible here!

Try to assess whether there are longer-term disputes, but acknowledge to each other that it is okay to disagree for the time being. If you can both admit that there are conflicts that must be resolved a little later (and, as discussed below, agree on mediation

as a method to resolve them), you will feel far more at ease—and less desperate to sort everything out the day you leave.

Ten Steps to Resolving Your Conflicts

After you've actually separated and each of you has reached some degree of emotional and physical stability, you should find it much easier to resolve any remaining areas of conflict. While each breakup comes with its unique disputes, there are a few general rules and procedures that you will probably want to follow.

It often helps to begin by conceptualizing the dissolution process as a series of tasks best handled over time (not as one impossibly large basket of jumbled tasks). True, even when approached sequentially, several of the component tasks may still seem daunting. But as long as you have confidence that you are making progress along a fairly predictable path, you are likely to feel less angry or discouraged. And remember, along with the freedom of not being married comes the responsibility of managing one's breakup without the burdensome legal rules of divorce.

Here, then, are the major paths (and some alternative steps) you can follow to resolve disputes:

1. The first big step is to make a clear list of the remaining issues each of you believes need to be resolved—from who owns what furniture to who gets to keep the apartment.

TIP

Never argue over what to argue over. At this beginning stage, any item that is on either partner's list should be treated as a problem that needs to be resolved. There will be plenty of time to eliminate seemingly trivial issues later.

2. The easiest and most direct way to resolve your conflicts is to negotiate with each other directly. See "The Power of Talk," below.

3. Decide which of several available procedures you are going to use to attempt to resolve the disputes you can't work out without help (for example, mediation or arbitration). Once you agree on the method you'll use to resolve your disputes, put your plans in writing and sign the document so you can move on to tackle the substantive issues. The Agreement to Mediate and Arbitrate form, shown below, can get you started.

4. Take stock of the emotional barriers that may prevent resolution (maybe you blame your ex for the breakup), and try as hard as you can to overcome them. In addition to mediation, this may require formal separation counseling or meeting at a "safe place" with a trusted mutual friend who can work to calm your anger.

The Power of Talk

Whether you choose to meet face to face or to communicate in writing, by phone, or by email, direct negotiation is likely to be the cheapest and quickest approach if—and only if—you are both able to follow these simple rules:

- Schedule face-to-face discussions ahead of time, being careful to pick a location and method that ensures privacy, concentration, and a calm interchange. Don't talk about heavy topics in the middle of the workday or when one of you is tired or stressed.

- Do your homework in advance (for example, arrange to have your house appraised before you meet), and don't be afraid to postpone a discussion if you need more information. But don't delay for more than a few days—or cancel meetings without a good reason—or your former partner is likely to jump to the conclusion that you are stalling.

- Keep good notes of your discussions, and promptly write down and sign any agreements you reach, even if you use a coffee-stained paper napkin to record the agreement.

5. Figure out a realistic pace and timetable for resolving your substantive disputes. Commit to a schedule of meetings, phone calls, or emails, and then make a conscious effort to keep the ball rolling.

6. Attempt to limit your discussions to practical items such as who will get to keep certain property. Focus on finding solutions, not allocating blame. Don't view your meetings as an opportunity to try to resolve the emotional rifts of your dissolution (any separation counseling should take place at another time).

7. Educate and empower yourselves to handle property disputes rationally and competently.

For example, for house-related disputes you may need to get an appraisal or learn the exact process of transferring title. For automobile disputes, you will want to determine the car's actual sales value and obtain a form from the state for transferring ownership. For couples with major assets (especially those that have increased in value), a visit to a tax consultant or financial adviser may be necessary.

SEE AN EXPERT

Check out the possible tax implications of your separation. Separating couples are often tempted to value assets and divide them 50-50 (or according to some other percentage that they agree is fair). But before you do this, consider the tax consequences. If your assets have appreciated (for example, the value of your stock in XYZ Corp. has tripled), the person who gets the asset will have to pay tax on it when sold. This can result in an unfair distribution between the partners because the other partner doesn't bear the tax burden. Also, if one partner transfers an asset to the other partner, the partner making the transfer may be subject to gift tax and the recipient may be subject to capital gains tax—taxes that married couples transferring assets don't face. In some states, significant tax penalties are imposed whenever real estate interests are transferred between unmarried partners.

The bottom line: Before splitting assets, get tax advice from an expert. For an overview of the issues involved when splitting assets that have appreciated, see *Divorce and Money*, by Violet Woodhouse (Nolo)—though geared towards divorcing couples, this book provides valuable advice for unmarried couples as well.

8. Figure out a starting negotiating position. Do this by evaluating the likely outcomes for each area of dispute in the context of what it could cost to mount a serious court battle; for example, you may decide that accepting 40% instead of 50% of the amount in dispute makes more sense than engaging in protracted litigation. Once you determine your own

bottom line, it's usually best to keep it to yourself—at least for a while. It's often unwise to offer too big a compromise too soon—unless your ex is really willing to settle all disputes quickly and reasonably. Better to offer a series of small concessions, hoping your partner will begin to do the same, allowing you to work together to find common ground.

9. Assuming you agree on at least some things, start by writing them down. Then, as you work out the rest of the issues in dispute, add these to your "agreed-upon" list so that you gradually build a comprehensive agreement. If your agreement is fairly short, a simple exchange of letters or emails is perfectly legal, as long as it is clear at the end of the day what you both agreed to.

Once you have settled a number of issues, prepare a written settlement agreement, such as the one shown in "Putting It All Together: Preparing a Settlement Agreement."

10. Last, but certainly not least, you need to conscientiously implement your agreement. This means promptly completing and signing all the paperwork required to record and carry out its provisions. For items such as furniture and art objects, it may simply be a matter of hiring a mover. For financial accounts, a joint letter to the bank or the stock broker will usually be sufficient. For real estate transfers, a more formal set of tasks awaits you, as discussed below.

Mediation, Arbitration, and Other Ways to Resolve Disputes

Some couples can do all the heavy lifting of separating their lives themselves with no help from outsiders, while others may need to use one or two formal dispute resolution methods at different stages of their separation. It should go almost without saying that the more jointly owned property you have, the longer it can take to pull everything apart—particularly if you're starting from scratch and you have no written agreement spelling out ownership issues.

If either of you has trouble staying focused on the practical issues involved in your breakup or you can't avoid gut-wrenching psychodramas, you will probably need to ask a neutral third party—or sometimes two neutral parties—to moderate and structure your conversation. This can be done in several different ways. The major factors to consider in choosing the right approach are:

- cost
- time (avoiding long delays)
- available dispute-resolution resources, and
- the need for special expertise (for example, dividing ownership of a good-sized business).

This section discusses alternatives to traditional court proceedings, such as mediation and arbitration. These are commonly known as alternative dispute resolution or ADR.

Informal Negotiation Through Third Parties

If either of you believes it's too emotionally difficult to negotiate directly with each other, each of you can select an advocate or representative who will then talk to each other without either of you being present. The advocates can exchange letters or phone calls or meet face to face. This kind of shuttle diplomacy is basically what lawyers do, but there is nothing wrong with having a trusted (and clearheaded) friend, real estate broker, or accountant play this role. Of course, all key decisions must eventually be made, or at least ratified, by you and your former partner. While turning negotiations over to representatives can be a slow process, it can work very well when your dispute centers on just a few practical issues (for example, the value of a business or real estate). But be sensitive to the fact that, especially if you hire

lawyers to do this task, you want peacemakers, not warriors, and you need to watch the clock (legal fees can mount up fast).

Mediation

Mediation is a nonadversarial process where a neutral person (a mediator) helps you settle your differences. Mediation is often used to help separating couples work out problems concerning division of property and issues involving children.

With mediation, the two of you get together to talk face to face about your disagreements, with a neutral mediator working to help you find realistic solutions. No one has the power to impose a solution—rather, you must work out your own agreement voluntarily. Unlike a judge, the mediator's role is to help you and your partner find common ground. When this happens, both parties usually feel like their dispute was resolved fairly, and a good foundation is laid for future cooperation. This approach is especially important if you have children. In addition, mediation often costs less than either an arbitration or court proceeding and, unlike going to court, is conducted in private.

Each of you can come into the mediation solo, or you can each bring an advocate along—either a friend or an attorney, depending on how complex your disagreements are. You also may want to bring along an advocate if your ex has better negotiation skills or more financial savvy.

Mediation—which allows disputants to express personal and emotional issues, but eventually focus on practical ones—can produce great results, and it almost always moves more quickly than a protracted exchange of written communications. The key is to have a good mediator and to allow enough time to air your conflicts and find solutions. In this context, a series of shorter mediation sessions works best for some people, while half-day or even daylong sessions may be very useful if complicated property ownership issues must be resolved.

If your partner is refusing to try mediation, you might try to emphasize that agreeing to mediation is not an agreement to any particular outcome. It doesn't even guarantee that an agreement will be reached, although mediation is very often successful. Your partner should simply understand that mediation is the cheapest and quickest—and most humane—way to resolve conflicts.

Make sure to select a mediator you both have confidence in (or at least believe is neutral)—someone with the background and experience necessary to help you settle the issues in your case. The needs of a couple trying to resolve a dispute about real estate will differ from those of a couple fighting over the car and a few household possessions or from a couple grappling with custody issues. To find a good mediator, get references from people you trust—friends, relatives, colleagues, or a trusted attorney. Depending on your situation, you may want to contact a community agency that offers mediation, usually by trained volunteers. Private practice mediators are another option.

Remember to document any settlement you reach in a clear written agreement. Once you do, this contract is enforceable in court just like any other binding agreement.

RESOURCE

Mediation requires advance preparation and thought. From jointly agreeing on a good mediator, through planning your mediation strategy (for example, understanding your bottom line), to writing up the final agreement, you need to understand exactly what is happening and why. Information about mediation is available online from Nolo's website at www.nolo.com, under the heading "Rights and Disputes". An excellent source of more thorough information is *Mediate, Don't Litigate*, by Peter Lovenheim and Lisa Guerin, available as an eBook at www.nolo.com. Also, *Divorce Without Court: A Guide to Mediation & Collaborative Divorce*, by Katherine Stoner (Nolo), provides excellent advice on mediation that applies to unmarried couples as well as a married couple going through a divorce. While the legal aspects of your breakup will not be the same as those faced by married people, many of the practical and financial issues are the same. Finally, if you have children, be sure to see *Building a Parenting Agreement That Works: How to Put Your Kids First When Your Marriage Doesn't Last*, by Mimi Lyster (Nolo). This book includes valuable advice on how mediation can help resolve custody and visitation disputes.

Arbitration

If mediation fails to resolve a dispute, arbitration often is the next best choice. Arbitration is best understood as a kind of private trial, but one that is quicker, less formal, and almost always cheaper than courtroom litigation. You sign an agreement to submit your dispute to a neutral decision maker (called an "arbitrator"), and agree to abide by the arbitrator's decision. Normally, arbitration awards are binding and not appealable. In order to make arbitration effective, you will need to reach agreement on the following before the arbitration hearing:

- **Set a timeline.** Agree on a rough timetable for bringing the disputes to a conclusion. Even though the precise date of the arbitration hearing can't be set until you select your arbitrator, try to get a clear sense of how many weeks or possibly months this process is going to take.

- **Select the arbitrator.** You can delegate the process of selecting an arbitrator to a friend or an attorney, use a local arbitration business that will propose a list of arbitrators (with each party having the right to strike those who seem unfair or unqualified), or jointly pick a person. If you don't know much about a proposed arbitrator, check the person's references and level of expertise in handling your type of dispute.

- **Set the rules.** Sign a written agreement stating that you will abide by the arbitrator's decision, and agree to waive any rights to appeal. In most states, arbitration agreements can be enforced through the local courts, so you have a practical and cost-effective remedy if your ex doesn't comply with the arbitrator's order.

- **Decide on advocates.** Decide whether you can each bring an attorney or advocate with you to the arbitration hearing. Most folks prefer to retain the right to bring an attorney or an advocate to the hearing, even if at the last minute they decide not to. If you are easily intimidated by your ex or have trouble expressing yourself in a stressful situation, having an advocate will help. But if you are able to represent your position effectively and want to avoid the expense and adversarial climate that can result from bringing a lawyer, consider handling the hearing on your own.

- **Agree on the issues in dispute.** Before you go into arbitration, if at all possible, make a list of the principal issues that need to be resolved. Acknowledge that new issues may arise later, but try to be as specific as you can about what it is you are fighting over.

- **Conduct your investigation.** Decide whether either of you needs to conduct any investigation or obtain copies of documents or other information before the hearing. For example, if only one of you has access to the real estate, financial, or business-related documents, you may need to agree to full disclosure of all key information as part of your agreement to arbitrate.

- **Decide who pays.** The arbitrator will probably charge by the hour, and typically will ask each party to foot half the bill. Often it's best for each side to pay their own fees, but this may not be the case if one party feels particularly aggrieved. An alternative is to empower the arbitrator to award attorneys' fees or arbitration costs to the prevailing party.

How to Make an Agreement to Use Mediation and Arbitration

After you have decided what procedures the two of you are going to use to resolve your conflicts, you should prepare an agreement setting out how you want to move forward and what disputes you will be resolving. A sample Agreement to Mediate and Arbitrate is shown below. You can tailor it to your own situation.

CD-ROM

The forms CD includes a copy of the Agreement to Mediate and Arbitrate, and Appendix B includes a blank tear-out version of this form.

Lawyers and Lawsuits: Going to Court

If you can't even agree about setting up a mediation or arbitration procedure to settle your dispute or if one party is particularly aggressive, the courts may be your only resort. Litigation (an adversarial legal proceeding) is likely to be expensive, ugly, time-consuming, and very depressing, so only take this route if all else fails. But when nothing else works and there is a lot of money or property in dispute, going to court at least provides a way to resolve your conflicts.

TIP

Small claims court may be an option—if your suit involves a relatively small amount of money (generally, less than $7,500). For an overview of small claims court, see the "Rights and Disputes" topic of Nolo's website at www.nolo.com. Nolo also publishes a complete book on the subject of bringing or defending a small claims court case, *Everybody's Guide to Small Claims Court*, by Ralph Warner. California residents can use *Everybody's Guide to Small Claims Court in California*, also by Ralph Warner (Nolo).

Agreement to Mediate and Arbitrate

_____Eric Stall_____ and _____Kate Pulis_____ agree as follows:

1. We have agreed to submit the following disputes to mediation, and if mediation is unsuccessful, to arbitration:

   a. Ownership of our residence in Orlando, Florida, including the disposition of the residence and our mutual claims for reimbursement for contributions made to the purchase and upkeep of the residence

   b. Ownership of our one automobile (2002 Toyota Corolla), including disposition of the automobile and our mutual claims for reimbursement for contributions made to its purchase and upkeep

   c. Kate's claim for reimbursement for money paid to City College in connection with Eric's education, and

   d. Eric's claim for a partial ownership interest in Kate's accounting business
   _____ .

2. We agree to discuss these areas of dispute in mediation, as follows:

   a. We will try to select a mediator jointly, and if no mediator is selected by ___April 1, 20xx___, each one of us will nominate one friend, and the two of them shall select the mediator.

   b. We shall meet no fewer than ___three___ times to mediate, within ___6 weeks___ of the selection of a mediator, with all costs of mediation split equally between us. The mediator will determine the time and place of each meeting. Each session will be at least two hours long.

   c. Until we reach an agreement, compromise offers or proposals presented by either of us shall be confidential and, if mediation fails, will not to be disclosed to anyone else or used in any subsequent arbitration or court proceeding.

   d. If an agreement is reached, it shall be set out in writing and signed by both of us. If one of us fails to abide by it and an attorney is needed to enforce its terms in court, the prevailing party shall have the right to reimbursement of attorney's fees.

3. If after we mediate on ___three___ occasions no settlement is reached and we elect not to schedule any more mediation sessions, either of us may require arbitration by sending a written arbitration request to the other. If this occurs:

   a. We will jointly select an arbitrator who will conduct an arbitration under the rules of the American Arbitration Association. If for any reason we can't agree on an arbitrator within ___one month___ of the written demand for arbitration, ___Judge Marilyn Strauss of our local county court___ will select the arbitrator. By agreeing to arbitration, we each agree to give up the right to a jury trial.

   b. The costs of the arbitration will be split equally between the two of us. If either of us wishes to, she or he may bring an attorney to the hearing; however, each of us will be solely responsible for any attorneys' fees we incur.

   c. Each of us will provide the other with copies of all documents relevant to these disputes at least ___two weeks___ prior to the arbitration proceeding. At the same time, each of us will supply the other with a list of all witnesses who will be asked to testify at the arbitration hearing.

   d. The decision of the arbitrator will be binding, and either of us may enforce it through the local trial court if the other does not comply with its terms. If an attorney is needed to enforce the arbitration decision, the prevailing party will have the right to reimbursement of the attorney's fees incurred specifically for this purpose.

_Eric Stall_____ _March 20, 20xx_____
Signature   Date

_Kate Pulis_____ _March 20, 20xx_____
Signature   Date

! **CAUTION**

Avoid battles of principle. Oftentimes, one or both partners may be inclined to be very rigid, greedy, or vindictive in a breakup. Take our advice and avoid this tendency, no matter how much resentment you might have about past wrongs. Looking back at your breakup even a few years from now, you'll be very grateful if you can say, "We settled our disputes quickly and decently and got on with our lives." It follows that you should look out for any reasonable opportunity to make a deal and move on, even if this means you compromise a little more than you originally intended. If you are using an attorney who wants to win at any cost, find a more conciliatory attorney!

Typical Legal Claims in an Unmarried Dissolution

Here's a brief rundown of the types of claims commonly raised in court in an unmarried dissolution:

- **Breach of contract.** Was the contract (agreement) for sharing funds, debts, or assets written, oral, or implied? Which partner breached the contract?

- **Partition of real and personal property.** Who owns what real estate and personal property? How is it to be divided up or sold, and who is to receive what share of the proceeds?

- **Post-separation support.** Does either person claim that an oral or written agreement states that the other owes him or her post-separation financial support? If so, how much, for how long, and what is the proof that an agreement for the payment of support exists?

- **Personal injury and financial compensation.** Does either partner have valid claims for personal injuries or financial harm, such as the destruction of a valuable possession, the wrongful withdrawal of money from a bank account, or an injury during a domestic violence episode?

Basic Rules for Going to Court

If, despite your best efforts at working out a reasonable compromise, you end up in court, here are a few basic guidelines:

- Find a good attorney experienced in unmarried dissolutions to represent you. Chapter 11 explains how.

- Try to evaluate how your ex is going to respond to the prospect of litigation. With some people the mere mention of going to court will bring them to the bargaining table. But with others it is likely to greatly increase tensions.

- Learn how the litigation process is likely to work to resolve your particular problems. If you are fighting over your house, find out whether there is a local protocol for appraising and dividing up real estate, and how it may affect the outcome. If your dispute concerns joint bank accounts or claims for post-separation support, research how the local courts deal with these issues (in many states, by law, alimony-type support is not ever awarded to unmarried partners). Try to evaluate how the litigation process will actually proceed for your particular case: Do you need to file any papers immediately? (You might, especially if your name isn't on the title to a property you claim is part yours.) How much pretrial paperwork will there be; how will the trial be handled; will there be a jury? The more you know ahead of time, the better your decision making will be.

- Make it clear to your lawyer—and frequently remind yourself—that while you are initiating litigation out of frustration or desperation, you always remain open to compromise. Even after court papers are filed or a trial begins, it is not too late to put the litigation on hold and schedule a mediation session.

Solutions for Property Division Problems

This section presents an overview of legal rules that cover the types of property-related disputes that most frequently arise in unmarried dissolutions. The law governing property division for unmarried couples differs in several important respects from the laws that control how married couples divorce. Even so, the basic issues unmarried people fight over (property ownership and support) are pretty much the same as those that arise in any divorce court.

If you have prepared a written living together or property agreement as we recommend in earlier chapters, many issues involving who owns what and how your property will be divided at separation should already be addressed.

Tenants

For those of you who are renters, your home division process should be fairly simple. You will need to decide who is staying and who is moving on, how you are going to deal with your landlord, who gets the security deposit, and who will pay any debts that arise in the process. If you both plan to move out, be sure to give your landlord proper notice (typically 30 days for a month-to-month rental agreement).

What if you both want to keep the rental? Unless you had an agreement beforehand, generally there is no legal preference for who gets to keep the apartment. As discussed in more detail in Chapter 5, you need to act fairly and rationally (ideally, you should reach your agreement long before the time of separation).

If you lived in the place first, or are the only one who has signed the lease or rental agreement with the landlord and actually pays the monthly rent to the landlord, you probably have first claim on the apartment. If you both have signed the lease or you both regularly pay rent, your rights to remain in the apartment are probably equal (unless you have a written agreement to the contrary), even if one of you got there first.

Try to talk about your situation, with an eye to allowing the person who genuinely needs the place the most to stay. Bend over backwards to be reasonable about the last month's rent and damage deposits. Sometimes it's fair to agree that the person staying will make a financial contribution to the departing partner's moving costs and perhaps even a portion of the new rent payment (especially if it is significantly higher). The security deposit should be returned to the partner who paid it, or split equally. Even if you end up paying a little more than you think is equitable, it will be well worth it if it helps keep the peace. We've found that the best compromises are made when both people feel they've gone more than halfway. Mediation may help resolve disputes over the rental, as it will give you a chance to reach a mutually satisfactory agreement.

If both of you have signed the lease, you should jointly talk with the landlord and have the lease rewritten in the name of the remaining party alone. Be sure that the person moving out has a reasonable amount of time to leave, such as three or four weeks. Each person has the right to keep all his or her personal belongings, even if one person is behind in his or her share of the rent. Never lock up or toss out the other person's property.

! **CAUTION**

Don't deny your ex access to your shared home except in extreme circumstances. If you're going to lock a person out, be ready to sign a police complaint, because it may come to that if your former partner uses force to try and get in. Except where a person has no legal right to live on the premises (in other words, the person hasn't signed a rental agreement or lease, hasn't been living with you long, and hasn't paid rent), locking a person out is illegal, and you can be sued for money damages.

What if one person moves out without paying their share of the rent? As a general rule, each cotenant is 100% liable to the landlord, meaning that if one of you disappears in a huff, the other is on the legal hook for all the rent—but may be able to claim contribution from the other partner/ owner. See "Cotenants' Legal Obligations to the Landlord" in Chapter 5 for more on the issue of tenants' "joint and several" liability for paying rent and complying with the lease.

Homeowners

Life is more complex for separating couples who own a home. If the two of you didn't sign a joint house ownership agreement that sets forth your intentions in case of dissolution, you have two choices. You can either follow the legal procedures that apply in your state—typically this means the court will order the property to be sold, and the net proceeds (after paying mortgages, liens, and costs of sale) to be divided—or you can reach your own compromise settlement.

In order to sort out who gets what regarding your house, you will need to resolve a few basic issues.

Who Owns the House?

Your first possible conflict may be over who owns what percentage of your house or other real property. Especially if one of you believes he or she owns a larger share, or if only one partner is listed on the deed, this can be difficult if you haven't previously signed a house ownership agreement. Remember that in just about every state, having both names on the deed to the house creates a legal presumption that you are 50-50 owners, and anyone claiming a different percentage has to prove the existence of an agreement saying so (often in writing).

Fights frequently arise when your contributions to the property have been unequal. Often a partner who has contributed less financially (say, to the down payment) believes that he or she chipped in something else of equivalent value to the property, such as labor to fix up the house. Take into consideration whether either of you has made any significant extra monetary or labor contributions to the property (for example, one of you just paid $15,000 for a new roof, built a garage, or paid the entire mortgage payment for the last three months). If so, be ready to award that person appropriate additional compensation, most often in the form of a reimbursement rather than a greater share of the equity. When trying to reach an agreement, put aside the most extreme arguments of either person, and acknowledge that there is merit to each side's more rational demands. If conflicts arise over house ownership, it's best to try the following approach to reach a fair settlement regarding these claims:

- Read the discussion on contracts for equal and unequal ownership of a house in Chapter 6 for ideas on how to adjust ownership fairly when one person contributes more to the down payment and the other makes other contributions (money or labor).

- One possibility is to reduce each partner's total contribution (down payments, mortgage payments, labor, improvements) to a dollar figure. By comparing the two figures, you can come up with what percentage of the house each of you owns. If you can't resolve disputes over the value of your contributions, it often makes sense to get the help of a real estate professional.

- Narrow the financial gap between the two of your positions by compromising on other demands or making other financial concessions.

- Compare the benefit of splitting the difference to the cost of fighting over every last penny. Hopefully, looking at what will happen if you don't settle will encourage you to come to a compromise figure. If you still can't reach an agreement, convene a single mediation session where you limit your discussion to this one point of disagreement. In most instances you will reach a compromise by the end of the day. If you are still at odds, convene a single short arbitration session where you empower the arbitrator to resolve this financial dispute quickly.

If One Partner Will Sell to the Other

Next, you've got to decide whether you will jointly sell the house to a third party or whether one of you will buy out the other's interest. Usually, it is much easier and cheaper for both of you if one of you sells to the other (rather than selling it to a third party) because you avoid all the costs that accompany a market sale. So if either or both of you are interested in holding on to the real estate you own together, it makes sense to attempt to negotiate a mutually agreeable solution.

Assuming you haven't already agreed (pre-breakup) that one person will have first dibs on buying out the other's share in the house, you may use a coin flip or some other simple mechanism to determine who stays and who goes. (These options are included in our house ownership contracts in Chapter 6.) Or, if both of you want to keep the house, you can conduct an informal "auction," where the partner who is willing to pay the most gets to keep the place. You can also use mediation or arbitration to resolve the conflict. An arbitrator can be given the power to decide who should stay (after hearing whatever arguments you each make) and perhaps award the selling partner financial compensation for having to move.

If you can agree on who is going to buy the house but can't agree on a sale price, the best way to set the price is to get an appraisal from an experienced real estate appraiser familiar with the local market. If you can't agree on an appraiser, each of you can get your own appraisal and you can average the results. Or, you can get a less formal opinion from an experienced real estate broker—cheaper, but often less accurate.

Understand that most appraisals estimate the sale price, but do not take into account the cost of selling the property. If you have your jointly owned real estate appraised and then agree that one of you will buy out the other, you may want to reduce the price by the amount of the real estate commission that would be charged if you sold the place to a third party. In other words, even though you won't have to pay a commission when one of you sells to the other, the buying partner will need to do this eventually, so the buyout evaluation probably should reflect this.

In coming up with a buyout price, make sure, in addition to deducting the amount of the broker's commission, you also figure out and deduct the cost of any deferred maintenance that would have to be done if the place was put on the market. Next, of course, subtract the remaining mortgage amount to arrive at your combined "equity." Assuming this is a positive number, this is the sum that you should use to determine the buyout price (which will be 50% of that number if you own the property in equal shares).

EXAMPLE:

If the appraiser says your house is worth $400,000 and you still owe $220,000 on your loan, subtract $24,000 for the eventual 6% broker's commission, $15,000 for the necessary pre-sale repairs, and $220,000 for the loan. The resulting amount ($141,000) is the equity which you will need to divide up; if you each own 50% of the place, the buying partner should pay the selling partner half that amount, or $70,500.

Find out from a local broker or attorney what the procedures are for doing an internal buyout, and make sure you take into account the costs of transfer. Some states impose transfer taxes or recordation fees, and these need to be allocated between the two of you. Often it's best to forestall possible disputes by agreeing to pay transfer costs and taxes 50-50. In addition, obtain the proper deeds and forms and, if necessary, have a professional help you fill them out. You may not need to use a title company or buy title insurance if your transfer is relatively straightforward and you aren't worried about the selling partner's ability to deliver title to his or her share free of any liens or judgments. If you are worried about possible liens, you will have to go through a title company and purchase title insurance—which can add more than $500 to the cost of transferring title. Either way, once the property has been deeded to one of you, this person will need to record the transfer deed with your local property recorder's office.

Finally, figure out your options regarding your mortgage. Quite often, the selling partner will agree to keep his or her name on the loan, at least for a year or two, in which case the buying partner would not need to obtain a new mortgage; of course, in this case the buying partner should give the selling partner written assurance that the mortgage will get paid each month, to help prevent the selling partner from ending up with a

---

Home Buyout Agreement
(One Co-Owner Sells to the Other)

__Bill Thomas__ and __Teresa Garcia__ have agreed to settle the ownership of their house at __4 Greenwood Road, Albany, New York__, [hereafter property], as follows:

1. __Bill__ will purchase __Teresa's__ interest in the property by paying ~~him or~~ her $ __42,000__, no later than __April 1, 20xx__. Within __three days__ of this payment, __Teresa__ shall deliver to __Bill__ a signed and notarized quitclaim deed to the property. __Bill__ will handle the recordation of the deed and pay all costs of transfer.

2. __Bill__ agrees to purchase __Teresa's__ interest knowing that __there are structural and roof problems in the property, and that there is a dispute with the neighbor over the use of the common driveway__. __Bill__ releases __Teresa__ from these or any other claims arising out of the condition of the property or the title to the property.

3. __Teresa__ agrees to keep ~~his/~~her name on the current mortgage for at least __one year__, by which time __Bill__ shall either obtain a new mortgage that does not involve __Teresa__ or sell the property.

4. __Bill__ will be responsible for any and all costs and obligations regarding the property, including all mortgage debt, as of __April 1, 20xx__.

5. Either party may compel enforcement of this agreement by arbitration, at which the arbitrator may award attorneys' fees and costs to the prevailing party.

__Bill Thomas__
Signature

__February 15, 20xx__
Date

__Teresa Garcia__
Signature

__February 15, 20xx__
Date

tarnished credit rating or facing a bank's demand for payment. If one partner takes his or her name off the loan, in some states and with some banks, the remaining partner can retain the existing loan in his or her own name even after a buyout. (With some loans the selling partner can even be absolved of any further liability.) But in other areas and situations, the buying partner may have to get a new loan. To present a financial statement strong enough to qualify for a new mortgage, the buying partner may need to defer making payments to the selling partner (or make very low payments) for a period of time. If this isn't acceptable to the selling partner, it may be possible for the buying partner to obtain a home equity loan in addition to the first mortgage.

Even if the buyout is amicable and all deed forms have been signed and recorded, be sure to write up a simple agreement stating what you've agreed to. This way you will have a document setting forth your entire agreement, in case a dispute arises later.

A sample Home Buyout Agreement you can tailor to your own situation is shown above.

CD-ROM

The forms CD includes a copy of the Home Buyout Agreement, and Appendix B includes a tear-out copy of this form.

SEE AN EXPERT

Have your Home Buyout Agreement reviewed by a local broker or real estate attorney. You'll want to make sure that any special rules covering internal buyouts are covered in your agreement.

If Both Partners Will Sell the Property to a Third Party

If neither of you wants the house, you will probably sell it on the market (most likely with a broker's help). Be sure to select a qualified broker who is sensitive to the fact that you are splitting up. The broker can handle the delicate arrangements of fixing up and showing the home, knowing that things may be tense between the two of you. But given that it's in both partners' interest to sell the property for the best possible price, try to work cooperatively.

Once you've sold the place, you still need to divide up the proceeds according to your respective percentages of ownership. Fortunately, a dispute about how much each of you owns need not slow up a sale. You can simply agree in advance to put the disputed portions of the sale proceeds into a joint account requiring both signatures; include a proviso that the funds will not be disbursed until you jointly decide on the division and put your decision in writing. If you do not decide within some defined period of time how to divide the profit, agree that the dispute will be mediated and, if no agreement is reached, arbitrated.

If you can't resolve this dispute by negotiation or mediation, consider submitting it to binding arbitration. You can use a real estate broker (if the dispute is primarily about the value of each party's contribution) or an attorney (if the dispute is primarily legal) as your arbitrator.

TIP

Take advantage of capital gains tax breaks. If you sell your home, either to your partner or to a third party, you can probably shield $250,000 of your profits from capital gains tax. See "Check Out Legal and Tax Issues Before Transferring a Share of Your House" in Chapter 6 for details.

Dividing Other Real Estate

If you own other real estate, such as an investment property or a vacation home, you need to go through the same process as with your primary residence. Decide whether either of you is going to buy out the other's share or whether you are going to sell the place to a third party. Then figure out the property's value and resolve any competing claims for reimbursement for extras. Once the dust settles, you may even be able to continue owning the property jointly as an investment. This is especially likely if you agree to hire a professional management company so you don't have to deal with each other over the details. But if you go this route, be sure to have a written management agreement for the property—you are business partners now, not lovers, so you need to act in a businesslike manner.

Other Financial Assets and Liabilities

Joint bank accounts, stock accounts, and savings accounts also must be distributed when you separate. The same joint ownership rules that apply to real estate apply here—having both names on the account creates a legal presumption that it's owned 50-50, and whoever claims a larger share normally has to prove an agreement (such as the ones in Chapter 4) stating otherwise. Once again, if disagreements arise, try to reach a compromise. But if you can't, consider mediating or, if necessary, submitting the dispute to binding arbitration. In the meantime, make sure you instruct the bank or stockbroker to hold all the funds pending a jointly signed release, to do away with worries that either party will abscond with all of the money.

SEE AN EXPERT

See a financial consultant (in addition to your lawyer) if substantial assets are involved. This is particularly important if you have no written agreement, you have lived together a long time, and the breakup is not amicable.

You also need to make arrangements to allocate any joint debts. Your first task is to close all joint credit accounts immediately. Do this even if you have to act unilaterally (but, of course, inform your partner). Next, if possible, the two of you should promptly pay outstanding balances. (If you made an agreement to share assets and can't agree about

Dividing a Small Business

If one or both of you have built up a small business during the course of your relationship, you may face a battle over who owns what share of it. If the business is considered a shared asset, or you can prove that there was an implied agreement between the two of you to share ownership, most courts will try to evaluate the current value of the business and determine the percentage interest of each partner. If only one partner is the true owner but the other one has contributed time or money to the business beyond what he or she has been compensated for, the courts may be willing to evaluate the situation based upon the reasonable value—called "quantum meruit"—of the nonowner's contribution. Unlike a married couple, you aren't entitled to a share of your partner's business unless you can prove that you had some kind of agreement regarding the business or performed lots of uncompensated work for it. If the business is valuable and you can't resolve your dispute, you may both need to consult lawyers experienced in small business matters.

who owes how much, one possibility is to divide your debts according to the same percentages as in your agreement.)

If one of you doesn't have the cash to pay his or her share of joint debts, consider having the richer one pay them up front, with the poorer one signing a promissory note promising to repay his or her ex the appropriate share of debt. (Chapter 6 includes a promissory note you can use for this purpose.) Be careful here, though, as the "creditor" partner can only collect if the "debtor" partner has the funds to pay the debt. If you don't pay off all joint debts, and the debtor partner doesn't come through, your bank will not forgive your obligation just because you had a private agreement that your partner would reimburse you later on. And even if both names aren't listed as debtors on a particular debt, if you had an agreement between you to share the debt you should honor that agreement and figure out how to allocate the debt.

Putting It All Together: Preparing a Settlement Agreement

Your final agreement should be a clearly written document covering the details of your separation. Be as specific and clear as possible and list each key provision (Who gets the car? The piano? The cat?) separately. A sample settlement agreement is shown below. You can use this as a model and substitute or incorporate clauses and sections from other agreements in this book.

Be sure you both date and sign your settlement agreement and each keep a copy. It's a good idea to have your signed agreement notarized, just in case there's a future need (in court or arbitration) to prove that the signatures on the agreement are not forged.

Your signed agreement is enforceable in court in the same way as is any other binding agreement—assuming the agreement doesn't call for an illegal action.

SEE AN EXPERT

As recommended many times throughout this book, have an attorney review your agreement, especially if children, a lot of money, or property are involved.

Children: Custody, Visitation, and Support

The law can sometimes be very unfair to unmarried parents—both as it is written and as it is sometimes applied by prejudiced judges. Making matters even

messier is the fact that although unmarried parents have far more rights than in the past, the law in many states is still in great flux.

But married or not, one thing never changes—when you split up, it's vital for your kids' current and future well-being that you try, try, try to reach a compromise about issues of custody, visitation, and support. Doing this in a constructive, humane way may be a great challenge. But, your ability to get along civilly—if not cheerfully—is the biggest gift you can give your children. Sometimes this can be accomplished through open discussions between the two of you. In other situations it will require counseling, therapy, or mediation. No matter how scary or messy breaking up can sometimes be, as long as you are each determined to avoid a contested court battle and willing to put your egos aside in an effort to work together in the best interests of your child, you should be able to work out even the toughest parenting issues. One thing is sure—if you do, your children will thank you for it.

CROSS REFERENCE

The basics of the law regarding the children of unmarried couples are covered in Chapter 7, and Chapter 8 covers issues involving children from a prior relationship, including the impact of living together on custody of children from a prior marriage. If you and your partner are arguing about your children, go back and reread these chapters for an overview of how the law generally regards your nonmarital family. While the discussion in Chapter 8 is focused on custody issues when a married couple separates, much of the general advice also applies to custody of children of an unmarried couple.

If you can't reach an early compromise on the issues of custody (who has legal authority over the child and where does the child live), visitation (how often and under what conditions does the noncustodial parent spend time with the child), and child support (whether the noncustodial

Sample Settlement Agreement

Arnie Woo and Alice Isaacs agree as follows:

1. In exchange for the promises described in this agreement dated April 10, 20xx, we agree to settle all our disputes arising out of our personal relationship and the co-ownership of our residence at 997 Pine Road, Boston, Massachusetts (hereafter residence).

2. Arnie shall purchase Alice's interest in our residence under a separate Home Buyout Agreement signed this same date.

3. Alice shall have sole ownership of the Audi automobile currently registered in her name, and Arnie shall have sole ownership of the Jeep Cherokee currently in both parties' names, with no equalization payment due from or to either party. Alice shall sign the required transfer document for the Jeep, which Arnie shall prepare. Arnie shall be solely responsible for all transfer costs and taxes for the Jeep Cherokee.

4. We have divided and distributed all items of shared or co-owned personal property, and any items left remaining in the residence as of the date of this agreement shall be the property of Arnie.

5. Any disputes arising out of this agreement or out of our relationship shall be discussed in mediation, as follows:

   a. We will try to select a mediator jointly, and if no mediator is selected within two weeks of any demand for mediation, each one of us will nominate one friend, and the two of them shall select the mediator.

   b. We will meet no fewer than three times to mediate, in two-hour sessions, within one month of the selection of a mediator, with all costs of mediation split equally between us. The mediator will determine the time and place of each meeting.

   c. Until we reach an agreement, compromise offers or proposals presented by either of us will be confidential and, if mediation fails, will not be disclosed to anyone else or used in any subsequent arbitration or court proceeding.

   d. If we reach an agreement, it will be set out in writing and signed by both of us. If one of us fails to abide by it and an attorney is needed to enforce its terms in court, the prevailing party will have the right to reimbursement for his or her attorney's fees.

6. If, after we mediate on three occasions, no settlement is reached and we elect not to schedule any more mediation sessions, either of us may require arbitration by sending a written arbitration request to the other. If this occurs:

   a. We will jointly select an arbitrator who will conduct the arbitration under the rules of the American Arbitration Association. If for any reason we can't agree on an arbitrator within one month of the written demand for arbitration, Judge Marilyn Strauss of our local county court will select the arbitrator. By agreeing to arbitration, we each agree to give up the right to a jury trial.

   b. The costs of the arbitration will be split equally between the two of us. If either of us wishes to, she or he may bring an attorney to the hearing; however, each of us will be solely responsible for any attorneys' fees incurred.

   c. Each of us will provide the other with copies of all documents relevant to these disputes at least two weeks prior to the arbitration proceeding. At the same time, each of us will supply the other with a list of all witnesses who will be asked to testify at the arbitration hearing.

   d. The decision of the arbitrator will be binding, and either of us may enforce it through the local trial court if the other does not comply with its terms. If an attorney is needed to enforce the arbitration decision, the prevailing party will have the right to reimbursement of the attorney's fees incurred specifically for this purpose.

7. Contingent upon the implementation of the provisions of this agreement and the resolution of any disputes that arise in enforcing the terms of this agreement, we agree to release each other from any and all claims arising out of or relating to our personal relationship, including any claim for financial compensation or property ownership.

Arnie Woo	_April 10, 20xx_
Signature	Date
Alice Isaacs	_April 10, 20xx_
Signature	Date

parent contributes anything to the costs of raising the child), you will have to submit your dispute to the court system.

While the specific rules for child custody and visitation differ from state to state, here is a general overview.

Your Rights Under the Law

Your rights vary depending on whether one or both of you are legal parents of the child.

If Both of You Are Legal Parents

If both of you are legal parents of the child—either because you are both biological parents, because you have jointly adopted your child, or because the nonbiological parent has been able to obtain a legally valid stepparent or second-parent adoption—your child-related disputes will normally be handled in the same way as if you were a divorcing married couple. You may be required to attend mediation sessions or submit to an investigative process with county personnel. After listening to a county social worker's report about each of your parenting abilities and home situations, the local family court judge will have great discretion to make child custody and visitation decisions. The legal standard the judge will always follow is the "best interests of the child." In most states you can propose your own custody and visitation arrangements. If the judge believes these to be sensible (and especially if you both agree to follow them), the court will often approve your proposal. But if the judge doesn't agree with your proposal, the judge can substitute a modified or even completely different arrangement.

Where Paternity Is an Issue

Sometimes there is a disagreement over whether the male partner is really the father of a child raised by an unmarried couple. If a paternity or parenthood statement has not been signed when a breakup seems imminent, do it right away. (Chapter 7 discusses this in detail and provides a form.) It's important to everyone's interests (most especially the father's) that this step be accomplished. If for any reason the father refuses to sign, this is a strong indication that he may not support his child, and the mother will want to seriously consider going to court to get a judgment of paternity and a child support order.

Custody. In many states the court will order that both legal parents retain custody (sometimes called joint, or shared, legal custody). This means each parent has equal authority over the key decisions in the child's life (such as education and medical care), as well as a legal obligation to care for and support the child. Physical custody (where the child lives) is typically shared, with the child spending some days or weeks with one parent and living with the other parent at other times. In other states the court will award both parents "joint legal custody," but stipulate that one parent will be the "primary physical custodian." In still other states, it is far more common for the court to award one parent "primary physical custody," while the other is given "reasonable rights of visitation." But no matter what the legal description, the usual practical result is that the parent who isn't the primary caretaker during the school week is granted liberal rights to spend weekends or other time with the child (called visitation) unless there is a strong reason why this would be detrimental to the child.

Visitation. Like custody, you and your former partner can make visitation arrangements voluntarily. However, if your efforts are frustrated by the actions of the other parent (or someone else with physical custody of the child), you will have to file a court action and request that a judge order visitation.

Support. In every state, both legal parents are required to support their children, regardless of whether they were married when the child was born. When it comes to supporting a child financially, if parental incomes are unequal—or if one parent is shouldering most of the costs of taking care of the child—the family law court will order the noncustodial parent to contribute a specified sum of money to the costs of childrearing (called child support), often by referring to published guidelines establishing minimum levels of support. The family law court will retain the right to modify this amount should parental incomes or the needs of the children change.

The amount of child support awarded will depend on how much each parent makes and spends on housing, health care, and other necessary child-related expenses, including dental bills and private school tuition. The monthly amount can vary widely, and each state has its own child support guidelines that are set by statute. We encourage you to learn what the court would likely order in your particular situation, so that you have an idea of where to start in the negotiation process. Most family law practitioners are familiar with the standard child support formulas in your area, and there's lots of information available online as well. You can use a search engine to look for child support calculators for your state and get a general idea of how much support is appropriate in your case.

If support isn't paid voluntarily, the parent with custody or someone acting on the child's behalf (such as the welfare department) can sue the noncustodial parent to obtain a court order setting the amount of child support the noncustodial parent must pay. If the father doesn't pay, but has the ability to do so, the district attorney can prosecute him under criminal laws. County jails are full of fathers who don't take their support obligations seriously.

For more details on legal requirements regarding child support, see Chapter 8.

If Only One of You Is the Legal Parent

Where only one parent is the legal parent (for example, you came along after your partner's child was born and did not adopt the child), the legal situation is very different. In most states, the nonlegal parent has few legal rights, and in a few states, none at all. This is usually true even if the nonlegal parent has helped raise the child for many years and is a primary giver of care and emotional support.

In many states, the hard truth is that the nonlegal parent has no legal standing to seek custody, either partial or full. And, as if this isn't unfair enough, in some states the nonlegal parent doesn't even have the right to request court-ordered visitation privileges—no matter how emotionally close that parent had been to the child. A decision of the U.S. Supreme Court in 2000 (*Troxel v. Granville*, 530 U.S. 57 (2000)) denied grandparents the right to obtain legal visitation of their grandchildren over the mother's objection, and a similar outcome might result in a legal claim by a former partner.

Fortunately, an increasing number of states are beginning to recognize the right of nonlegal parents to visit the children they have helped raise; Ohio, Virginia, and Wyoming allow "any interested person" to bring an action for visitation, and Arizona allows visitation to persons who act as parents to a child. A few courts have even awarded custody to the nonlegal parent, especially where that person was the primary caregiver. And when the natural parent is unfit or deceased, it is more likely for courts to give the nonlegal parent a major child-rearing role (and sometimes to prefer the nonlegal parent to grandparents or other blood relatives).

Because the law does not fully recognize their relationship with the child, nonlegal parents rarely have any financial obligations to their partner's children. And where a nonlegal parent offers to help support the children in exchange for visitation or custody rights, most courts say no.

In some states, second-parent adoption may be available even if you and your partner are not living together any more. If the legal parent is willing to formalize the nonlegal parent's relationship with the child, consult a lawyer about whether a second-parent adoption is a possibility. If it is, you can incorporate a paragraph to the effect that you intend to complete a second-parent adoption into the parenting agreement shown below.

If you are being denied the right to continue actively participating in the life of a child you have helped raise, your first step should be to attempt to work with the legal parent to create a practical arrangement that meets the child's needs as well as yours. Failing this, you will need to consider whether it makes sense to attempt to achieve your goals by going to court. But before you do, you'll want to do the necessary legal research in your state or consult a lawyer to answer the following questions:

- Does your state allow you to present a claim for visitation or partial custody if you are not a legal parent? If so, what are the procedures you must follow? And what legal standards does the court follow in deciding whether to grant your request?

- If no such procedures have been established in your state or if the law is hostile to unmarried couples, are you willing to be a "test case" and try to forge new law?

TIP

The legal parent should put the child's interests first. If you are the legal parent and you are facing a custody and visitation challenge from your former partner, make your children's emotional needs—not yours—the highest priority. If your children want to remain in close contact with your ex (who they may have lived with for many years), put their wishes before your own. Of course, if you truly believe that your former partner's interaction with your kids will be seriously harmful, by all means resist his or her claims for custody or visitation.

Parenting Agreements

Because unmarried couples don't get divorces, judges and lawyers aren't necessarily involved in the child-raising issues. Unmarried couples can make their own parenting agreements covering support, custody, and visitation issues, either on their own or with the help of a mediator or family law counselor. If it's possible, this is the best approach. Be mindful, however, that if the physical or financial well-being of your child is at risk, most courts will not consider themselves bound by your agreement, and may order modifications or additional obligations. Also, if court proceedings are likely, you're unclear about your rights, or there's conflict between you and the other parent over key issues involving your child, consult an attorney.

Remember that each of your circumstances regarding jobs, residence, and relationships are likely to change, so it's a good idea to approach your agreement with a spirit of flexibility and openness. Also, no custody, support, or visitation agreement—even one ordered by a judge—is ever permanently binding. An amount of child support that seems fair and adequate today may not be enough tomorrow. Custody with one parent may work brilliantly for a year and then sour. Your agreement must be a living document, not a museum piece frozen under glass. It should be a statement of needs and expectations that lays a solid foundation for the changes and additions that will surely come.

Below are examples of two parenting agreements you can use as models to write your own:

- Parenting Agreement (Both Parents Are Legal Parents), and
- Parenting Agreement (Only One Parent Is a Legal Parent).

Be sure you both date and sign any agreement you reach and each keep a copy. It's a good idea to have your signed agreement notarized if you anticipate any future need (in court or arbitration) to prove that the signatures on the agreement are not forged.

CAUTION

Arbitration clauses may be unenforceable. In some states, you cannot make an agreement to arbitrate child custody. Check this out before including this provision in your agreement.

RESOURCE

Building a Parenting Agreement That Works: How to Put Your Kids First When Your Marriage Doesn't Last, **by Mimi Lyster (Nolo), is an excellent resource for preparing and negotiating a comprehensive parenting agreement covering custody and visitation.** We highly recommend you read this when preparing your own agreement.

Sample Parenting Agreement
(Both Parents Are Legal Parents)

Sam Matlock and Chris Woodling make this agreement because they have decided to stop living together, but wish to provide for the upbringing and support of their children, Natasha and Jason. Sam and Chris agree as follows:

1. Until Jason and Natasha are both in school, Chris will have primary responsibility for child care during the week and Sam shall pay child support to Chris in the amount of $800 per month per child.

2. Jason and Natasha will spend most weekends and at least one month during the summer with Sam; Sam will be available for babysitting at least two weekday nights.

3. All major decisions regarding Jason and Natasha's physical location, support, visitation, education, and the like will be made jointly by Sam and Chris; Jason and Natasha will be involved in the decision making to an extent consistent with their ages.

4. When both Natasha and Jason are in school, Chris intends to return to her career as a marketing consultant at least part-time and Sam intends to return to school to finish his Ph.D. Sam and Chris contemplate that during this period, Chris will earn enough to support the children and Sam will take on a larger share of the child care duties.

5. Both Sam and Chris commit themselves to conduct their affairs without resorting to lawyers and courts. If communication becomes difficult, they promise to participate in a program of joint counseling. If any issue becomes impossible to compromise, they will submit the dispute to binding arbitration.

6. Any dispute arising out of this agreement will be mediated by a third person mutually acceptable to both Sam and Chris. The mediator's role will be to help the parties arrive at a solution, not to impose one. If good faith efforts to arrive at a solution with the help of a mediator prove to be fruitless, either party may make a written request to the other that the dispute be arbitrated.

Sam Matlock _____   _May 4, 20xx_ _____
Signature   Date

Chris Woodling _____   _May 4, 20xx_ _____
Signature   Date

Sample Parenting Agreement
(Only One Parent Is a Legal Parent)

This agreement is made on January 1, 20xx, between Edward Donato and Sarah Friedan of Cincinnati, Ohio, regarding the parenting of the minor child Brenda Sue Donato.

We agree as follows:

1. This agreement concerns the parenting of Brenda, who was adopted legally by Ed on July 15, 20xx, six months before he met Sarah. Because Brenda has been raised equally in our home for the last several years and is equally bonded to both of us, we intend that Brenda shall continue to be raised by both of us.

2. We agree to work cooperatively to share physical custody of Brenda, and we agree that it is in Brenda's best interests that we continue to do so for the foreseeable future.

3. We shall each contribute equally to the financial costs of raising Brenda.

4. We agree that each of us will either maintain our current residence or will live within twenty (20) miles of the other's current residence until such time as Brenda reaches the age of 18, and that if either of us changes our residence outside of this distance without the other person's written consent, the person moving will lose the right to have Brenda in his or her physical custody (but not the right to visit with her frequently).

5. We agree that Sarah shall have the same rights and obligations to Brenda as if she were her legal parent. Should any dispute arise between the parties, Ed may not at any time assert that Sarah is not a parent of Brenda or that she has any lesser parental status than any other party, by virtue of the lack of legal parentage by Sarah.

6. In the event of any dispute between us regarding the custody, care, financial support, or upbringing of Brenda, we hereby agree that we will in good faith attend at least four mediation sessions, to be held weekly, with the cost of mediation to be shared equally by us.

7. We agree that the District Court of the State of Ohio will have jurisdiction to resolve all matters regarding the enforcement of this agreement and the custody, visitation, and support of Brenda. Specifically, Ed willingly agrees to allow the court to determine the custody, visitation, and/or support of Brenda without asserting as a defense Sarah's nonlegal parental status.

8. If any attorneys' fees or costs are incurred by either of us in a court proceeding regarding the custody, visitation, or child support of Brenda, then the court will have jurisdiction to award attorneys' fees and costs as provided by the relevant sections of this state's family code, even though the proceedings may be in a parentage or other action rather than in a dissolution or separation proceeding.

9. Sarah is hereby nominated by Ed as the guardian for the person and estate of Brenda, in the event that Ed becomes unable to care for Brenda, to serve without bond. If Sarah cannot serve as Brenda's guardian, then Ed's mother, Elaine Meritt, will be nominated to serve as guardian.

10. This agreement is the only agreement between us with respect to Brenda. It can only be changed if we both agree, and changes must be in writing. In the event that any part of this agreement is held to be invalid, the remainder of the agreement will be in full force and effect.

Edward Donato	_January 1, 20xx_
Signature	Date
Sarah Friedan	_January 1, 20xx_
Signature	Date

Lawyers and Legal Research

Although this book explains many of the legal issues faced by unmarried couples living together, here are some suggestions for those of you who wish to expand on what you learned here or get additional help from an expert.

The best ways to get more information are:

- **Legal research.** When you want more information on a specific legal issue, such as your state rules on common law marriage.

- **Do-it-yourself legal resources.** When you're ready to begin a routine legal proceeding, such as an uncontested divorce or child support modification, and want to use a book or other resource to help you do it yourself.

- **Small claims court.** When your dispute with your former partner concerns a relatively small amount of money, as might be the case when you don't agree about how to divide a rental deposit. Depending on the state, you can normally sue in small claims court for an amount between $2,500–$10,000 without the need for a lawyer.

- **Legal advice.** When you want specific information from a lawyer or want a lawyer to review a form you've prepared, such as a living together contract or will.

- **Mediation.** When you and your partner (or former partner) are disputing who owns what, how to divide jointly owned property, or another issue, such as child custody, and you want help in attempting to work out a solution.

- **Legal representation.** When you want to explore the possibility of initiating a lawsuit, or you're defending a lawsuit and want a lawyer to represent you. For example, if you claim that you and the person you lived with had an oral contract to share property, but that person denies it, formal legal help may be necessary. You will also need to hire a lawyer if you are going through a contested child custody case or are adopting a child with your partner.

Doing Your Own Legal Research

This book gives you a good start toward solving most of the legal issues facing unmarried couples. But many questions, especially specifics of state law, may not be answered here. This section explains how to research the law yourself.

Library Research

If you need to visit a law library to answer your question, don't overlook librarians as valuable guides. Most librarians in public law libraries are very helpful, as long as you don't expect them to do the research for you. They are usually happy to help you locate the materials you need.

Here's what you should find in an average law library:

- the text of your state's laws

- published court opinions interpreting your state's laws, and

- legal articles containing explanations of laws.

This means you can typically find and read any statute or case we've referred to in this book.

Finding a Law Library

To do legal research, you need to find a law library that's open to the public. Public law libraries are often housed in county courthouses, public law schools, and state capitals. If you can't find one, ask a public library reference librarian, court clerk, or lawyer. If there is no law library in your area that is open to the public, start your research at the largest nearby public library. Public libraries often have state codes and some major legal treatises.

This section explains the basic steps to researching a legal question.

RESOURCE

Nolo's website at www.nolo.com provides
an overview of legal research. For more in-depth help,
see *Legal Research: How to Find & Understand the Law*,
by Stephen Elias and Susan Levinkind (Nolo). This
nontechnical book gives easy step-by-step instructions
on how to find legal information.

Statutes and Regulations

Once you get to the library, ask a librarian to help
you locate the laws of your state—called "codes,"
"laws," or "statutes," depending on the state. You'll
want the annotated version, which contains the
statutes, excerpts from relevant cases, and cross-
references to related articles. You can also easily find
the statutes online—see "Online Legal Resources,"
below.

If you know the statute's number or citation, you
can go directly there. If you don't know the statute
number, and you're checking the laws online,
you can enter a "keyword" that is likely to be in
your state's law such as "unmarried couples" or
"custody." If you just want to browse through the
statutes, you can search the table of contents.

If you're looking at a hard copy of the statutes,
check the index to find the subject you are looking
for. State statutes are often divided into sections.
The major section is the Civil Code, which usually
contains laws relating to contracts, living together,
divorce, custody, adoption, and credit. In some
states there is a separate Family Code that deals
with the divorce and custody laws. The Probate
Code contains laws relating to wills. There are
other codes as well—insurance codes, real property
codes, criminal codes, and welfare codes. The
sections in each code are numbered sequentially,
and once you get the code number from the index,
it's easy to find the statute you need. If you have
trouble, ask the law librarian for help.

Once you look at the statute in the hardcover
volume, check the "pocket part" (annual update)
at the back of the book for any amendments.

Then skim the summaries of recent court decisions
contained in the Annotation section immediately
following the statute itself. If any summary looks
helpful, you'll want to read the entire case from
which the summary was taken.

Case Decisions

Judicial cases are printed in books called Reports.
In this book, we've included citations to some
important legal cases, in the event you want to read
the entire text. Interpreting a case citation is easy
once you learn the abbreviations.

A case citation normally has five elements:

1. The case name (names of the people or
   companies involved)
2. The specific volume of the series of books
   where the case is located
3. The name of the series (set) of books where the
   case is located
4. The page number
5. The year the case was decided

The California case that established the right of
unmarried couples to contract about their rights
and obligations is cited as:

1	2	3	4	5
Marvin v. Marvin,	557	P.2d	106	(1976).

Each state has its own "official" reporter for
appellate and Supreme Court cases, and each
official reporter has its own form of citation. For
example, California's official reports of the Supreme
Court are called the "California Reports" and
are abbreviated as Cal., Cal. 2d, Cal. 3d, or Cal.
4th, in order from the very first published case in
the first series (Cal.) to the most recent series of
books (Cal. 4th). Appellate court cases are called
"California Appellate Reports" and are reported as
Cal.App., Cal.App.2d, etc.

In addition to the official reports, private
companies publish unofficial books with the same

cases, as an alternative reference source. West Publishing Company puts out many of these alternate reporters. Some of these are regional, such as the Pacific Reporter (abbreviated P. or P.2d) and the Atlantic Reporter (abbreviated A. or A.2d). Some are specific to a state, such as the California Reporter (which is different from the California Official Reports, and which contains both appellate and Supreme Court opinions).

Often, case citations list every possible reference where you can find a copy of the case, so that whichever type of reporter your law library has, you will be able to find the case. For example, a complete citation for *Marvin v. Marvin* would be 18 Cal.3d 660, 557 P.2d 106, 134 Cal.Rptr. 815 (1976). The *Marvin* decision is the same, word for word, in each of these three books.

Family Law Resources

To find answers to legal questions involving unmarried couples, it helps to locate a good background resource specific to the legal area of family law. Here are several:

- *Family Law Reporter*—a newsletter, published by the Bureau of National Affairs, containing the text and synopses of important cases as they're decided. Older copies are bound together in volumes, with a subject index at the back to help you find what you need.
- *Family Law Quarterly*—a journal published by the American Bar Association. Every year in the winter issue, the journal summarizes family law in an article, "Family Law in the 50 States—An Overview," which lays out trends and new developments and contains much material on cohabitation.
- *American Law Reports*—a series of articles, published in five sets. Each article is about a particular point of law, and attempts to survey the field and gather all relevant cases on the topic. If you check the index under

"cohabitation," you'll find many articles. These volumes contain pocket parts that discuss new cases not included in the articles.

- *Clark's Hornbook on Domestic Relations, 2nd edition*—a one-volume "hornbook," meaning a book that summarizes the law in a given area. This book covers the basics of family law and includes cohabitation issues.

Online Legal Resources

The Internet can be a fabulous source of legal knowledge. Sites that may help with your legal research include:

- www.law.cornell.edu, a site maintained by Cornell Law School. You can find the text of federal court decisions and some state court decisions. There are also excellent summaries of law by topic.
- www.statelocalgov.net is a good source for finding local ordinances online and has links to many resources.
- www.unmarried.org, the website of the Alternatives to Marriage Project, includes updates on key rulings that affect unmarried couples.
- www.findlaw.com provides free access to legal resources, including some state and federal statutes.
- Nolo's website at www.nolo.com has free articles and information about issues affecting unmarried couples, as well as legal research tools.

Hiring a Lawyer

As a general rule, you should consider hiring an attorney if the amount at stake is high enough to justify the legal fees or if there is something the lawyer can do for you that you can't do or choose not to do yourself. There are many reasons you might want a hire a lawyer:

- to review documents you've prepared using this book, such as your living together agreement

- to complete more complex forms than we've provided—for example, if you have complicated estate planning needs

- to check your state laws or give you more information on a particular subject—for example, to confirm that you have a good case against an ex-partner

- to assist you in an adoption or real estate transaction, or

- to represent you in a breakup or help you obtain rights to a child you helped raise—whether in court or in a mediation session.

What Lawyers Can Do for You

There are three basic ways a lawyer can help you.

Consultation and advice. A lawyer can analyze your situation and advise you on your best plan of action. Ideally, the lawyer will explain all of your options so you can make the choice—for example, if you have a lot of assets and need a high-end estate plan. But keep on your toes. Some lawyers may subtly steer you in the direction they want you to go, and sometimes that will be the one that nets them the largest fee.

Negotiation. The lawyer can help you negotiate —perhaps if you and your ex are in the midst of a nasty breakup. Many lawyers excel at negotiating—especially if they use that skill a lot in their practice.

Representation. You'll need a lawyer to represent you if you believe your rights are being seriously violated or if there's a lot of money at stake. For example, if you and your living together partner have only an oral contract to share all property, and your partner dies with no will or other estate plan, you'll likely need a lawyer to help you assert your claim that a portion of the property in your deceased partner's name actually belongs to you. Also, for almost any situation involving children—like adoption (other than stepparent adoption), or

a fight to see a child you've been coraising—you will undoubtedly need a lawyer to represent you. You might also need representation if you've unsuccessfully tried every possibility to settle your breakup issues.

RESOURCE

If you do end up fighting in court, read *Represent Yourself in Court: How to Prepare & Try a Winning Case,* **by Paul Bergman and Sara J. Berman-Barrett (Nolo).** This book will help you pursue your own lawsuit or can help you understand and monitor what your lawyer is doing.

How to Find a Lawyer

If you do need a lawyer, realize that only a few lawyers know enough about living together issues to be worthy of serious consideration. Unfortunately, lawyers who don't know much about the law in this area (or who are even hostile to the idea of living together) can't always be trusted to decline this type of work. In short, it's up to you to be sure any lawyer you consult has the skills and experience you need.

There are several ways to find a good lawyer:

- **Personal referrals.** This is your best approach. If you know someone whose judgment you respect who was pleased with a lawyer who helped with a family law problem, call that lawyer first. Even if the lawyer can't take on your case or doesn't have the experience necessary, he or she will likely be able to recommend someone else who is experienced, competent, and available.

- **Prepaid legal help.** If you're a member of a prepaid legal plan that offers a certain amount of free advice for a yearly fee, your membership fee will normally entitle you to several free consultations. Obviously, you'll want to take advantage of this time, especially if you only need a document reviewed or want advice on a fairly routine issue.

Unfortunately, there's no guarantee that the lawyers available through these plans will know about the problems of unmarried couples. Also, whenever you use any service offered by a prepaid insurance plan, be forewarned: The lawyer is probably getting only a modest payment from the plan for dealing with you and may have agreed to this minimal amount in the hope of selling other legal services not covered by the monthly premium. So if a plan lawyer immediately recommends an expensive legal procedure, get a second opinion before you say yes.

- **Group legal practice.** Some unions, employers, and consumer action organizations offer group legal plans to their members or employees. These plans are provided by companies such as Prudential, LawPhone, Midwest Legal Services, and others. As with prepaid legal plans, the idea behind these programs is to allow members to obtain comprehensive legal assistance free or at low rates. If you're a member of such a plan, and the service you need is covered for free, start there. But some of these plans offer only a few free services, with the rest covered at a supposedly reduced rate. This can be a poor consumer deal. You may be referred to a lawyer who is not an expert in the problems of unmarried couples, or a lawyer who is overburdened with a large number of clients.

- **Lawyer referral panels.** Most county bar associations will provide the names of at least some attorneys who practice in the area. Typically, you can get a referral to an attorney who claims to specialize in family law, and an initial consultation, either for free or a low fee. A problem is that the bar association referrals usually provide only minimal screening of the attorneys listed, meaning that the lawyers who participate may not be the most experienced or competent in your area. Indeed, many lawyers who are well regarded in your community don't list with these services, because they already have more than enough business. Of course, you may find a skilled attorney willing to work for a reasonable fee this way, but before you become anyone's client, check out that lawyer's credentials, experience, and references.

- **Self-help clinics.** Many county bar associations and some law schools set up do-it-yourself clinics at little or no cost. These clinics often provide an overview of the procedure involved, assistance in completing forms, and help preparing to appear in court in areas such as obtaining temporary restraining orders, uncontested divorces, and guardianships. Many of these clinics are open only to low-income people, and most are limited to serving residents of a particular geographical area.

- **Yellow pages and Internet.** The yellow pages and Internet have extensive lists of attorneys, both by specialty and alphabetical order. Many of the ads quote initial consultation rates. If all else fails, let your fingers do the walking (or typing). But before you get extensively involved with a lawyer you don't know, ask for and check his or her references.

- **Online lawyer directories.** There are quite a few online lawyer directories that will help you find a lawyer in your area. Most of them are not very different from the yellow pages, in that they'll just provide you with a name, address, and telephone number. Nolo's lawyer directory is different, in that it provides detailed profiles of each lawyer who advertises there. Find the directory at www.lawyers.nolo.com.

What to Look for in a Lawyer

No matter what approach you take to finding a lawyer, here are some suggestions on how to make sure you have the best possible working relationship:

- **Determine the type of lawyer you need.** There's no such thing as a lawyer for all occasions. Some lawyers specialize in one narrow type of law (bankruptcy, for example), some are good negotiators, and a few pride themselves on being "fang dog" litigators. To avoid the serious initial mistake of hiring the wrong lawyer, determine exactly what you need done. The best lawyer to review a document may be different from the best lawyer to mediate a dispute or represent you in court.

- **Look for a family law specialist.** Keep in mind that lawyers learn mostly from experience and special training, not from law school, which rarely imparts any practical information. Start by asking any lawyer you're considering hiring what percentage of the lawyer's practice is in family law and how experienced the lawyer is in dealing with the problems of unmarried couples.

- **Work with a lawyer who advocates trying to settle disputes using nonadversarial techniques, such as mediation.** Only rarely does it make sense to take family disputes to court without first making a serious effort to mediate. (See Chapter 10 for more on how mediation works.)

- **Do some personality testing.** You should be personally comfortable with any lawyer you hire. When making an appointment, ask to talk directly to the lawyer. If you can't, this may be a hint as to how accessible he or she is. When you talk to or meet with the lawyer, ask specific questions. Do you get clear, concise answers? If the lawyer says little except to suggest that you let the firm handle the problem, watch out. Don't be a passive client or deal with a lawyer who wants you to be one.

- **Pay particular attention to how the lawyer responds to your already having considerable information.** Just by reading this book, you're far better informed about the law concerning unmarried couples than are most clients.

Some lawyers are threatened when a client is knowledgeable, while others are pleased to deal with an informed person. Find out which type you're dealing with at the outset.

- **Look for a lawyer coach.** Often what you need is a helping hand with paperwork or a bit of advice, but not formal legal representation. The good news is that there are far more lawyers who will help you help yourself than there used to be. The bad news is that most lawyers still do not embrace this "lawyer coach" model, and therefore you may have to conduct a fairly extensive search to find one.

- **Money matters.** Fees—how much you'll pay for legal services—are one of the biggest bones of contention and biggest areas of misunderstanding between a lawyer and client. Don't be afraid to bring up the subject. In many states, a lawyer must give you a written fee agreement (contract) if your bill is expected to be more than a certain amount—often $1,000. That contract must explain the fees and charges, define the services to be provided, and describe the lawyer's, and your, responsibilities. Even if your state doesn't require a lawyer to do this, it's a good idea to request such a fee agreement.

  If you're in doubt about what you are being charged for, ask direct questions about what the quoted fee covers. For example, many lawyers will charge you separately for the costs of filing and serving legal documents and often for other things, like copying charges; others will include this in their overall fee. You should be able to find an attorney willing to represent you for either a flat rate or an hourly rate of, say, $175–$250, depending on where the lawyer's office is (city lawyers tend to be pricier) and how complex your case is (extensive court time will cost). Contingency fee cases, where the lawyer takes money only if your case is won, are generally prohibited in family law cases.

- **Think it over.** Once you find a lawyer you like, make a one- or two-hour appointment to fully discuss your situation. Be ready to pay on the spot, and then go home and think about what the lawyer recommends and how much it will cost. If the lawyer's advice doesn't make complete sense, or you have other reservations, call someone else.

Firing a Lawyer

One major problem people often have when dealing with lawyers is knowing when and how to fire them. Basically, you have the right to fire a lawyer at any time, although, of course, you're obligated to pay for any authorized services that have already been performed.

Sometimes when a lawyer is fired, it's because a client believes the lawyer has provided incompetent or unethical service or has overcharged. If this is your situation, immediately call your state bar association and ask for information on how to file a formal complaint against the lawyer.

How to Use the CD-ROM

The tear-out forms in Appendix B are included on a CD-ROM in the back of the book. Please read this appendix and the ReadMe.txt file included on the CD-ROM for instructions on using it.

In accordance with U.S. copyright laws, the CD-ROM and its files are for your personal use only.

The CD-ROM can be used with Windows computers. It is not a standalone software program. It installs files that use software programs that need to be on your computer already.

Note to Mac users: This CD-ROM and its files should also work on Macintosh computers. Please note, however, that Nolo cannot provide technical support for non-Windows users.

How to View the README File

To view the file ReadMe.txt, insert the CD-ROM into your computer's CD-ROM drive and follow these instructions:

- **Windows 2000, XP, and Vista:** (1) On your PC's desktop, double click the My Computer icon; (2) double click the icon for the CD-ROM drive into which the CD-ROM was inserted; (3) double click the ReadMe.txt file.
- **Macintosh:** (1) On your Mac desktop, double click the icon for the CD-ROM that you inserted and (2) double click on the ReadMe.txt file.

Installing the Form Files Onto Your Computer

Before you can do anything with the files on the CD-ROM, you need to install them onto your computer.

Insert the CD-ROM and do the following.

Windows 2000, XP, and Vista

Follow the instructions that appear on the screen.

If nothing happens when you insert the CD-ROM, then (1) double click the My Computer icon; (2) double click the icon for the CD-ROM drive that you inserted the CD-ROM into; (3) double click the file Setup.exe.

Macintosh

If the "Living Together CD" window is not open, open it by double clicking the "Living Together CD" icon.

(1) Select the "Living Together Forms" folder icon and (2) drag and drop the folder icon onto your computer.

Where Are the Files Installed?

Windows 2000, XP, and Vista

- RTF files are installed by default to a folder named \Living Together Forms in the \Program Files folder of your computer.

Macintosh Users

- RTF files are located in the "Living Together Forms."

Using the Word Processing Files to Create Documents

The CD-ROM includes word processing files that you can open, complete, print, and save with your word processing program. All word processing forms come in rich text format and have the extension ".RTF." For example, the form for the Will discussed in Chapter 9 is on the file Will.rtf. RTF files can be read by most recent word processing programs including MS Word, Windows WordPad, and recent versions of WordPerfect.

The following are general instructions. Because each word processor uses different commands to open, format, save, and print documents, refer to your word processor's help file for specific instructions.

Do not call Nolo's technical support if you have questions on how to use your word processor or your computer.

Opening a File

You can open word processing files with any of the three following ways:

1. Windows users can open a file by selecting its "shortcut." (1) Click the Windows "Start" button; (2) open the "Programs" folder; (3) open the "Living Together Forms" folder; (4) click the shortcut to the form you want to work with.

2. Both Windows and Macintosh users can open a file by double clicking it. (1) Use My Computer or Windows Explorer (Windows 2000, XP, or Vista) or the Finder (Macintosh) to go to the Living Together Forms folder and (2) double click the file you want to open.

3. Windows and Macintosh users can open a file from within their word processor. (1) Open your word processor; (2) go to the File menu and choose the Open command. This opens a dialog box where (3) you will select the location and name of the file. (You will navigate to the version of the Living Together Forms folder that you've installed on your computer.)

Editing Your Document

Here are tips for working on your document.

Refer to the book's instructions and sample agreements for help.

Underlines indicate where to enter information, frequently including bracketed instructions. Delete the underlines and instructions before finishing your document.

Signature lines should appear on a page with at least some text from the document itself.

Editing Forms That Have Optional or Alternative Text

Some forms have check boxes that appear before text. Check boxes indicate:

- Optional text that you can choose to include or exclude.
- Alternative text that you select to include, excluding the other alternatives.

If you are using the tear-out forms in Appendix B, mark the appropriate box to make your choice.

If you are using the CD-ROM, we recommend doing the following:

Optional text

Delete optional text you do not want to include and keep the text that you do want to use. In either case, delete the check box and the italicized instructions. If you choose to delete an optional numbered clause, renumber the subsequent clauses after deleting it.

Alternative text

Delete the alternatives that you do not want to include first. Then delete the remaining check boxes, as well as the italicized instructions that you need to select one of the alternatives provided.

Printing Out the Document

Use your word processor's or text editor's "Print" command to print out your document.

Saving Your Document

Use the "Save As" command to save and rename your document. You will be unable to use the "Save" command because the files are "read-only." If you save the file without renaming it, the underlines that indicate where you need to enter your information will be lost, and you will be unable to create a new document with this file without recopying the original file from the CD-ROM.

Forms on the CD-ROM

The following files are in rich text format (RTF):

File Name	Form Title
NoCommonLaw.rtf	Agreement of Joint Intent Not to Have a Common Law Marriage
PropertySeparate.rtf	Agreement to Keep Property Separate
AttachmentA.rtf	Attachment A—Separately Owned Property
ShareProperty.rtf	Agreement to Share Property
AttachmentB.rtf	Attachment B—Jointly Owned Property
JointPurchase.rtf	Agreement for a Joint Purchase
RentedSpace.rtf	Agreement Covering Rented Living Space
AddRoommate.rtf	Letter Requesting Permission to Add a Roommate
EqualOwnership.rtf	Contract for Equal Ownership of a House
PromissoryNote.rtf	Promissory Note
UnequalOwnership.rtf	Contract for Unequal Ownership of a House
ImmediateCo-Owner.rtf	Agreement for One Person to Move Into the Other's House and Become an Immediate Co-Owner
GradualCo-Owner.rtf	Agreement for One Person to Move Into the Other's House and Become a Co-Owner Gradually
Parenthood.rtf	Acknowledgment of Parenthood
Will.rtf	Will
Codicil.rtf	Codicil
SeparationHousing.rtf	Short-Term Agreement Regarding Separation and Housing
ProtectProperty.rtf	Agreement to Protect Property During a Breakup
Mediate.rtf	Agreement to Mediate and Arbitrate
HomeBuyout.rtf	Home Buyout Agreement

Tear-Out Forms

Chapter	Form Name
2	Agreement of Joint Intent Not to Have a Common Law Marriage
3	Agreement to Keep Property Separate
3	Attachment A (Separately Owned Property)
3	Agreement to Share Property
3	Attachment B (Jointly Owned Property)
3	Agreement for a Joint Purchase
5	Agreement Covering Rented Living Space
5	Letter Requesting Permission to Add a Roommate
6	Contract for Equal Ownership of a House
6	Promissory Note
6	Contract for Unequal Ownership of a House
6	Agreement for One Person to Move Into the Other's House and Become an Immediate Co-Owner
6	Agreement for One Person to Move Into the Other's House and Become a Co-Owner Gradually
7	Acknowledgment of Parenthood
9	Will
9	Codicil
10	Short-Term Agreement Regarding Separation and Housing
10	Agreement to Protect Property During a Breakup
10	Agreement to Mediate and Arbitrate
10	Home Buyout Agreement

Agreement of Joint Interest Not to Have a Common Law Marriage

_____ and _____

agree as follows:

We have been and plan to continue living together as two free, independent beings and neither of us
has ever intended to enter into any form of marriage, common law or otherwise.

_____   _____

Signature   Date

_____   _____

Signature   Date

Agreement to Keep Property Separate

_____ and _____

agree as follows:

1. This contract sets forth our rights and obligations toward each other. We intend to abide by its provisions in a spirit of cooperation and good faith.

2. All property owned by either of us as of the date of this agreement will remain the separate property of its owner and cannot be transferred to the other person unless this is done in writing. We have each attached a list of our major items of separate property to this contract. (See Attachment A, Separately Owned Property.)

3. The income each of us earns—as well as any items or investments either of us purchases with our income—belongs absolutely to the person who earns the money unless there is a written joint ownership agreement as provided in Clause 6.

4. We will each maintain our own separate bank, credit card, investment, and retirement accounts, and neither of us will in any way be responsible for the debts of the other (if we register as domestic partners in a community that makes this option available and, by so doing, the law requires us to be responsible for each other's basic living expenses, we agree to assume the minimum level of reciprocal responsibility required by the law).

5. Expenses for routine household items and services, which include groceries, utilities, rent, and cleaning supplies, will be shared equally.

6. From time to time, we may decide to keep a joint checking or savings account for a specific purpose (for example, to pay household expenses), or to own some property jointly (for example, to purchase a television). If so, the details of our joint ownership agreement will be put in writing (either in a written contract or a deed, title slip, or other joint ownership document).

7. Should either of us receive real or personal property by gift or inheritance, the property belongs absolutely to the person receiving the gift or inheritance and cannot be transferred to the other except in writing.

8. In the event we separate, each of us will be entitled to immediate possession of our separate property.

9. Any dispute arising out of this contract will be mediated by a third person mutually acceptable to both of us. The mediator's role will be to help us arrive at our solution, not to impose one on us. If good faith efforts to arrive at our own solution to all issues in dispute with the help of a mediator prove to be fruitless, either of us may make a written request to the other that the dispute be arbitrated. In that case, our dispute will be submitted to arbitration under the rules of the American Arbitration Association, and one arbitrator will hear our dispute. The decision of the arbitrator will be binding on us and will be enforceable in any court that has jurisdiction over the controversy. By agreeing to arbitration, we each agree to give up the right to a jury trial.

10. This agreement represents our complete understanding regarding our living together and replaces any and all prior agreements, written or oral. It can be amended, but only in writing, and any amendments must be signed by both of us.

11. If a court finds any portion of this contract to be illegal or otherwise unenforceable, the remainder of the contract is still in full force and effect.

_____   _____
Signature   Date

_____   _____
Signature   Date

Attachment A

Separately Owned Property

The following is the separate personal property of _____:

_____

_____

_____

_____

_____

_____

_____

_____

_____

_____

_____

_____

_____

_____

_____

_____

_____

_____

The following is the separate personal property of _____:

_____

_____

_____

_____

_____

_____

_____

_____

_____

_____

_____

_____

_____

_____

_____

_____

_____

_____

Agreement to Share Property

_____ and _____

agree as follows:

1. This contract sets forth our rights and obligations toward each other. We intend to abide by this agreement in a spirit of cooperation and good faith.

2. All earned income received by either of us after the date of this contract and all property purchased with this income belongs in equal shares to both of us with the following exceptions:

   _____

   _____

   _____ .

3. All real or personal property earned or accumulated by either of us prior to the date of this agreement (except jointly owned property listed in Attachment B of this agreement), including all future income this property produces, is the separate property of the person who earned or accumulated it and cannot be transferred to the other except in writing. Attached to this agreement in the form of Attachments A, Separately Owned Property, and B, Jointly Owned Property, are lists of the major items of property each of us owns separately and both of us own jointly as of the date of this agreement.

4. Should either of us receive real or personal property by gift or inheritance, that property, including all future income it produces, belongs absolutely to the person receiving the gift or inheritance and cannot be transferred to the other except in writing.

5. In the event we separate, all jointly owned property will be divided equally.

6. Any dispute arising out of this contract will be mediated by a third person mutually acceptable to both of us. The mediator's role will be to help us arrive at our solution, not to impose one on us. If good faith efforts to arrive at our own solution to all issues in dispute with the help of a mediator prove to be fruitless, either of us may make a written request to the other that the dispute be arbitrated. In that case, our dispute will be submitted to arbitration under the rules of the American Arbitration Association, and one arbitrator will hear our dispute. The decision of the arbitrator will be binding on us and shall be enforceable in any court that has jurisdiction over the controversy. By agreeing to arbitration, we each agree to give up the right to a jury trial.

7. This agreement represents our complete understanding regarding our living together and replaces any and all prior agreements, written or oral. It can be amended, but only in writing, and any amendments must be signed by both of us.

8. If a court finds any portion of this contract to be illegal or otherwise unenforceable, the remainder of the contract is still in full force and effect.

_____   _____
Signature   Date

_____   _____
Signature   Date

Attachment B

Jointly Owned Property

The following property is jointly owned by _____ and _____
in equal proportions except as other noted:

_____

_____

_____

_____

_____

_____

_____

_____

_____

_____

_____

_____

_____

_____

_____

_____

_____

_____

_____

_____

_____

_____

_____

_____

_____

_____

_____

_____

_____

_____

_____

_____

Agreement for a Joint Purchase

_____ and _____

agree as follows:

1. We will jointly acquire and own a _____ (the Property) at a cost of $_____ .

2. We will own the Property in the following shares:

   _____ will own _____ % of the Property and _____ will own _____ % of the Property.

3. Should we separate and cease living together, one of the following will occur:

   a. If one of us wants the Property and the other doesn't, the person who wants the Property will pay the other the fair market value (see Clause 4) of his or her share of the Property.

   b. If both of us want the Property, the decision will be made in the following way [_choose one_]:

   ☐ (1) Right of First Refusal. _____ shall have the right of first refusal and may purchase _____ share of the Property for its fair market value (see Clause 4). _____ will then become sole owner of the Property.

   ☐ (2) Coin Toss Method. We will flip a coin to determine who is entitled to the Property. The winner, upon paying the loser for his or her share of ownership, will become the sole owner of the Property.

   ☐ (3) Other. _____ .

4. Should either of us decide to end the relationship, we will do our best to agree on the fair current value of the Property. If we can't agree on a price, we will jointly choose a neutral appraiser and abide by that person's decision.

5. Should we separate and neither of us wants the Property—or if we can't agree on a fair price—we will advertise it to the public, sell it to the highest bidder, and divide the money according to our respective ownership shares as set forth in Clause 2.

6. Should either of us die while we are living together, the Property will belong absolutely to the survivor. (If either of us makes a will or other estate plan, this agreement shall be reflected in that document.)

7. This agreement can be changed, but only in writing, and any changes must be signed by both of us.

8. Any dispute arising out of this contract will be mediated by a third person mutually acceptable to both of us. The mediator's role will be to help us arrive at our solution, not to impose one on us. If good faith efforts to arrive at our own solution to all issues in dispute with the help of a mediator prove to be fruitless, either of us may pursue other legal remedies.

9. If a court finds any portion of this contract to be illegal or otherwise unenforceable, the remainder of the contract is still in full force and effect.

_____   _____
Signature   Date

_____   _____
Signature   Date

Agreement Covering Rented Living Space

_____ and _____ agree that:

1. We will jointly rent _____. We have both signed a _____ with the landlord, _____, and have each paid $_____ towards the security deposit of $_____ .

2. Each of us will pay one-half of the rent and one-half of the utilities, including the basic monthly telephone, cable, and DSL charges. We will each keep track of and pay for our own long distance calls. Rent will be paid on the first of each month and utilities within ten days of when the bill is received. Utilities will be in the name of

   _____ .

3. If either of us wants to move out, the one moving will give the other and the landlord 30 days' written notice and will pay his/her share of the rent for the entire 30-day period even if he/she moves out sooner.

4. No third person will be invited to stay in the apartment without the agreement of both.

5. If one of us no longer wishes to live with the other, but both want to keep the apartment, the following will occur:

   ☐ _____ has first rights to stay in the apartment and _____ will move out.

   ☐ We will ask a third person to flip a coin to see who gets to stay.

   ☐ The person who needs the apartment most will retain it. Need will be determined by a third party whom we agree is objective, within two weeks of the date when one informs the other that he/she wishes to separate. In making this decision, the third party will consider each person's relative financial condition, proximity to work, the needs of any minor children, and _____ _[list any other important factors]_____ .

   ☐ Other. _____ .

   The person who is to leave will do so within _____ of when that decision is made, and will have an additional _____ to pay his/her obligations for rent, utilities, and any damage to the apartment.

6. Any dispute arising out of this agreement will be mediated by a third person mutually acceptable to both of us. The mediator's role will be to help us arrive at a solution, not to impose one on us. If good faith efforts to arrive at our own solution with the help of a mediator prove to be fruitless, either of us may make a written request to the other that the dispute be arbitrated. If such a request is made, our dispute will be submitted to arbitration under the rules of the American Arbitration Association, and one arbitrator will hear our dispute. The decision of the arbitrator will be binding on us and shall be enforceable in any court that has jurisdiction over the controversy. By agreeing to arbitration, we each agree to give up the right to a jury trial.

7. Additional agreements: _____ .

8. This agreement represents our complete understanding regarding our living together and replaces any prior agreements, written or oral. It can be amended, but only in writing, and any amendments must be signed by both of us.

9. If a court finds any portion of this contract to be illegal or otherwise unenforceable, the remainder of the contract is still in full force and effect.

_____   _____
Signature   Date

_____   _____
Signature   Date

Letter Requesting Permission to Add a Roommate

_____

_____

_____

_____

_____

_____

Dear _____ :

     I live at the above address and regularly pay rent to your office. I would like to add a second person, _____ , to my _____ beginning _____ . He/She will be glad to complete a rental application and provide a recent copy of his/her credit report and references.

     I will call you soon to discuss this further. Thank you very much for considering this request.

Very truly yours,

_____

Signature

Contract for Equal Ownership of a House

_____ and _____ make the

following agreement to jointly purchase and own the house at _____

_____ (hereafter house):

1. We will purchase the house for $_____ (including closing costs).

2. We will take title as:

   ❏ tenants in common, or

   ❏ joint tenants with right of survivorship.

3. We will each contribute one-half of the down payment and closing costs and pay one-half of the required payments for the mortgage, homeowners' insurance, property taxes, costs for needed repairs and routine maintenance, and _____ . Any improvements to the house costing more than $_____ will be made by mutual consent with each of us agreeing to pay half for all such improvements.

4. Should either of us decide to end the relationship and cease living together, one of the following will occur:

   (a) If one person wants to stay and the other wants to move on, the person staying will pay the person leaving fair market value (see Clause 5) for his or her share within 90 days. When payment is made, the person selling his or her share will deed the house to the person buying the house. The person buying the house will ensure that the selling partner's name is taken off the mortgage. If the lender refuses to remove the selling partner's name from the mortgage, the buying partner will obtain a new loan in his or her name only. If the buying partner cannot obtain a new loan in his or her name only, the house shall be sold.

   (b) If both of us want to keep the house, we will try to reach a mutually satisfactory agreement for one to buy out the other. If by the end of two weeks we can't, the decision will be made as follows:

   ❏ (1) Right of First Offer. _____ shall have the right of first offer. This means that _____ may purchase _____ share of the house within 90 days for its fair market value (see Clause 5). If _____ does not make full payment during this 90-day period, _____ shall have an additional 90 days in which to buy out _____ share for its fair market value. When payment is made, the person leaving will deed the house to the person retaining it in his or her name alone. The person buying the house will ensure that the selling partner's name is taken off the mortgage. If the lender refuses to remove the selling partner's name from the mortgage, the buying partner will obtain a new loan in his or her name only. If neither person exercises his or her buyout right, or if the buying partner cannot obtain a new loan in his or her name only, the house shall be sold.

   ❏ (2) Coin Toss Method. A friend will be asked to flip a coin within 60 days of our decision to separate. The winner of the coin toss is entitled to buy out the loser's share, provided the winner pays the loser fair market value (see Clause 5) within 90 days. If full payment isn't made during this period, the loser of the coin toss will have an additional 90 days in which to buy out the winner's share of the property at fair market value (see Clause 5). When payment is made, the person leaving will deed the house to the person retaining it in his or her name alone. The person buying the house will ensure that the selling partner's name is taken off the mortgage. If the lender refuses to remove the selling partner's name from the mortgage, the buying partner will obtain a new loan in his or her name only. If the buying partner cannot obtain a new loan in his or her name only, the house shall be sold.

❑ (3) Other. _____

_____ .

(c) If neither of us wants to own the house or payment isn't made within 90 days, the house will be sold and the profits divided as follows: _____ .

(d) We are both responsible for our share of the mortgage, insurance, and taxes until the house is sold or it changes ownership. If one of us moves out of the house before it is sold, the remaining person will make a good faith effort to find a tenant who will pay a fair market rent. Assuming a tenant is found, the rental amount will be credited against the departing partner's payment for shared housing costs.

5. Should either of us decide to end the relationship, we will do our best to agree on the fair market value of our house. However, if we can't agree, we will jointly choose and pay for the services of a licensed real estate appraiser to conduct an appraisal, and abide by the result. If we can't agree on an appraiser in the first place, each of us will independently retain and pay for the services of a licensed real estate appraiser. The fair market value of the house will be the average of the two appraisals. "Fair market value" for one person's share of the property is defined as an amount equal to the fair market value of the entire property, less the then-current mortgage amount, multiplied by that person's percentage ownership interest in the property.

6. Should either of us die, the survivor, if he or she has not become the owner of 100% of the deceased person's share through joint tenancy or a will, has the right to purchase the portion of the property given or left to someone else at the fair market value (to be arrived at under the terms of Clause 5) within 200 days of the date of death.

7. If either of us is unable or unwilling to pay his or her share of the mortgage, taxes, or insurance payments in a timely manner, the other may make those payments. The extra payments will be treated as a personal loan to be paid back by the person on whose behalf they are made within six months, including _____% interest per annum. If the loan isn't repaid in six months, the debtor must vacate the house and either sell his or her interest to the other party (in which case the buying partner must ensure that the selling partner's name is removed from the mortgage, as set forth in Clause 4) or agree to sell the entire property at fair market value which will be established by appraisal as set out in Clause 5.

8. This contract is binding on our heirs and our estates.

9. Any dispute arising out of this agreement will be mediated by a third person mutually acceptable to both of us. The mediator's role will be to help us arrive at a solution, not to impose one on us. If good faith efforts to arrive at our own solution with the help of a mediator prove to be fruitless, either of us may make a written request to the other that the dispute be arbitrated. If such a request is made, our dispute will be submitted to arbitration under the rules of the American Arbitration Association, and one arbitrator will hear our dispute. The decision of the arbitrator will be binding on us and will be enforceable in any court that has jurisdiction over the controversy. By agreeing to arbitration, we each agree to give up the right to a jury trial.

_____   _____
Signature   Date

_____   _____
Signature   Date

Promissory Note

(Loan Repayable in Installments With Interest)

Name of Borrower: _____

Name of Lender: _____

1. For value received, Borrower promises to pay to Lender the amount of $ _____
   at _____
   [address where payments are to be sent] at the rate of _____% per year from the date this note was
   signed until the date it is paid in full no later than _____ .
   Borrower will receive credits for prepayments, reducing the total amount of interest to be repaid.

2. Borrower agrees that this note shall be paid in installments, which include principal and interest, of
   not less than $_____ per month, due on the first day of each month, until such time as the principal
   and interest are paid in full.

3. If any installment payment due under this note is not received by Lender within _____ days of its
   due date, the entire amount of unpaid principal shall become immediately due and payable at the option of
   Lender without prior notice to Borrower.

4. In the event Lender prevails in a lawsuit to collect on it, Borrower agrees to pay Lender's attorney fees in an
   amount the court finds to be just and reasonable.

_____   _____

Borrower's signature   Date

_____

Print name

Contract for Unequal Ownership of a House

_____ and _____ make the
following agreement to jointly purchase and own the house at _____
(hereafter house):

1. We will purchase the house for $_____ (including closing costs).

2. We will take title as tenants in common with the following shares:

   _____   _____%

   _____   _____%

3. _____ will contribute _____% and _____ will contribute _____% of the down
   payment and closing costs. _____ will pay _____% and _____ will pay _____%
   of the required payments for the mortgage, homeowners' insurance, property taxes, and
   _____. All use-related expenses and maintenance will be paid equally. Any
   improvements to the house costing more than $_____ will be made by mutual consent with each of
   us agreeing to pay half, and each shall contribute equally to all such improvements.

4. Should either of us decide to end the relationship and cease living together, one of the following will occur:

   (a) If one person wants to stay and the other wants to move on, the person staying will pay the person leaving
       fair market value (see Clause 5) for his or her share within 90 days. When payment is made, the person
       selling his or her share will deed the house to the person buying the house. The person buying the house
       will ensure that the selling partner's name is taken off the mortgage. If the lender refuses to remove the
       selling partner's name from the mortgage, the buying partner will obtain a new loan in his or her name
       only. If the buying partner cannot obtain a new loan in his or her name only, the house shall be sold.

   (b) If both of us want to keep the house, we will try to reach a mutually satisfactory agreement for one to
       buy out the other. If by the end of two weeks we can't, the decision will be made as follows:

   ❏ (1) Right of First Offer. If both of us want to keep the house, _____ will have the right of
      first offer. This means that _____ may purchase _____ share of the house within 90
      days for its fair market value (see Clause 5). If _____ does not make full payment during
      this 90-day period, _____ will have an additional 90 days in which to buy out _____
      share for its fair market value. When payment is made, the person leaving will deed the house to the
      person retaining it in his or her name alone. The person buying the house will ensure that the selling
      partner's name is taken off the mortgage. If the lender refuses to remove the selling partner's name
      from the mortgage, the buying partner will obtain a new loan in his or her name only. If neither person
      exercises his or her buyout right, or if the buying partner cannot obtain a new loan in his or her name
      only, the house shall be sold.

   ❏ (2) Coin Toss Method. A friend will be asked to flip a coin within 60 days of our decision to separate.
      The winner of the coin toss is entitled to buy out the loser's share, provided the winner pays the loser
      fair market value (see Clause 5) within 90 days. If full payment isn't made during this period, the loser
      of the coin toss will have an additional 90 days in which to buy out the winner's share of the property
      at fair market value (see Clause 5). When payment is made, the person leaving will deed the house to
      the person retaining it in his or her name alone. The person buying the house will ensure that the selling
      partner's name is taken off the mortgage. If the lender refuses to remove the selling partner's name from
      the mortgage, the buying partner will obtain a new loan in his or her name only. If the buying partner
      cannot obtain a new loan in his or her name only, the house will be sold.

❑ (3) Other. _____

_____

_____

    (c) If neither of us wants to own the house or payment isn't made within 90 days, the house will be sold and the profits divided as follows: _____ and _____ .

    (d) We are both responsible for our share of the mortgage, insurance, and taxes until the house is sold or it changes ownership. If one of us moves out of the house before it is sold, the remaining person will make a good faith effort to find a tenant who will pay a fair market rent. Assuming a tenant is found, the rental amount will be credited against the departing partner's payment for shared housing costs.

5. Should either of us decide to end the relationship, we will do our best to agree on the fair market value of our house. However, if we can't agree, we will jointly choose and pay for the services of a licensed real estate appraiser to conduct an appraisal, and we will abide by the result. If we can't agree on an appraiser in the first place, each of us will independently retain and pay for the services of a licensed real estate appraiser. The fair market value of the house will be the average of the two appraisals. "Fair market value" for one person's share of the property is defined as an amount equal to the fair market value of the entire property, less the then-current mortgage amount, multiplied by that person's percentage ownership interest in the property.

6. Should either of us die, the survivor, if he or she has not become the owner of 100% of the deceased person's share through a will, has the right to purchase the portion of the property given or left to someone else at the fair market value of that share (to be arrived at under the terms of Clause 5) within 200 days of the date of death.

7. If either of us is unable or unwilling to pay his or her share of the mortgage, taxes, or insurance payments in a timely manner, the other may make those payments. These payments will be treated as a personal loan to be paid back by the person on whose behalf they are made within six months, including _____ % interest per annum. If the loan isn't repaid in six months, the debtor must vacate the house and either sell his or her interest (in which case the buying partner must ensure that the selling partner's name is removed from the mortgage, as set forth in Clause 4) or agree to sell the entire property at fair market value which will be established by appraisal as set out in Clause 5.

8. This contract is binding on our heirs and our estates.

9. Any dispute arising out of this agreement will be mediated by a third person mutually acceptable to both of us. The mediator's role will be to help us arrive at a solution, not to impose one on us. If good faith efforts to arrive at our own solution with the help of a mediator prove to be fruitless, either of us may make a written request to the other that the dispute be arbitrated. If such a request is made, our dispute will be submitted to arbitration under the rules of the American Arbitration Association, and one arbitrator will hear our dispute. The decision of the arbitrator will be binding on us and will be enforceable in any court that has jurisdiction over the controversy. By agreeing to arbitration, we each agree to give up our right to a jury trial.

_____   _____

Signature   Date

_____   _____

Signature   Date

Agreement for One Person to Move Into the Other's House and Become an Immediate Co-Owner

_____ and _____ agree as follows:

1. _____ now owns the house at _____ (hereafter house).

2. The fair market value of the house is currently $_____ .

3. Equity in the house (fair market value less mortgage and other house-related indebtedness) is $_____ .

4. _____ hereby sells _____% of the equity in the house to _____ for $_____ , retaining a _____% interest in the house.

5. We will take title as [_choose one_]:

   ❏ tenants in common with the following shares:

   _____   _____%

   _____   _____%

   ❏ joint tenants with right of survivorship.

6. Payment is due as follows [_choose one_]:

   ❏ full payment of $_____ is due upon signing of this agreement.

   ❏ beginning with the first of the month after this contract is signed, payment will be made in equal monthly installments, including simple interest of _____% per year, and this agreement will be recorded in a separate promissory note.

7. All future housing costs, including payments for the mortgage, homeowners' insurance, property taxes, and _____ , will be split as follows: _____ . All use-related expenses (including utilities and the cost of routine repairs) and maintenance will be split as follows: _____ . Any improvements to the house costing more than $_____ will be made by mutual consent with each of us agreeing to pay half, and each shall contribute equally to all such improvements.

8. Should either of us decide to end the relationship and cease living together, one of the following will occur:

   (a) If one person wants to stay and the other wants to move on, the person staying will pay the person leaving fair market value (see Clause 9) for his or her share within 90 days. When payment is made, the person selling his or her share will deed the house to the person buying the house. The person buying the house will ensure that the selling partner's name is taken off the mortgage. If the lender refuses to remove the selling partner's name from the mortgage, the buying partner will obtain a new loan in his or her name only. If the buying partner cannot obtain a new loan in his or her name only, the house will be sold.

   (b) If both of us want to keep the house, we will try to reach a mutually satisfactory agreement for one to buy out the other. If by the end of two weeks we can't, the decision will be made as follows:

      ❏ (1) Right of First Offer. If both of us want to keep the house, _____ shall have the right of first offer. This means that _____ may purchase _____ share of the house within 90 days for its fair market value (see Clause 9). If _____ does not make full payment during this

90-day period, _____ shall have an additional 90 days in which to buy out _____ share for its fair market value. When payment is made, the person leaving will deed the house to the person retaining it in his or her name alone. The person buying the house will ensure that the selling partner's name is taken off the mortgage. If the lender refuses to remove the selling partner's name from the mortgage, the buying partner will obtain a new loan in his or her name only. If neither person exercises his or her buyout right, or if the buying partner cannot obtain a new loan in his or her name only, the house shall be sold.

❑ (2) Coin Toss Method. A friend will be asked to flip a coin within 60 days of our decision to separate. The winner of the coin toss is entitled to buy out the loser's share, provided the winner pays the loser fair market value (see Clause 9) within 90 days. If full payment isn't made during this period, the loser of the coin toss will have an additional 90 days in which to buy out the winner at fair market value (see Clause 9). When payment is made, the person leaving will deed the house to the person retaining it in his or her name alone. The person buying the house will ensure that the selling partner's name is taken off the mortgage. If the lender refuses to remove the selling partner's name from the mortgage, the buying partner will obtain a new loan in his or her name only. If the buying partner cannot obtain a new loan in his or her name only, the house shall be sold.

❑ (3) Other. _____
_____ .

(c) If neither of us wants to own the house or payment on a buyout isn't made within 90 days, the house will be sold and the profits divided as follows: _____ .

(d) We are both responsible for our share of the mortgage, insurance, and taxes until the house is sold or it changes ownership. If one of us moves out of the house before it is sold, the remaining person will make a good faith effort to find a tenant who will pay a fair market rent. Assuming a tenant is found, the rental amount will be credited against the departing partner's payment for shared housing costs.

9. Should either of us decide to end the relationship, we will do our best to agree on the fair market value of our house. However, if we can't agree, we will jointly choose and pay for the services of a licensed real estate appraiser to conduct an appraisal, and we will abide by the result. If we can't agree on an appraiser in the first place, each of us will independently retain and pay for the services of a licensed real estate appraiser. The fair market value of the house will be the average of the two appraisals. "Fair market value" for one person's share of the property is defined as an amount equal to the fair market value of the entire property, less the then-current mortgage amount, multiplied by that person's percentage ownership interest in the property.

10. Should either of us die, the survivor, if he or she has not become the owner of 100% of the deceased person's share through joint tenancy or a will, has the right to purchase the portion of the property given or left to someone else at the fair market value of that share (to be arrived at under the terms of Clause 9) within _____ days of the date of death.

11. If either of us is unable or unwilling to pay his or her share of the mortgage, taxes, or insurance payments in a timely manner, the other may make those payments. These payments will be treated as a personal loan to be paid back by the person on whose behalf they are made within _____ months, including _____% interest per annum. If the loan isn't repaid in six months, the debtor must vacate the house and either sell his or her interest (in which case the buying partner must ensure that the selling partner's name is removed from the mortgage, as set forth in Clause 4) or agree to sell the entire property at fair market value, which will be established by appraisal as set out in Clause 9.

12. This contract is binding on our heirs and our estates.

13. Any dispute arising out of this agreement will be mediated by a third person mutually acceptable to both of us. The mediator's role will be to help us arrive at a solution, not to impose one on us. If good faith efforts to arrive at our own solution with the help of a mediator prove to be fruitless, either of us may make a written request to the other that the dispute be arbitrated. If such a request is made, our dispute will be submitted to arbitration under the rules of the American Arbitration Association, and one arbitrator will hear our dispute. The decision of the arbitrator will be binding on us and will be enforceable in any court that has jurisdiction over the controversy. By agreeing to arbitration, we each agree to give up the right to a jury trial.

_____   _____
Signature   Date

_____   _____
Signature   Date

Agreement for One Person to Move Into the Other's House and Become a Co-Owner Gradually

_____ and _____ agree as follows:

1. _____ owns the house at _____ , (hereafter house) subject to a mortgage with the _____ in the amount of $_____ .

2. The fair market value of the house is currently $_____ .

3. _____ equity in the house (fair market value less mortgage or other house-related indebtedness) is $_____ .

4. Beginning with the date this contract is signed, _____ will pay all monthly expenses for the mortgage, homeowners' insurance, property taxes, utilities, and necessary repairs and maintenance, estimated to be $_____ per month, and will continue to do so until his or her total payments equal $_____ or until we separate or agree to modify this agreement, after which the payments will be split equally.

5. _____ share of the total net equity of the house shall be figured at the rate of _____ for every month that he or she pays all of the expenses as set out in Clause 4, based on $_____ of the monthly payment contribution counted as the equity buy-in amount. For example, if _____ pays all the expenses for two years, his or her interest in the house equity shall be _____%.

6. _____ shall deed the house to _____ as "Tenants in Common" and record the deed and this contract, upon the signing of this agreement.

7. Should we separate prior to the time that _____ contributes $_____ , _____ shall have first right to remain in the house and buy out _____ equity share as determined by Clause 5. _____ shall leave within 30 days of the decision to separate.

8. Once _____ contributes $_____ , the house shall be owned equally by both of us, and all expenses for taxes, mortgage, insurance, and repairs shall be shared equally.

9. Should we separate after the time that _____ contributes $_____ , one of the following will occur:

    (a) If one person wants to stay and the other wants to move on, the person staying will pay the person leaving fair market value (see Clause 10) for his or her percentage share at the time, within 90 days. When payment is made, the person selling his or her share will deed the house to the person buying the house. The person buying the house will ensure that the selling partner's name is taken off the mortgage. If the lender refuses to remove the selling partner's name from the mortgage, the buying partner will obtain a new loan in his or her name only. If the buying partner cannot obtain a new loan in his or her name only, the house shall be sold.

    (b) If both of us want to keep the house, we will try to reach a mutually satisfactory agreement for one to buy out the other. If by the end of two weeks we can't, the decision will be made as follows:

    ❏ (1) Right of First Offer. If both of us want to keep the house, _____ shall have the right of first offer. This means that _____ may purchase _____ share of the house within 90 days for its fair market value (see Clause 10). If _____ does not make full payment during this 90-day period, _____ shall have an additional 90 days in which to buy out _____ share for its fair market value. When payment is made, the person leaving will deed the house to the person retaining it in his or her name alone. The person buying the house will ensure that the selling partner's name is taken off the mortgage. If the lender refuses to remove the selling partner's name from the mortgage, the buying partner will obtain a new loan in his or her name only. If neither person exercises his or her buyout right, or if the buying partner cannot obtain a new loan in his or her name only, the house shall be sold.

❏ (2) Coin Toss Method. A friend will be asked to flip a coin within 60 days of our decision to separate. The winner of the coin toss is entitled to buy out the loser's share, provided the winner pays the loser fair market value (see Clause 10) within 90 days. If full payment isn't made during this period, the loser of the coin toss will have an additional 90 days in which to buy out the winner's share of the property at fair market value (see Clause 10). When payment is made, the person leaving will deed the house to the person retaining it in his or her name alone. The person buying the house will ensure that the selling partner's name is taken off the mortgage. If the lender refuses to remove the selling partner's name from the mortgage, the buying partner will obtain a new loan in his or her name only. If the buying partner cannot obtain a new loan in his or her name only, the house shall be sold.

❏ (3) Other. _____
_____ .

(c) If neither of us wants to own the house or payment isn't made within 90 days, the house will be sold and the profits divided as follows: _____ .

(d) We are both responsible for our share of the mortgage, insurance, and taxes until the house is sold or it changes ownership. If one of us moves out of the house before it is sold, the remaining person will make a good faith effort to find a tenant who will pay a fair market rent. Assuming a tenant is found, the rental amount will be credited against the departing partner's payment for shared housing costs.

10. Should either of us decide to end the relationship, we will do our best to agree on the fair market value of our house. However, if we can't agree, we will jointly choose and pay for the services of a licensed real estate appraiser to conduct an appraisal, and abide by the result. If we can't agree on an appraiser in the first place, each of us will independently retain and pay for the services of a licensed real estate appraiser. The fair market value of the house will be the average of the two appraisals. "Fair market value" for one person's share of the property is defined as an amount equal to the fair market value of the entire property, less the then-current mortgage amount, multiplied by that person's percentage ownership interest in the property.

11. Should either of us die, the survivor, if he or she has not become the owner of 100% of the deceased person's share through joint tenancy or a will, has the right to purchase the portion of the property given or left to someone else at the fair market value of that share (to be arrived at under the terms of Clause 10) within _____ days of the date of death.

12. This contract is binding on our heirs and our estates.

13. Any dispute arising out of this agreement will be mediated by a third person mutually acceptable to both of us. The mediator's role will be to help us arrive at a solution, not to impose one on us. If good faith efforts to arrive at our own solution with the help of a mediator prove to be fruitless, either of us may make a written request to the other that the dispute be arbitrated. If such a request is made, our dispute will be submitted to arbitration under the rules of the American Arbitration Association, and one arbitrator will hear our dispute. The decision of the arbitrator will be binding on us and will be enforceable in any court that has jurisdiction over the controversy. By agreeing to arbitration, we each agree to give up the right to a jury trial.

_____   _____
Signature   Date

_____   _____
Signature   Date

Acknowledgment of Parenthood

_____ and _____ hereby acknowledge that

they are the biological parents of _____ ,

born _____ , in _____ .

_____ and _____ further state that they have

welcomed _____ into their home and that it's their

intention and belief that _____ is fully legitimate for

all purposes, including the right to inherit from and through both parents.

_____ and _____ further expressly acknowledge

their duty to raise and support _____ .

We declare under penalty of perjury that the information set forth in this document is true and correct.

_____   _____

Signature   Date

_____   _____

Signature   Date

Will

Will of _____

I, _____ , a

resident of _____ County,

_____ , declare that this is my will.

I. Revocation

I revoke all wills and codicils that I have previously made.

II. Children

A.   I have _____ children now living, whose names and dates of birth are:

_____   _____

Name   Date of Birth

[repeat as needed]

The terms "my children" as used in this will shall include any other children hereafter born to or adopted by me.

B.   I have the following grandchildren who are the children of my deceased child:

_____   _____

Name   Date of Birth

[repeat as needed]

C.   If at my death any of my children are minors, and a guardian is needed, I nominate _____ _____ as personal guardian of my minor children. If he/she cannot, or declines to, serve, I nominate _____ as personal guardian. I nominate _____ to be appointed guardian of the property of my minor children. If _____

cannot, or declines to, serve, I nominate _____ to

be appointed guardian of the property of my minor children.

III. Gifts

A. I make the following gifts of money or personal property:

    1. I give the sum of $_____ to _____

       if he/she/it survives me by 30 days; if he/she/it doesn't, this gift shall be made to

       _____ .

[repeat as needed]

    2. I give _____

       to _____

       if he/she/it survives me by 30 days; if he/she/it doesn't, the gift shall be made to

       _____ .

[repeat as needed]

    3. I forgive and cancel the debt of $_____ owed to me by

       _____ .

[repeat as needed]

B. I make the following gifts of real estate:

    1. I give my interest in the real estate in _____

       commonly known as _____ ,

       to _____

       if he/she/it survives me for 30 days. If he/she/it doesn't survive me for 30 days, that property shall

       be given to _____ .

[repeat as needed]

IV. Residue

I give the residue of my property subject to this will as follows:

A. To _____

    if he/she/it survives me by 30 days.

B. If not, to _____

    if he/she/it survives me by 30 days.

C. If neither _____

    nor _____ survives me by

    30 days, then to _____ .

V. Executor

A. I nominate _____ as executor of this

    will, to serve without bond. If _____ for any reason

    fails to qualify or ceases to act as executor, I nominate _____ to serve

    without bond.

B. I grant to my executor the right to place my obituary of her/his choosing in the papers she/he thinks

    appropriate.

VI. No Contest

If any person named to receive any of my property under my will, in any manner contests or attacks
this will or any of its provisions, that person shall be disinherited and shall receive none of my property,
and my property shall be disposed of as if that contesting beneficiary had died before me leaving no
children.

///

///

///

VII. Simultaneous Death

If _____ and I should die simultaneously, or under such circumstances as to render it difficult or impossible to determine who predeceased the other, I shall be conclusively presumed to have survived _____ for purposes of this will.

Signature

I subscribe my name to this will this _____ day of _____ , _____ , at _____ , _____ , _____ , and declare that I sign and execute this Will willingly and as my free and voluntary act and that I am under no constraint or undue influence.

_____

Signature

Witnesses

On this _____ day of _____ , _____ , _____ declared to us, the undersigned, that this instrument, consisting of _____ pages, was his/her will, and requested us to act as witnesses to it. He/She thereupon signed this will in our presence, all of us being present at the time. We now, at his/her request, in his/her presence and in the presence of each other, subscribe our names as witnesses and declare we understand this to be his/her will, and that to the best of our knowledge the testator is competent to make a will, and under no constraint or undue influence.

We declare under penalty of perjury that the foregoing is true and correct.

_____

Witness's Signature

_____

Address

_____

Witness's Signature

_____

Address

_____

Witness's Signature

_____

Address

Codicil

_____ Codicil to the Will of _____ dated

_____ , _____ .

I, _____ , a resident

of _____ County, _____ , declare this to be

the first codicil to my will dated _____ , _____ .

First. I revoke Item _____ of Clause _____ , and substitute the following:

_____

_____

_____

_____

_____ .

Second. I add the following new Item _____ to Clause _____ :

_____

_____

_____

_____

_____ .

Third. In all other respects I confirm and republish my will dated _____ , _____ .

I subscribe my name to this codicil this _____ day of _____ ,

_____ , at _____ , and declare that I sign and execute

this codicil willingly and as my free and voluntary act and that I am under no constraint or undue

influence.

_____

Signature

On the date written below,_____

declared to us, the undersigned, that this instrument, consisting of _____ pages, including this

page signed by us as witnesses, was the _____ codicil to his/her will and requested us to act as

witnesses to it. He/she thereupon signed this codicil in our presence, all of us being present at the same

time. We now, at his/her request, in his/her presence and in the presence of each other, subscribe our

names as witnesses, and declare we understand this to be his/her codicil, and that to the best of our

knowledge the testator is competent to make a will, and under no constraint or undue influence.

Executed on _____ , _____ , at _____ ,

_____ .

We declare under penalty of perjury that the foregoing is true and correct.

_____
Witness's Signature

_____
Address

_____
Witness's Signature

_____
Address

_____
Witness's Signature

_____
Address

Short-Term Agreement Regarding Separation and Housing

_____ and _____ agree as follows:

1. We have agreed to live apart, effective _____ .

2. _____ will remain in our apartment at _____ , and _____ agrees to move out no later than _____ . If _____ elects to leave any of his or her personal belongings behind, he or she will remove them no later than _____ , at his or her expense, giving _____ prior notice of time of pickup. Any of _____ personal belongings that he or she does not remove prior to _____ may be retained or disposed of by _____ , unless we jointly agree in writing to another plan.

3. Any household expenses incurred prior to _____ will be split between us, following our usual allocation. Any household expenses incurred after _____ will be the sole responsibility of _____ , even if _____ remains until _____ .

4. Housing costs will be split as follows:

   ❑ (a) Renters

   _____ will be solely responsible for any and all rent due on or after _____ . The security deposit in the sum of $_____ will be retained by _____ , in exchange for the agreement to pay the utility bills, telephone bills, and insurance incurred on or after _____ .

   ❑ (b) Homeowners

   Bills and expenses. Effective _____ , since _____ will be living in the residence, he or she will pay all monthly bills, including mortgage payments, insurance, utilities, and day-to-day maintenance costs (to unplug a toilet, for example). Property taxes and all necessary major repairs (to fix a leak in the roof or replace the furnace, for example) will be split by us equally. So long as we both continue to pay our share of these major expenses, we both shall be entitled to half of any increase in property values between _____ and the time the house is sold.

   House ownership. We both agree to make a good faith effort to promptly resolve the issue of which of us will own the residence long-term (or whether it will be sold). _____ agreement to vacate the residence at this time shall not be interpreted as a waiver of his or her claim to an equal share of the equity, either through a buyout or a market sale. Unless an agreement is reached by _____ or we agree jointly in writing to extend this agreement, the property shall be listed for sale on _____ and, after paying off the mortgage and other house-related debts, the proceeds of sale shall be split equally between us.

5. Any disputes arising out of this agreement will be submitted first to mediation. We both agree to meet in good faith with a mediator for no fewer than _____ meetings in a month's time, with expenses to be shared equally. If any disputes remain unresolved after the mediation, the disputes will be submitted to binding arbitration, with the costs of the arbitration split equally between us. By agreeing to arbitration, we each agree to give up the right to a jury trial.

_____   _____
Signature   Date

_____   _____
Signature   Date

Agreement to Protect Property During a Breakup

_____ and _____ agree as follows:

1. We disagree over who has the right to retain the following items of personal property: _____
    _____ .

2. In order to resolve this dispute, we have agreed to place these items in storage at the _____
    _____ . _____ will pay the monthly cost of storage, and our friend
    _____ will retain the only key. Neither of us will attempt to gain access to this locker or
    remove any items from it until we have resolved this dispute.

3. If we are unable to resolve this dispute within _____ of today, we will attempt
    to resolve the dispute in mediation, meeting with a mediator chosen by _____ and
    approved by both of us. If mediation does not result in a settlement, we will submit the dispute to
    binding arbitration, with the arbitrator chosen by _____ and approved by both of
    us.

4. Upon settlement of the dispute or receipt of the arbitrator's decision, _____ will
    open the locker and we will each take the items awarded to us or as agreed upon by us.

_____   _____
Signature   Date

_____   _____
Signature   Date

Agreement to Mediate and Arbitrate

_____ and _____ agree as follows:

1. We have agreed to submit the following disputes to mediation, and if mediation is unsuccessful, to arbitration:

   _____

   _____

   _____

   _____

   _____

   _____

   _____

   _____ .

2. We agree to discuss these areas of dispute in mediation, as follows:

   a. We will try to select a mediator jointly, and if no mediator is selected by _____ , each one of us will nominate one friend, and the two of them shall select the mediator.

   b. We shall meet no fewer than _____ times to mediate, within _____ of the selection of a mediator, with all costs of mediation split equally between us. The mediator will determine the time and place of each meeting. Each session will be at least two hours long.

   c. Until we reach an agreement, compromise offers or proposals presented by either of us shall be confidential and, if mediation fails, will not to be disclosed to anyone else or used in any subsequent arbitration or court proceeding.

   d. If an agreement is reached, it shall be set out in writing and signed by both of us. If one of us fails to abide by it and an attorney is needed to enforce its terms in court, the prevailing party shall have the right to reimbursement of attorney's fees.

3. If after we mediate on _____ occasions no settlement is reached and we elect not to schedule any more mediation sessions, either of us may require arbitration by sending a written arbitration request to the other. If this occurs:

   a. We will jointly select an arbitrator who will conduct an arbitration under the rules of the American Arbitration Association. If for any reason we can't agree on an arbitrator within _____ of the written demand for arbitration, _____ will select the arbitrator. By agreeing to arbitration, we each agree to give up the right to a jury trial.

   b. The costs of the arbitration will be split equally between the two of us. If either of us wishes to, she or he may bring an attorney to the hearing; however, each of us will be solely responsible for any attorneys' fees we incur.

c. Each of us will provide the other with copies of all documents relevant to these disputes at least

_____ prior to the arbitration proceeding. At the same time, each of us will supply

the other with a list of all witnesses who will be asked to testify at the arbitration hearing.

d. The decision of the arbitrator will be binding, and either of us may enforce it through the local trial court

if the other does not comply with its terms. If an attorney is needed to enforce the arbitration decision,

the prevailing party will have the right to reimbursement of the attorney's fees incurred specifically for

this purpose.

_____   _____

Signature   Date

_____   _____

Signature   Date

Home Buyout Agreement
(One Co-Owner Sells to the Other)

_____ and _____ have agreed to settle

the ownership of their house at _____ , as follows:

1. _____ will purchase _____ interest in the house by paying him or her

    $_____ , no later than _____ . Within _____ of this payment,

    _____ shall deliver to _____ a signed and notarized quitclaim deed to the

    property. _____ will handle the recordation of the deed and pay all costs of transfer.

2. _____ agrees to purchase _____ interest knowing that _____

    _____ .

    _____ releases _____ from these or any other claims arising out of the condition

    of the property or the title to the property.

3. _____ agrees to keep his/her name on the current mortgage for at least

    _____ , by which time _____ shall either obtain a new mortgage that does

    not involve _____ or sell the property.

4. _____ will be responsible for any and all costs and obligations regarding the property,

    including all mortgage debt, as of _____ .

5. Either party may compel enforcement of this agreement by arbitration, at which the arbitrator may
    award attorneys' fees and costs to the prevailing party.

_____   _____

Signature   Date

_____   _____

Signature   Date

Index

A

CATALOG

BUSINESS

	PRICE	CODE
Business Buyout Agreements (Book w/CD)	$49.99	BSAG
The California Nonprofit Corporation Kit (Binder w/CD)	$69.99	CNP
California Workers' Comp: How to Take Charge When You're Injured on the Job	$34.99	WORK
The Complete Guide to Buying a Business (Book w/CD)	$24.99	BUYBU
The Complete Guide to Selling a Business (Book w/CD)	$34.99	SELBU
Consultant & Independent Contractor Agreements (Book w/CD)	$29.99	CICA
The Corporate Records Handbook (Book w/CD)	$69.99	CORMI
Create Your Own Employee Handbook (Book w/CD)	$49.99	EMHA
Dealing With Problem Employees	$44.99	PROBM
Deduct It! Lower Your Small Business Taxes	$34.99	DEDU
Effective Fundraising for Nonprofits	$24.99	EFFN
The Employer's Legal Handbook	$39.99	EMPL
The Essential Guide to Family and Medical Leave (Book w/CD)	$39.99	FMLA
The Essential Guide to Federal Employment Laws	$39.99	FEMP
The Essential Guide to Workplace Investigations (Book w/CD)	$39.99	NVST
Every Nonprofit's Guide to Publishing (Book w/CD)	$29.99	EPNO
Form a Partnership (Book w/CD)	$39.99	PART
Form Your Own Limited Liability Company (Book w/CD)	$44.99	LIAB
Home Business Tax Deductions: Keep What You Earn	$34.99	DEHB
How to Form a Nonprofit Corporation (Book w/CD)—National Edition	$49.99	NNP
How to Form a Nonprofit Corporation in California (Book w/CD)	$49.99	NON
How to Form Your Own California Corporation (Binder w/CD)	$59.99	CACI
How to Form Your Own California Corporation (Book w/CD)	$39.99	CCOR
How to Run a Thriving Business	$19.99	THRV
How to Write a Business Plan (Book w/CD)	$34.99	SBS
Incorporate Your Business (Book w/CD)	$49.99	NIBS
Investors in Your Backyard (Book w/CD)	$24.99	FINBUS
The Job Description Handbook (Book w/CD)	$29.99	JOB
Legal Guide for Starting & Running a Small Business	$34.99	RUNS
Legal Forms for Starting & Running a Small Business (Book w/CD)	$29.99	RUNSF
LLC or Corporation?	$24.99	CHENT
The Manager's Legal Handbook	$39.99	ELBA
Marketing Without Advertising	$20.00	MWAD
Music Law: How to Run Your Band's Business (Book w/CD)	$39.99	ML
Negotiate the Best Lease for Your Business	$24.99	LESP
Nolo's Quick LLC	$29.99	LLCQ
Patent Savvy for Managers: Spot & Protect Valuable Innovations in Your Company	$29.99	PATM
The Performance Appraisal Handbook (Book w/CD)	$29.99	PERF
The Progressive Discipline Handbook (Book w/CD)	$34.99	SDHB
The Small Business Start-up Kit (Book w/CD)—National Edition	$24.99	SMBU
The Small Business Start-up Kit for California (Book w/CD)	$24.99	OPEN
Starting & Building a Nonprofit: A Practical Guide (Book w/CD)	$29.99	SNON
Starting & Running a Successful Newsletter or Magazine	$29.99	MAG
Tax Deductions for Professionals	$34.99	DEPO
Tax Savvy for Small Business	$36.99	SAVVY
Wow! I'm in Business	$19.99	WHOO
Working for Yourself: Law & Taxes for Independent Contractors, Freelancers & Consultants	$39.99	WAGE
Working With Independent Contractors (Book w/CD)	$29.99	HICI
Your Limited Liability Company: An Operating Manual (Book w/CD)	$49.99	LOP
Your Rights in the Workplace	$29.99	YRW

Prices subject to change.

CONSUMER

	PRICE	CODE
How to Win Your Personal Injury Claim	$29.99	PICL
Nolo's Encyclopedia of Everyday Law	$29.99	EVL
Nolo's Guide to California Law	$24.99	CLAW
Your Little Legal Companion (Hardcover)	$9.95	ANNI

ESTATE PLANNING & PROBATE

	PRICE	CODE
8 Ways to Avoid Probate	$19.99	PRAV
The Busy Family's Guide to Estate Planning (Book w/CD)	$24.99	FAM
Estate Planning Basics	$21.99	ESPN
The Executor's Guide: Settling a Loved One's Estate or Trust	$34.99	EXEC
Get It Together: Organize Your Records (Book w/CD)	$21.99	GET
How to Probate an Estate in California	$49.99	PAE
Make Your Own Living Trust (Book w/CD)	$39.99	LITR
Nolo's Simple Will Book (Book w/CD)	$36.99	SWIL
Plan Your Estate	$44.99	NEST
Quick & Legal Will Book (Book w/CD)	$19.99	QUIC
Special Needs Trust: Protect Your Child's Financial Future (Book w/CD)	$34.99	SPNT

FAMILY MATTERS

	PRICE	CODE
Always Dad: Being a Great Father During & After a Divorce	$16.99	DIFA
Building a Parenting Agreement That Works	$24.99	CUST
The Complete IEP Guide	$34.99	IEP
Divorce & Money: How to Make the Best Financial Decisions During Divorce	$34.99	DIMO
Divorce Without Court: A Guide to Mediation & Collaborative Divorce	$29.99	DWCT
Do Your Own California Adoption: Nolo's Guide for Stepparents & Domestic Partners (Book w/CD)	$34.99	ADOP
Every Dog's Legal Guide: A Must-Have for Your Owner	$19.99	DOG
Get a Life: You Don't Need a Million to Retire Well	$24.99	LIFE
The Guardianship Book for California	$34.99	GB
A Judge's Guide to Divorce (Book w/CD)	$24.99	JDIV
A Legal Guide for Lesbian and Gay Couples (Book w/CD)	$34.99	LG
Living Together: A Legal Guide for Unmarried Couples (Book w/CD)	$34.99	LTK
Nolo's Essential Guide to Divorce	$24.99	NODV
Nolo's IEP Guide: Learning Disabilities	$29.99	IELD
Parent Savvy	$19.99	PRNT
Prenuptial Agreements: How to Write a Fair & Lasting Contract (Book w/CD)	$34.99	PNUP
Work Less, Live More: The Way to Semi-Retirement	$17.99	RECL
The Work Less, Live More Workbook (Book w/CD)	$19.99	RECW

GOING TO COURT

	PRICE	CODE
Becoming a Mediator	$19.99	BECM
Beat Your Ticket: Go To Court & Win!—National Edition	$21.99	BEYT
The Criminal Law Handbook: Know Your Rights, Survive the System	$39.99	KYR
Everybody's Guide to Small Claims Court—National Edition	$29.99	NSCC
Everybody's Guide to Small Claims Court in California	$29.99	CSCC
Fight Your Ticket & Win in California	$29.99	FYT
How to Change Your Name in California	$34.99	NAME
Legal Research: How to Find & Understand the Law	$39.99	LRES
Nolo's Deposition Handbook	$34.99	DEP
Represent Yourself in Court: How to Prepare & Try a Winning Case	$39.99	RYC
Win Your Lawsuit: A Judge's Guide to Representing Yourself in California Superior Court	$39.99	SLWY

HOMEOWNERS, LANDLORDS & TENANTS

	PRICE	CODE
Buying a Second Home (Book w/CD)	$24.99	SCND
The California Landlord's Law Book: Rights & Responsibilities (Book w/CD)	$44.99	LBRT
The California Landlord's Law Book: Evictions (Book w/CD)	$44.99	LBEV
California Tenants' Rights	$29.99	CTEN
Deeds for California Real Estate	$27.99	DEED
Every Landlord's Legal Guide (Book w/CD)	$44.99	ELLI
Every Landlord's Guide to Finding Great Tenants (Book w/CD)	$19.99	FIND
Every Landlord's Tax Deduction Guide	$34.99	DELL
Every Tenant's Legal Guide	$29.99	EVTEN

	PRICE	CODE
For Sale by Owner in California (Book w/CD)	$29.99	FSBO
How to Buy a House in California	$34.99	BHCA
Leases & Rental Agreements (Book w/CD)	$29.99	LEAR
Neighbor Law: Fences, Trees, Boundaries & Noise	$26.99	NEI
Nolo's Essential Guide to Buying Your First Home (Book w/CD)	$24.99	HTBH
Renters' Rights: The Basics	$24.99	RENT

IMMIGRATION

	PRICE	CODE
Becoming A U.S. Citizen: A Guide to the Law, Exam and Interview	$24.99	USCIT
Fiancé & Marriage Visas	$34.99	IMAR
How to Get a Green Card	$29.99	GRN
U.S. Immigration Made Easy	$39.99	IMEZ

MONEY MATTERS

	PRICE	CODE
101 Law Forms for Personal Use (Book w/CD)	$29.99	SPOT
Chapter 13 Bankruptcy: Repay Your Debts	$39.99	CHB
Credit Repair (Book w/CD)	$24.99	CREP
How to File for Chapter 7 Bankruptcy	$29.99	HFB
IRAs, 401(k)s & Other Retirement Plans: Taking Your Money Out	$34.99	RET
Lower Taxes in 7 Easy Steps	$16.99	LTAX
The New Bankruptcy: Will It Work for You?	$21.99	FIBA
Solve Your Money Troubles	$19.99	MT
Stand Up to the IRS	$29.99	SIRS
Surviving an IRS Tax Audit	$24.95	SAUD

PATENTS & COPYRIGHTS

	PRICE	CODE
All I Need Is Money: How to Finance Your Invention	$19.99	FINA
The Copyright Handbook: What Every Writer Needs to Know (Book w/CD)	$39.99	COHA
Getting Permission: How to License and Clear Copyrighted Materials (Book w/CD)	$34.99	RIPER
How to Make Patent Drawings	$29.99	DRAW
The Inventor's Notebook	$24.99	INOT
Legal Guide to Web & Software Development (Book w/CD)	$44.99	SFT
Nolo's Patents for Beginners	$24.99	QPAT
Patent, Copyright & Trademark: An Intellectual Property Desk Reference	$39.99	PCTM
Patent It Yourself	$49.99	PAT
Patent Pending in 24 Hours	$34.99	PEND
Patent Savvy for Managers: Spot & Protect Valuable Innovations in Your Company	$29.99	PATM
Profit from Your Idea (Book w/CD)	$34.99	LICE
The Public Domain	$34.99	PUBL
Trademark: Legal Care for Your Business and Product Name	$39.99	TRD
What Every Inventor Needs to Know About Business & Taxes (Book w/CD)	$21.99	ILAX

SENIORS

	PRICE	CODE
Long-Term Care: How to Plan & Pay for It	$19.99	ELD
Social Security, Medicare & Goverment Pensions	$29.99	SOA

SOFTWARE Call or check our website at www.nolo.com for special discounts on Software!

	PRICE	CODE
LLC Maker—Windows	$89.95	LLP1
Patent Pending Now!	$119.99	PP1
PatentEase—Windows	$349.00	PEAS
Personal RecordKeeper 5.0 CD—Windows	$59.95	RKD5
Quicken Legal Business Pro 2008—Windows	$109.99	SBQB8
Quicken WillMaker Plus 2008—Windows	$79.99	WQP8

Order Form

Name
Address
City
State, Zip
Daytime Phone
E-mail

Our "No-Hassle" Guarantee

Return anything you buy directly from Nolo for any reason and we'll cheerfully refund your purchase price. No ifs, ands or buts.

☐ Check here if you do not wish to receive mailings from other companies

Item Code	Quantity	Item	Unit Price	Total Price

Method of payment

☐ Check   ☐ VISA
☐ American Express
☐ MasterCard
☐ Discover Card

Subtotal	
Add your local sales tax (California only)	
Shipping: RUSH $12, Basic $6 (See below)	
"I bought 2, ship it to me FREE!"(Ground shipping only)	
TOTAL	

Account Number
Expiration Date
Signature

Shipping and Handling

Rush Delivery—Only $12

We'll ship any order to any street address in the U.S. by UPS 2nd Day Air* for only $12!

* Order by 9:30 AM Pacific Time and get your order in 2 business days. Orders placed after 9:30 AM Pacific Time will arrive in 3 business days. P.O. boxes and S.F. Bay Area use basic shipping. Alaska and Hawaii use 2nd Day Air or Priority Mail.

Basic Shipping—$6

Use for P.O. Boxes, Northern California and Ground Service.

Allow 1-2 weeks for delivery.

U.S. addresses only.

For faster service, use your credit card and our toll-free numbers

Call our customer service group Monday thru Friday 7am to 6 pm PST

Phone
1-800-728-3555

Fax
1-800-645-0895

Mail
Nolo
950 Parker St.
Berkeley, CA 94710

NOLO

Order 24 hours a day @ www.nolo.com

Get the Latest in the Law

Nolo's Legal Updater
We'll send you an email whenever a new edition of your book is published!
Sign up at **www.nolo.com/legalupdater**.

Updates at Nolo.com
Check **www.nolo.com/update** to find recent changes in the law that
affect the current edition of your book.

Nolo Customer Service
To make sure that this edition of the book is the most recent one, call us at
800-728-3555 and ask one of our friendly customer service representatives
(7:00 am to 6:00 pm PST, weekdays only). Or find out at **www.nolo.com**.

Complete the Registration & Comment Card ...
... and we'll do the work for you! Just indicate your preferences below:

Registration & Comment Card

NAME   DATE

ADDRESS

CITY   STATE   ZIP

PHONE   EMAIL

COMMENTS

WAS THIS BOOK EASY TO USE?   (VERY EASY)   5   4   3   2   1   (VERY DIFFICULT)

☐ Yes, you can quote me in future Nolo promotional materials. *Please include phone number above.*

☐ Yes, send me **Nolo's Legal Updater** via email when a new edition of this book is available.

Yes, I want to sign up for the following email newsletters:

  ☐ **NoloBriefs** (monthly)
  ☐ **Nolo's Special Offer** (monthly)
  ☐ **Nolo's BizBriefs** (monthly)
  ☐ **Every Landlord's Quarterly** (four times a year)

☐ Yes, you can give my contact info to carefully selected
partners whose products may be of interest to me.

LTK14